GOALS FOR SOCIAL WELFARE 1973-1993

Other books by HARLEIGH B. TRECKER

Social Group Work: Principles and Practices

Social Work Administration: Principles and Practices

Education for Social Work Administration *(with Frank Z. Glick and John C. Kidneigh)*

Group Services in Public Welfare

Citizen Boards at Work: New Challenges to Effective Action

GOALS FOR
SOCIAL WELFARE
1973-1993

An Overview of the Next Two Decades

EDITED BY

HARLEIGH B. TRECKER

University Professor of Social Work
School of Social Work
The University of Connecticut

ASSOCIATION PRESS / *NEW YORK*

GOALS FOR SOCIAL WELFARE 1973–1993

Copyright © 1973 by Harleigh B. Trecker

Association Press, 291 Broadway, New York, N.Y. 10007

Library of Congress Cataloging in Publication Data

Main entry under title:

Goals for social welfare, 1973–1993.

Celebrating the 100th anniversary of the National Conference on Social Welfare.
    Bibliography: p.
    1. Social service—United States—Addresses, essays, lectures. I. Trecker, Harleigh Bradley, 1911–   ed.
HV95.G56   361'.973   73–1284

International Standard Book Number: 0-8096-1857-5
Library of Congress Catalog Card Number: 73-1284

PRINTED IN THE UNITED STATES OF AMERICA

Dedicated with appreciation to the
National Conference on Social Welfare, for
100 years a forum of concern for improving
the human condition.

Contents

PART II

New Ways To Meet Needs: Goals for the Future

Introduction

Goals for Social Welfare 1973–1993: *An Overview of the Next Two Decades,* as the title indicates, is a book about the next twenty years and the goals toward which the workers in the field of social welfare should strive. In the thirteen chapters of the book it is the hope of the editor and the contributors that readers will get both a sense of direction and a sense of urgency as they set sights and targets for the period ahead. It is our intent to stimulate discussion and encourage readers to formulate their own aims for where they want the field to be twenty years hence.

The year 1973 was chosen as the year to release this book because at that time the National Conference on Social Welfare will observe one hundred years of leadership in social welfare thinking and planning. In a sense, this book is a salute to the Conference and to the thousands of persons who, over the century, have given of themselves to help the Conference become a vital part of the nation's conscience. One should hasten to add, however, that the book is in no way sponsored nor commissioned by the Conference. The idea for the book originated with the editor and he took responsibility for securing the volunteer contributors.

The sixteen people who have contributed chapters are listed in the back of the book along with brief biographical sketches. All of them are experienced leaders in the areas about which they have written. Most of them have at one time or another been prominent in the affairs of the Conference. Each writer was free to express his or her views without restriction. In fact, the only editing done was of an organizational nature. In every case the contributors speak only for themselves. The editor is grateful to them for the excellent job they have done.

It is hoped that many people will read this book, including both professional and volunteer workers in the broad field of social welfare. It should be particularly useful to policy planners and community leaders. For both beginning and experienced workers it may give guidance to their efforts to bring about changes in the field to which they are dedicated.

After the background prologue the book is divided into two parts. Part I: Social Welfare Needs and Challenges has six chapters which deal with Government and Social Welfare, Child Welfare Services, Services for Youth, Family Social Work, Services for the Aged, and Corrections in 1993. Part II: New Ways to Meet Needs—Goals for the Future has eight chapters, including one on Social Casework, Social Group Work, Community Organization, Social Work Research, Social Welfare Planning, Social Work Education, and Social Work Administration. An epilogue provides a convenient summary. Selected Readings are given to aid those who wish to do more in the way of exploring the future.

Some would argue that it is both foolish and futile to try to plan for the future. They would say there are too many unknowns about what will occur in the years ahead and the best one can do is to take things one day at a time! Yet it is our feeling that we *must* concern ourselves with the goals for the future because if we do not know to where we want to go we can scarcely map out routes for our journey. Furthermore, much of what will prevail in 1993 is going to be determined long before that date. Patterns set during the balance of the 1970's will be with us in the early 1990's. Twenty years is not a very long period of time. In fact, that sprightly little three-year-old of 1973 will be twenty-three in 1993, probably married, and will be taking on the opportunities and responsibilities of home, family, job, and community. For him and millions like him we have a responsibility to plan ahead and to set high goals.

Will all the goals listed here be achieved by 1993? Probably not. But by focusing on them now it seems reasonable to assume that the two decades ahead can be a period of vigorous striving for the betterment of humankind with some of the major targets reached.

It should be emphasized that none of the writers are presumptuous enough to ask the reader to agree with all, or even with anything, that has been said. But we *do* hope that each person, group, agency, and organization that is stimulated by this approach will devote some time to thinking about the future and to setting goals for themselves and for their organizations. For, as is said in Proverbs 29:18, "Where there is no vision the people perish."

HARLEIGH B. TRECKER

West Hartford, Connecticut

Prologue:
Why We Must Plan for the Future

During the period May 20–22, 1874, a small group of representatives from the State Boards of Charities of Massachusetts, Connecticut, New York and Wisconsin met in New York City under the auspices of the American Social Science Association and organized the Conference of Boards of Public Charities. This meeting was the beginning of the National Conference on Social Welfare as we know it today.

At this 1874 meeting the representatives heard papers on "The Duty of the States Toward Their Insane Poor," "The Laws of Pauper Settlement, and the Best Mode of Administering the Poor Law." Committees on Destitute and Delinquent Children, and on Uniformity of Statistics of Crime and Pauperism reported. Dr. R. T. Davis, discussing pauperism in the City of New York, said: "Pauperism is a matter which is daily becoming of more importance in our whole community. . . . Large numbers of workingmen, with their families, have, during the past year, been thrown out of employment without a sufficient fund of savings to fall back on."

In 1870 the population of the United States was 38,558,371. In writing about the third quarter of the nineteenth century, the period when the National Conference came into being, Harrison observed, "That was a period when population was growing rapidly in the United States, people were moving westward; a developing industrial economy was drawing multitudes of workers to congested population centers; a period when ideas, social theories and convictions were changing rapidly, and when technical knowledge and the exploitation of the natural resources of the national speedily advanced." [1] That was in 1874 when the Conference began. That small band of state leaders saw the need to confer nationally in 1874. The problems of that period demanded it. The need to confer is even greater in 1973 with a nation of over 200,000,000 persons caught in a maze of social problems far more complex and flowing from inter-related causes difficult if not impossible to pinpoint.

Certainly there is no shortage of problems in the early 1970's. Government at all levels has been cutting appropriations for social welfare. Children with special needs continue to be neglected. Many young people are alienated, confused, and in the grip of illnesses induced by drugs. Family life is undergoing serious strains and challenges. Older persons are shockingly ignored especially if they are alone and ill. The ancient corrections system in our country neither corrects nor rehabilitates. The poor continue to number in the millions and millions more exist marginally in economic terms. The so-called "affluent society" has turned out to be a myth and mirage for them as they struggle to rear their children and provide them with the education so necessary in today's world. As Reston puts it so well, "At the core and heart of life there is great uncertainty, self-doubt and even self-hate." [2]

As Schnapper put it, "America is clearly in trouble. At home the nation is plagued by crime, poverty, racial conflicts, deteriorating cities, educational inadequacies and dangerous inflation trends. Overseas, in Vietnam, hundreds of young Americans continue to lose their lives in an incredible quagmire that has cost more than a hundred billion dollars." [3]

Some Ways of Looking at the Future

In recent years many officials, scholars, commissions, and research groups have been looking at the future and seeking to predict what may happen.[4] There is wide variation in ways of viewing the future and reports of thoughts and projections tend to differ. An examination of a number of positions tends to bear this out.

Former Secretary of Commerce Maurice Stans has predicted that in twenty years our population will be approaching 300 million, with 70 per cent of this population living in twelve metropolitan areas. He expects our work week to decline, our fresh-water demands to double, and our Gross National Product to exceed $2 trillion.[5]

A university research center forecasts greatly improved life in our country in the 1980's. They project better medical care, more free time, higher incomes, more housing with conveniences, a cleaner environment and a partial solution to the transportation problem. They see "a possibility of a national health insurance plan" and better control over the mounting costs of medical care. They indicate that the hours people work each week will decline and that family income will increase markedly. They suggest that there will be a "more generally shared concern about the eradication of poverty." [6]

In spite of the persistent problems we face there is evidence that positive change is taking place even though such changes may be only in the beginning stages. Is there a fundamental shift away from the glorification of materialism to a more enduring goal of humanism? Some people think so and it is to be hoped that they are correct. Also, there seems to be greater interest in, concern about, and involvement in the affairs of government.[7] Perhaps this can be accounted for by the remarkable rise in the level of education of our people in the past half century. The conquest of disease continues to be a top priority in the health and medical field and much progress has been made. Spotty and not yet fully mobilized efforts are being made to clean up the environment. It is to be hoped that this movement will not only continue but will grow. The beginning of new cities is evident in a few places and while the scale is small the ideas have a grandeur that may yet be realized. There is much more use of the legal route for correcting society's abuses and this due process approach may have replaced the futile violent confrontations of an earlier time. There is much more information available for people today as the communication media continue to develop in the satellite age. There have been some wholesome efforts to decentralize government. The reshaping of international cooperation is certainly a positive. While "one world" is here in a geographical sense it is still to be achieved in a human sense.

At a management improvement conference conducted by the federal government in 1970 it was pointed out that:

> The lowest population projection for 1985 is 250 million people and for the year 2000 it is 300 million people. At least 71 per cent of these people are likely to be living in large urban areas. The defacto apartheid process that now exists will become even more pronounced. Seventy-five per cent of urban blacks will live in the central city; 70 per cent of urban whites will live in the suburbs. The suburbs will continue their phenomenal growth of the last decade during which they increased 25 per cent in population while the central cities were increasing only 1 per cent. Urban density will continue to decline as it has for the last 40 years. Consumer industries will follow the more affluent white populations to the suburbs. Unemployment and marginal employment, the latter being much more prevalent than the former, will continue to be a serious problem for us because it appears that over 20 per cent of the labor force in 1985 will not have completed high school. Concomitantly, society will have moved ahead rapidly into the cybernetics revolution: a revolution which will eliminate many jobs. In other words, if present trends are allowed to con-

tinue, chronic unemployment may be an even more severe problem in 1985 than it is today. It may be necessary to extend such programs as the Federal Assistance Program to even broader segments of the population. Many people will no longer be able to work and we will have to allocate some of our surplus productivity to their care.[8]

Population—Basic Factor in Planning

Thanks to the work of the Bureau of the Census and the significant report of the Commission on Population Growth and the American Future plus other ongoing studies and observations, we have some interesting and useful data regarding the population situation in our country in the period ahead. While it is not possible to predict with absolute certainty it appears that population will continue to increase and there will be more people in the United States twenty years from now. Exactly how many is not entirely clear. But the 1990 census could reveal that we are a nation of 250 million as contrasted with our present 208 million. While the present downturn in the birth rate may continue there is still reason to predict a 35 to 40 million increase in population in the next two decades. This is not exactly a "population explosion" but neither is it a decrease! Simply put, everything we need now will be needed by even more people in the future. The continued growth of population, even at a lesser rate, presents a great challenge to all of us.

In his historic message to the Congress on population President Nixon said:

In the United States our rate of population growth is not as great as that of developing nations. The present growth rate of about one per cent per year is still significant.

In 1917 the total number of Americans passed 100 million, after three full centuries of steady growth. In 1967—just half a century later—the 200 million mark was passed. If the present rate of growth continues, the third hundred million persons will be added in roughly a thirty-year period. This means that by the year 2000, or shortly thereafter, there will be more than 300 million Americans.

This growth will produce serious challenges for our society. I believe that many of our present social problems may be related to the fact that we had had only fifty years in which to accommodate the second hundred million Americans. In fact, since 1945 alone some 90 million babies have been born in this country. We have thus had to accomplish in a very few decades an adjustment to population growth which was once spread over centuries. And it now appears that we will have to provide for a third hundred million Americans in a period of just 30 years.

The great majority of the next hundred million Americans will be born to families which looked forward to their birth and are prepared to love them and care for them as they grow up. The critical issue is whether social institutions will also plan for their arrival and be able to accommodate them in a humane and intelligent way. We can be sure that society will *not* be ready for this growth unless it begins planning immediately.[9]

More people now live in metropolitan areas or urban regions and more people will be crowded into such areas during the period ahead. The United States is largely a nation of cities. But the central cites are declining in population or growing only slowly. The nonwhite population is more heavily concentrated in the central cities and most of the population growth for this group will take place there. Suburbs will continue to grow and their growth will be predominantly white.

The Commission on Population Growth and the American Future reports:

This country has experienced a demographic revolution in population distribution as well as in national population growth. Today, 69 per cent of the American people live in metropolitan areas—cites of 50,000 or more, and the surrounding county or counties that are economically integrated with the city. Between 1960 and 1970, the population of the United States grew 13 per cent, while the metropolitan population grew 23 per cent. Nearly all metropolitan growth took place through the growth of suburbs and territorial expension into previously rural areas. The United States has become mainly a nation of cities and their environs.[10]

In their demographic perspective on the twentieth-century United States the Commission on Population Growth and the American Future contrasted 1900 with 1970. In 1900 our population was 76 million; it was 205 million in 1970. In 1900 life expectancy was 47 years. In 1970 it was 70 years. In 1900 the median age was 23 years; it was 28 in 1970. In 1900 there were 32 births per 1,000 population but by 1970 that figure had declined to 18. Equally striking was the decline in deaths per 1,000 population. They were 17 in 1900 and only 9 in 1970. Immigrants also declined sharply, from 8 per 1,000 in 1900 to 2 per 1,000 in 1970. In 1900 the annual growth in population was 1¾ million or 2.3 per cent; in 1970 it was 2¼ million or 1.1 per cent.[11]

The Commission on Population Growth and the American Future

believes that the gradual stabilization of population—bringing births into balance with deaths—would contribute significanctly to the nation's ability to solve its problems, although such problems will not be solved by population stabilization alone. It would, however, enable our society to shift its focus increasingly from quantity to quality. . . . The Commission believes that slowing the rate of population growth would ease the problems facing the American government in the years ahead. Demands for governmental services will be less than they would be otherwise and resources available for public support of education, health and other governmental activities would be greater. However, it would be a serious error to read these conclusions as comforting and reassuring. Under the most optimistic assumptions, at least 50 million more people will be added to the United States population before the end of the century, increasing the demands on governmental services and making more difficult the achievement of a participatory political process responsive to contemporary conditions. More important, these added demands and complexities will fall on governmental structures and processes already severely burdened—many would say overburdened—by the problems facing the nation.

In this framework we must face the fact that Americans have suddenly become a metropolitan people. In 1970, nearly 70 per cent of the United States population was metropolitan—the figure will approach 85 per cent by the year 2000. For better or for worse, we are in the process of becoming an almost total urban society. Most metropolitan growth now results from natural increase, not migration. Thus, the trend toward bigness of metropolitan areas, if undesirable, cannot be substantially checked except as national growth is slowed down.

Migration is from low-income rural areas and abroad to metropolitan areas, from one metropolitan area to another, and from central cities to suburbs. Nearly 40 million or one in five Americans changes homes each year. About one in fifteen, a total of 13 million, migrate across county lines. What is needed is guidance and assistance.[12]

As one looks ahead it appears certain that there will be a considerable increase in the number of young adults; one-third of the expected total population increase in the next twenty years will be in the twenty-five to thirty year age group. There will be a corresponding lack of growth in the forty-five to sixty-four age group. The percentage of older persons in the population will increase.

Persons sixty-five and over now make up about one-tenth of our population, but their numbers are increasing more rapidly than the population as a whole. Furthermore, many aged persons are poor. They account for one-third of the poorest familes and one-half of the poorest one-person households. More than 50 per cent of the over 6 million families headed by a person sixty-five or over have incomes of less than $3,000 per year. Of the 3.6 million aged living alone, nearly half had incomes of less than $1,000 yearly. In addition, older people are often sick people. Although they make up only about 10 per cent of the population they spend 25 per cent of what all Americans spend on health care. Also, when hospitalized they stay in for a longer time than does the younger group of patients.[13]

In discussing the quality of life in America the Commission on Population Growth and the American Future pointed out:

> There are today, by official estimate 26 million Americans living in poverty conditions. This is 13 per cent of our population. Improvements in the average income of the population do something for these groups, but not enough. Their problem is that too many of them are not part of the system that generates and distributes income.
>
> Over six million poor people are working adults who simply do not make enough money to meet even the minimal official income standard. Over three million of the poor are persons aged 14 to 64 who are sick or disabled, in school, or unable to find work. Nearly five million are over age 65, and over eight million are children. Finally, more than two million are female heads of family whose responsibilities at home keep them from taking jobs.
>
> What this adds up to is that more than nine out of ten poor people are excluded—because of age, incapacity, poor training, family responsibilities, fiscal disincentives, or discrimination in the labor market—from the system that produces and distributes income and the things income buys. Real improvements in their lot will be reflected in a changing distribution of income. But while average income has risen dramatically and the number of poor has declined as a result, the relative distribution of income has changed little in the 25 years the Census Bureau has been measuring it.
>
> In a country as wealthy and resourceful as ours, there is no excuse for permitting deprivation. For the working poor and those who cannot find work, the solution is to eliminate racial and sex discrimination in employment, and to improve education and training. Beyond this, we need a serious reexamination of the status of the aged. Old people are healthier and better educated than ever before. They are often forced to stop working far before the end of their productive lives, because of outright discrimination and outdated restrictions against older workers, and because of fiscal disincentives against work built into our social security laws and other pension arrangements.
>
> Nevertheless, the country still has a number of people who cannot be helped by better access to the labor market. For these the answer should be an increased public responsibility for maintaining a decent standard of living.[14]

Sadly, the government has not yet made a firm commitment to the welfare of the nation's children. Bronfenbrenner and Bruner call attention to the need for such a commitment when they summarize the following facts:

> In 1971, 43 per cent of the nation's mothers worked outside the home. In 1948 the figure was only 18 per cent. One in every three mothers with children under six is working today. In 1948 the figure was one in eight.

There were more than 4.5 million mothers with children under six who were in the labor force last year.

In 1971, of all mothers of children under six, 10 per cent—1.3 million of them—were single parents bringing up children without a husband. Half of these mothers also held down a job.

Mothers in poor and near-poor families are much more likely to be gainfully employed, partly because so many of them are heads of families. Among families in poverty, 45 per cent of all children under six live in female-headed households; in non-poverty families the figure was only 3.5 per cent. In two-parent families where the husband earned $10,000 or over, only 20 per cent of the mothers worked; where the husband earned less than $7,000, 35 per cent of the mothers worked. These women work because they have to.

There are nearly six million pre-school children whose mothers are in the labor force. On these, one million live in families below the poverty line (e.g. income below $4,000 for a family of four). An additional one million children of working mothers live in near poverty (income between $4,000 and $7,000 for a family of four). All of these children would have to be on welfare if the mother did not work. Finally, there are about 2.5 million children under six whose mothers do not work, but where family income is below the poverty level without counting the many thousands of children in families above the poverty line who are in need of child care services, this makes a total of about 4.5 million children under six whose families need some help if normal family life is to be sustained.[15]

In addition to the need for greatly expanded child development services the growing population and the technological society will put heavy demands of higher education programs and facilities. As Grant points out, "Latest projections of the U.S. Office of Education and the Carnegie Commission on Higher Education estimate that enrollment in our colleges and universities will rise from 8.5 million in 1970 to 13.2 million in 1980, a 55 per cent increase. There will be a leveling off after 1980, but another upswing in the nineties. So, a lot more money will be needed for education, by students and the institutions they attend." [16]

Some Certainties About the Future

Noted scholars of the future see some things as being certain. Bell talks about the work of the Commission on the Year 2000. As he sees it:

... the world of the year 2000 has already arrived, for in the decisions we make now, in the way we design our environment and thus sketch the lines of constraints, the future is committed. Just as the gridiron pattern of city streets in the nineteenth century shaped the linear growth of the cities in the twentieth, so the new networks of radial highways, the location of new towns, the reordering of graduate school curricula, the decision to create or not to create a computer utility as a single system, and the like will frame the tectonics of the twenty-first century. The future is not an overarching leap into the distance; it begins in the present.

This is the premise of the Commission on the Year 2000. It is an effort to indicate now the future consequences of present public-policy decisions, to anticipate future problems, and to begin the design of alternative solutions so that our society has more options and can make a moral choice, rather than be constrained, as is so often the case when problems descend upon us unnoticed and demand an immediate response.[17]

As Michael observes:

. . . what happens over the years ahead in large degree will be outgrowths of present societal characteristics, forecasts about the next five to twenty-five years or so necessarily are based on implicit or explicit interpretations of what is happening now and why it is happening.[18]

Kostelanetz emphasizes that:

Social speculations are, essentially, articulated options, options which *may* be realized by people both inside politics and out; for a vision both comprehensive and detailed helps make human choices more considered and purposeful. As knowledge is power, so foreknowledge can be even greater power; and speculations, at their most relevant, propose alternatives that most of us would not be likely to consider on our own.[19]

So, even though they be speculations we must plan for the future. That we will be incorrect or even wrong in some of our plans and goals is inevitable but nonethelsess we must make the effort. We cannot leave social welfare planning and policy determination to chance and to drift.

As Kahn puts it so well:

Social planning involves a sequence of means-ends relationships. It is a process of policy determination for orderly development to achieve given objectives . . . the central goal of planning is not a blueprint but a series of generalized guides to future decisions and actions. It demands: *selection of objectives* in the light of assessment of interests, trends, or problems, social goals or values, and awareness of their broader implications; *a willingness to act in foresight,* based on more or less faith and rigorous projections; *constant translation of policies* into implications for specific objectives and for programs and action; *constant evaluation* and feedback.[20]

The needs and problems of people now are awesome. They will be even more perplexing, challenging, and difficult in the future. Planning

for their solution and goals for their resolution are of the utmost importance.

As Bell said:

> The only prediction about the future that one can make with certainty
> is that public authorities will face more problems than they have at any
> previous time in history. This arises from some simple facts: Social issues
> are more and more intricately related to each other because the impact of
> any major change is felt quickly throughout the national and even the
> international system. Individuals and groups, more conscious of these prob-
> lems as problems, demand action instead of quietly accepting their fate.
> Because more and more changes will be made in the political arena than in
> the market, there will be more open community conflict. The political
> arena is an open cockpit where decision points are more visible than they
> are in the impersonal market; different groups will clash more directly as
> they contend for advantage or seek to resist change in society.[21]

As the National Conference on Social Welfare convenes to observe
the one hundredth anniversary of its founding it is likely that the goals
of the past will be replaced by a new set of goals some of which are proposed in the chapters that follow. Taken together they say that we must
strive for a more humane and just society for all people everywhere.

As Banfield puts it:

> . . . the quality of a society must be judged by its tendency to produce
> desirable human types; the healthy society, then, is one that not only
> stays alive but also moves in the direction of giving greater scope and ex-
> pressions to what is distinctly human.[22]

PART I

SOCIAL WELFARE NEEDS
AND CHALLENGES

1

Government and Social Welfare Goals for 1993

WAYNE VASEY

The shape of a future even two decades from now is so uncertain that it is extremely difficult to project goals that might seem reasonably attainable in our tax-supported welfare system by that time. The kind of world in which we shall be living in 1993 will certainly determine the nature of the institutions and programs that we shall need. But we don't know what that world will be like. Furthermore, unless we develop a greater degree of wisdom than we have shown to date, we cannot be assured that we shall develop the kinds of programs that those times will require.

Our problem of projecting goals is further complicated by a question as to whether any of our institutions has the power to steer its own future course. Is the projection of institutional goals an exercise in futility? Is it possible that exponential changes in technology, demography, and in the social system will sweep our welfare and other institutions helplessly along in an irresistible tide of events? Is planning really feasible? Obviously, I think that it is. Even though change is so massive and so rapid that it "reduces the relevance of experience as a guide to public policy judgments" [1] it has not eliminated the past and present as a source of indicators for our future, and as the basis for some guidance as to what we should be aiming for in that not so distant period in the last decade of the present century. "The problem, of course," declare Kahn and Weiner, "is to sort out what changes from what continues and to discern what is continuous in the changes themselves."

I shall try to perform this difficult task. In doing so, I shall first indulge in some speculation about the society of 1993, take a look at our public welfare past and present in a search for cues, and then suggest what would seem to be relevant and reasonable goals.

Some Speculations About the Years Ahead

My view of the future is much less extreme than either the apocalyptic or utopian predictions of some of our current prophets who collectively give the impression that the years between now and the year 2000 will be a race between demise and paradise. I am not proceeding on the assumption that work will be obsolete in a completely automated society, and that we shall be "sitting under a cybernetic bread fruit tree," in the words of Elizabeth Wickenden. I do not assume that we shall have attained a completely classless society of equals, or that technological and biological revolutions will have made all of our present institutions obsolete and ourselves almost so.

There are possibilities for change which may be less dramatic than some of the more extreme possibilities, but which are significant enough in themselves, and certainly important in their implications for tax-supported welfare programs. By 1993, we could attain zero population growth. We may by then consider economic growth inimical to local, state, or national interests. We may adopt a new value system which stresses quality rather than quantity and environment rather than money. The public sector of society may be much larger and more influential with a corresponding decline in the size and significance of the private sector. Larger and politically stronger organized minorities may have great impact on the way the public allocates resources and benefits. We may be dealing seriously with our racial, ethnic, and other basic social problems, or we may be only trying to keep them at bay. There is a good chance that we shall have achieved equality in employment for women and for racial and ethnic minorities.

It isn't too hard to see what some of these changes might mean for governmental welfare institutions. For example, zero population growth will alter the balance among age groups and should change many of our priorities for social welfare. A proportionately larger number of elders will make their influence felt on policy makers and resource allocators.

The shift from the priority of economic growth could certainly reshape our views of welfare as a redistributive function of government. In comparison with other Western industrial countries, we have not been exactly lavish in our expenditures for public social services. In fact in per capita expenditures and in proportion to funds devoted to these services, we have consistently been at or near the bottom of the Western industrial heap. Gunnar Myrdal has cited the United States as "stingy." He declares, "America of all rich countries [is] the one which has the highest rate of unemployment, the worst and biggest slums, and which is least generous in giving economic security to its old people, its children, its sick people, and its invalids." [2]

The prospects are for a future in which hard decisions will have to be made. It will be less feasible for us to plan on financing welfare out of increases in the gross national product and without seriously disturbing the balance of commitments between our poor and our nonpoor. More than ever, strains may develop, especially between the poor and the middle class. The middle class will have to accept the prospect of being taxed more heavily to pay for better services to the poor. "Better schools for the poor and open admissions to college mean more competition and fewer resources for their own children, and a threat to the privileged advancement of their own children." [3] Similar invasions of other sanctuaries of privilege hold great possibilities for turbulence in the future.

The future is not an unattractive one, however, if we have the capacity for turning it to advantage for the people. It will call for our political system to change its habit of responding "with piecemeal archaisms rather than architectonic inventions." [4]

Even more fundamentally, it will demand a shift in our priorities. As Bayard Rustin declares, ". . . A humane culture as we have imagined it and dreamed of it in America, and which at certain periods of our history has appeared possible, seems today to be on the verge of being sacrificed to the special exigencies of the marketplace: that is to say, as the new technological and organizational obsession spreads, the possibility of our creating an engaged social conscience recedes further and further into the background, leaving more and more people, particularly our minorities, stranded and neglected in a deepening mire of social and economic problems." [5] This assessment of our present course calls for a basic change in our public morality before developments of the kind that would permit the commitment of a larger share of government resources to the poor and disadvantaged would be possible.

Our Welfare Past and Present

In the thirty-five years between the passage of the Social Security Act in 1935 and the beginning of the 1970's, the expanding role of government was most notable in its welfare policies and programs. We developed a large structure of welfare services "designed to eliminate or avoid the risks inherent in a market-oriented economy." [6] During this period, through government, we underwrote personal risks enacting old age and survivors insurance, unemployment insurance, public assistance, medical care for the aged, medical aid to the indigent, and other programs. At the same time we built protection against the risks of agricultural enterprise, and provided many programs designed to eliminate or ameliorate the risks of capital. Fusfeld declares, "It is fair to say that the modern economy could not survive without the socialization of risk that occurred in the last half century." [7]

At the beginning of the 1970's what did we have to show for three and one-half decades of effort in governmentally operated and supported welfare programs? What lessons does this experience provide that might be useful in planning for our future? What does it suggest for the future of government in social welfare?

To summarize, having breached or bypassed constitutional and traditional barriers to federal government action, we expanded the programs of the 1930's, added new ones, reached out to new classes of problems, and increased considerably our outlays for welfare at all levels of government.

We could show substantial gains in many areas. Using a fixed poverty line, we could show a decline in poverty from forty million persons in 1959 to twenty-five million in 1970.

We could point to increased federal commitments to the mentally retarded, to national support for mental health, to outlays for public housing over a period of three decades, to expanded support for vocational rehabilitation of the disabled, to federal funds for hospital construction, to the Older Americans Act of 1965, to Medicare and Medicaid, to child welfare and to many other evidences of our capacity to extend and expand the role of government in a wide range of social programs.

In all instances, these programs were responses to special needs acknowledged as valid public and national concerns. We demonstrate again and again that we can, when sufficiently moved, act with specific programs for explicit needs. We do not, however, acknowledge the role of government to underwrite a closely aritculated welfare structure in a comprehensive scheme of protective measures. It leaves government in a residual role, one of responding to the exigencies of the marketplace, and of supplementing but not pre-empting the function of the economy as the prime provider.

In the early part of the sixties, our collective conscience was stirred by one of our recurrent discoveries of poverty. History shows that we do, in fact, periodically discover poverty, lay our charitable offerings on the altar of conscience, and then move on to more gratifying and less disquieting pursuits.[8] Michael Harrington's *The Other America* pointed to the existence of a large number of people, not visible on the streets with clearly marked evidence of their condition, living in poverty in a society which assumed that its affluence reached out to all except an unfavored few living in "pockets of poverty." Oscar Lewis's studies of families living in destitution led him to the conclusion that there was in fact a "culture of poverty," coexisting with the dominant culture of the majority and with its own characteristics and habits. Robert Lampman pointed out the extent to which our system of income transfers, through our social insurance and public assistance programs, was failing to benefit the poor. We woke up to the shocking disclosure that in spite of economic affluence, and in spite of our outlays for income maintenance and other social services, one-fifth of our people were poor by officially defined standards.

What had happened? What was meant when people frequently referred to the "failure" of our welfare institutions? Was it a case of being too little and too late with our changes, or were our existing social policies inherently inadequate for the times? Let's look at the record.

Our system of old age insurance had undergone an impressive rate of institutional growth during that period. New classes of beneficiaries had been added, levels of payments had been improved, although not fast enough, and coverage had been extended to almost all classes of employment and self-employment. Our experience with this program demonstrated our ability to respond to needs which we acknowledge through methods we can accept, but it shows also that even under these favorable conditions, progress can lag behind expectations. As Elizabeth Wickenden suggests, "Its structure is admirably suited to American traditions and needs but it has not been used adequately to meet these needs." [9]

Progress in other programs was less favorable. Unemployment insurance in the various states remained meager in benefits, limited in coverage, and awkward to administer. Public assistance was a mélange of gaps in coverage, inadequacies in payment levels, and disparities in treatment from state to state. Our services to the disabled, the mentally retarded, and the mentally ill remained on the fringe of public concern and were meagerly supported.

Social scientists, including economists, anthropologists, sociologists, members of the health disciplines, lawyers, looked for solutions to the problem of poverty in the midst of plenty.

By the middle of the decade, the mood of the country had changed "from gloom to euphoria," to borrow a phrase from James Sundquist. As Sundquist states:

> In one of the most remarkable outpourings of major legislation in the history of the country, the Congress in 1964 and 1965 had expressed the national purpose in bold and concrete terms—to outlaw racial discrimination in many of its forms, to improve educational opportunity at every level, to eradicate poverty, to assure health care for old people to create

jobs for the unemployed, to cleanse the rivers and the air and protect and beautify man's environment.[10]

Buoyant confidence in our ability to solve our complex, nagging social problems of the day is certainly evident in this official statement:

> The United States is the first major nation in history which can look forward to victory over poverty. Our wealth, our income, our technical know-how, and our productive capacity put this goal within our grasp. As a nation, we clearly have the capacity to achieve this victory; what we need now is a commitment on the part of the people, the communities, private organizations, and all levels of government.[11]

Included in our "remarkable outpouring" was a wide range of federally sponsored measures. These included: (1) jobs for the unemployed; (2) opportunity for the poor; (3) schools for the young; (4) civil rights for minorities; (5) health care for the aged; (6) protection and enhancement of the outdoor environment.[12]

During the years of the Johnson Administration, the period of "The Great Society," the number of domestic welfare programs increased tenfold, from 40 to 400, while total expenditures doubled to over $18 billion. The keystone of these programs was the Economic Opportunity Act of 1964, the "war on poverty." Through its federally aided local community action programs, this measure was supposed to bring about coordination of federally supported new local programs, but also to induce older agencies to join in a concerted attack on poverty.[13]

In a concurrent and concomitant political development, the decade of the 1960's featured civil rights legislation on a scale unprecedented in our history. That history shows that civil rights for our minorities had lain dormant since the post-Civil War reconstruction period, until 1957. The Civil Rights Act of 1957 (PL85-315) prohibited action to prevent persons from voting in federal elections. Later laws in 1960, 1964, 1965, and 1968 were aimed at discrimination in employment, public accommodations, voting, education, and programs receiving public assistance. The 1968 law was designed to protect persons exercising their civil rights and to prevent discrimination in the sale and rental of housing.

It would seem then that the decade promised that the achievement of political equality through the free and untrammeled exercise of civil rights, like the goal of the elimination of poverty, was within the grasp of the American people.

What happened to the dream of civil rights?

The statistical picture is a mixed one, depending on what statistics are used. Some show progress, others no progress or even retrogression. For example, former Presidential Adviser to President Nixon, Daniel P. Moynihan, in a special memorandum, noted "extraordinary black civil rights progress," pointing to the doubling over an eight-year period of blacks earning $8,000 or more per year, and a four-year period rise in black enrollment at colleges of 85 per cent. He observed, on the gloomier side, the continuing low scores of black high school seniors in verbal tests, large-scale black teen-age urban unemployment, and increasing crime and arson rates in the black ghettos.

In education, an area not covered by Moynihan's memorandum, the picture is certainly mixed. The Nixon Administration has pointed with pride to the growth in the number of schools complying with desegregation deadlines or court orders. "But this did not mean that most blacks were attending schools in which the majority of the students were white. And it had no bearing on the situation in 'private white academies' in the South to which 400,000 white students had fled. In the North, continued white flight to the suburbs left the inner city schools primarily black. Nationwide, three of every four blacks attended schools which were primarily black."

While the numbers of blacks elected to public office rose, after the November 1970 elections, and was the highest since the Reconstruction era, it represented only .3 per cent of the 520,000 elected officials.

Racial violence, which flared in the city streets in the period from 1965 at Watts in Los Angeles, in 1967 in the riots in Detroit and Newark, and "the wave of fires and looting which struck Washington, Baltimore and Chicago" in the wake of the death of Martin Luther King, April 4, 1968, has subsided. Violence has continued "in a somewhat more selective and discriminating form." Individual attacks on white policemen, shootouts, clashes in colleges and courtrooms, integrated classrooms, and in prisons, and very recently in the ugly confrontations on school bussing, doesn't give too much room for encouragement. "And while the total quantity of blood actually shed in these incidents may be a bit less than in previous conflagrations, the question remains—what does the new trend mean? Is it a source for encouragement or concern? Have the majority of rioters turned away from rebellion to reconciliation, apathy, or despair?" [14]

Welfare and civil rights have common concerns. They affect the same people. The victims of failures of both include disproportionate numbers of black, chicano, and other racial minority peoples. Both are crucial to the attainment of equality. The right to travel, for example, is an empty one for the person without the money to do it. The right to attend a good school is connected with the right to live in a house in a neighborhood that has such a school. This in turn depends on whether one has the means to buy or rent such a house in such a neighborhood as well as whether the neighbors will let him move in. If you can't get a job, or are the first to be laid off, because of discrimination past or present, you can't earn much in the way of social insurance benefits. There are many, many ways in which it can be shown that civil rights and housing, manpower, education, public assistance, and other welfare programs are part of a closely linked chain of discrimination and inequality.

From Euphoria to Malaise

If the national mood had leaped to a euphoric state by 1965, it sagged again by 1970. It became quite the vogue to speak of our "national malaise" to denote a condition of despair over our capacity to solve our apparently intransigent social problems. John Gardner warned of a future in which our social institutions, caught between their "unloving critics and their uncritical lovers," were doomed.[15] Problems didn't disappear. Inner cities continued their inexorable decline. Rural poverty remained a nagging problem. Unemployment plagues the young, the poor, and members of racial minorities; for them the prosperity of the 1960's was called "a selective depression."

Between 1959 and 1970, there was an average annual decline of 4.9 per cent in the number of poor persons. Between 1969 and 1970, however, there was for the first time in ten years a reversal of the trend of reduction of the percentage of persons living in poverty. The number went up 1.2 million or to 5.1 per cent. In 1970, according to the Bureau of the Census Current Population Survey, in March, 1971, about 25.5 million people, or 13 per cent of the population were living in poverty.[16] The increase in 1970 could be attributed to the rise in unemployment during that period.

In the aggregate, over a decade, the figures are encouraging. But it is in the structure of remaining poverty that the difficulty lies. In 1970, the poverty rate for Negroes was more than three times that for whites. During the ten-year period, there was a decline of 53 per cent in the number of persons in households headed by males. By contrast, the numbers of poor persons in female-headed families showed no measurable decline. In 1970, according to the Census Report, persons in households headed by a woman constituted only 14 per cent of all persons, but about 44 per cent of poor persons.

Age and race combine as factors in continuing poverty. In 1970, children under eighteen years accounted for about 36 per cent of all white persons below the poverty level as compared to the 54 per cent of all Negroes who were poor. By contrast, aged persons made up about 19 per cent of all poor white persons but only 7 per cent of the Negro poor.

An interesting fact shows up in rural and urban poverty, respectively. Although approximately 64 per cent of the nation's families lived in metropolitan areas in 1970, poor families were about equally distributed between metropolitan and nonmetropolitan areas. About 50 per cent of poor white families living in metropolitan areas lived in the central city, as compared to 80 per cent of poor Negro families.[17]

Anyone reciting the record of our efforts to reduce poverty is in the position of telling first the good news, then the bad. The good news is that we have reduced poverty, at least in relation to a fixed line which is used to divide the poor from the nonpoor. But many people, members of minority groups, the aged, rural whites, members of families headed by women, are little if any better off than they were. We have had shocking disclosures of hunger, and of the existence of abject poverty in both town and country.

One of the crucial developments of the decade was what Piven and Cloward have called "The welfare explosion of the 1960's." [18] These authors note: "During the 1950's the AFDC (Aid to Families with Dependent Children) rolls rose by only 17 per cent. Between December 1960 and February 1969, the increase was 107 per cent.[19] But, they note as an "extraordinary fact," the rolls went up "all at once," with 71 per cent taking place in the four years after 1964.[20] Yet, in 1970, only half the people in poverty received public aid.

Many explanations have been offered for this rise, especially that part of it that occurred when times generally were good. To a people accustomed to thinking of the rise and fall of welfare as coincident with fluctuations in the economy this was hard to take. Piven and Cloward argue that the phenomenon was "a political response to a political disorder," that the welfare explosion was concurrent with the civil disorders of the late sixties, and with the turmoil produced by the civil rights struggle; they note further that it also coincided in time "with the enactment of a series of ghetto-placating federal programs (such as the anti-poverty program) which, among other things, hired thousands of poor people, social workers, and lawyers who, as it subsequently turned out, greatly stimulated people to apply for relief and helped them to obtain it." [21]

Whatever the explanation, the welfare rise is a baffling phenomenon. It has become a critical problem for mayors, governors, and other state and city officials. Discontent with public assistance has reached a new level of intensity as the number of persons receiving all forms of public assistance increased 9.5 to more than 14 million between 1969 and 1972. As the costs escalated, state and local officials, feeling the intolerable pressure on their beleaguered treasuries, began to look desperately for ways to control the welfare load. New York State, for example, proposed a "demonstration project," to cut off aid to nearly 25,000 persons in 7,000 families. These people would then have an "opportunity" to "earn back" what had been taken away through a system of "incentive points" for work and acceptable behavior, or what came to be called derisively "brownie points." This "solution" is a vivid example of our persistent efforts to regulate the size of the welfare load by controlling the behavior of the people who receive aid. This is not the only time in our history that we have sought answers in the programs designed to relieve poverty rather than in the conditions that have caused it. This, unfortunately, is one of the continuities of history.

The Nixon Administration, confronted by this picture of a rising welfare load, put welfare reform at the top of the agenda of its domestic policy proposals. When President Nixon offered the Family Assistance Plan in 1969, the climate for change could scarcely have been more favorable. The current welfare programs were under assault from all sides. Public assistance was alleged to be demeaning, inefficient, costly and unproductive. These were only a few of the pejorative terms used to condemn a system which had become almost universally unpopular. The President's Commission on Civil Rights in 1968 identified the welfare system as a factor in racial alienation. Reform seemed near.

But as the Nixon Plan became the subject of protracted congressional debate, it became evident that the consensus of discontent was not matched by a corresponding agreement on what to do. It was nearly impossible, it seemed, to design any measure that would meet the widely diverse criticisms that came from political right, left, and center. Alvin Schorr has aptly characterized the Nixon Plan as having been framed by "careful Calvinists and careless reformers." [22] Perhaps by trying to reconcile the views of people of widely different persuasions, the proposal inevitably included something for almost everyone to dislike.

Yet the very fact that such a proposal was made by a President of the United States, particularly one who had not been previously identified as a passionate advocate for social welfare, is in itself somewhat a hopeful sign for the future. A supposedly conservative President proposed a welfare system which included a national minimum income though a meager one, moved toward national standards, and proposed to extend aid to many previously excluded from the system, including families headed by underpaid workers. All these were once radical ideas. President Nixon brought them into the realm of conventional dialogue.

It is true that the President cloaked most of the new provisions in the austere garb of puritan rhetoric, and assured the Congress and the country that his aim was "workfare not welfare." The measure included provisions for compulsory registration for work or training, in deference to the common myth that welfare recipients prefer idleness on welfare to jobs with good pay. The federal minimum was below the level paid in most states, and successive proposed amendments in Congress emasculated all parts of the bill which would have compelled the states to maintain former standards. It is also true that the President had to reassure the Congress that the aim of more welfare was to produce less welfare.

In this sense, the bill embodies the persistent intent of federal policy, which Gilbert Steiner describes in these words: "Welfare is a public business whose liquidation under honorable conditions has been a stated goal of political leaders from President Roosevelt to President Nixon." [23] It is debatable whether it is as revolutionary as it seemed. In the bill's stalemate in the Senate, the restrictive provisions have seemed to be expressive of the dominant theme. Its work provisions are designed more to appeal to the ethical beliefs of the affluent than to respond to the needs of the poor. As someone has commented, the effect of the compulsory job training programs would be to help acquaint people with the jobs they are out of.

Thus far, I have sought to identify some continuities in the recent history of governmental social welfare. These include the persistence of a solid core of poverty at the end of a period of unprecedentedly widespread governmental development of its welfare enterprise; failure to stem the tide of general discontent; concentration of problems among certain segments of the population; failure to find a solution to our problems of inequality; inability to agree on welfare proposals for the future. Others could be cited, but these are representative.

The result has been a considerable amount of disenchantment with the role of government in this sphere of activity. Some have gone so far as to suggest that efforts by government to deal with problems of poverty, dependency and inequality are doomed to futility, and probably can only make things worse.

In the concluding chapter of a recent book, Edward Banfield predicts that our problems will persist for at least twenty years before being overcome "by accidental forces of economic growth, demographic changes, a general upper-and-middle classification." Government's planned efforts to hasten or alter these forces are alleged to be doomed. [24]

Lowi refers to "a spectacular paradox." He states, "We witness governmental action of gigantic proportion to solve problems forthwith and directly. Yet we also witness expressions of personal alienation and disorientation increasing, certainly not subsiding, in frequency and intensity." [25]

Does our actual experience justify this feeling of futility? Can we only offer prescriptions to keep the patient comfortable until he dies or recovers? This would be a gloomy prospect, indeed, for there is nothing in our past experience to justify Banfield's faith in the possibility that "accidental forces" will take care of poverty and inujstice. Historically, such incidents just haven't happened.

There is a growing body of opinion which holds that our policy, while not one of neglect, benign or otherwise, should be focused on mitigating the harshness of alienation and exclusion, and of contenting ourselves with incremental inroads on the problems. This may well be a current reaction to the frustrations and alleged "failures" of the past decade.

First, what do we mean by "failure"? What are some of the factors which contribute to what we deem to be such failure?

The National Urban Coalition has suggested that "the American Malaise . . . has its roots in the distance between national ideal and national reality." [26] It would seem to be a question not so much that nothing has been accomplished as that we have expected much more. We can point to some solid achievements: more people receiving hospital care; more disabled persons rehabilitated to gainful employment; reduction of infant mortality; more adults enrolled in federally assisted programs. Even the much maligned programs of public assistance over the years have helped to keep many families intact. Social Security has made the difference for many older retired persons living on the margin of poverty. Service programs for children and older persons and for the disabled have helped. It is wrong to dismiss the efforts of the past decades since 1935 as utterly worthless and unproductive.

Paradoxical as it may seem, the very fact that more was being done has led to the frustration and disappointment. When people's expectations are raised, they become less tolerant of their condition, and more demanding. In the last decade, Gans suggests, "the traditional faith in the ability of private enterprise to run the nation's economy has declined, and people now routinely expect Government to be the solver of last resort of America's problems." [27]

The painful dilemma that becomes apparent in a discourse on governmental action on social problems is this: While we are more and more inclined to look to government, we are doing so with less and less faith in its remedies.

Where and how have our remedies fallen short? If we see the problem as one of a revolt of rising expectations, what has thwarted our efforts to achieve them? Several suggestions have been made by different analysts. Space permits only a summary treatment of this complex subject.

One is the failure to match promises with adequate support. The War on Poverty is an oft-cited example. Critics of this "war" acknowledge the success of many of the service programs, but point to the gap between promise and performance.

Another is our habit of working at cross purposes. Mitchell Ginsberg gave one of the most succinct statements on this point when he stated that the welfare system is designed to save money and people and tragically winds up doing neither. With reference to public housing, to look at another area of governmental action, Gilbert Steiner observes: "The ambivalence between a brick and mortar activity and a social welfare activity ends in castigation from the supporters of each who feel, quite properly, that the program has not made sufficient progress in either area." [28]

A program may have an excessive number of goals, some explicit and others implicit. A program may break down under the burden of a mission overload. Roland Warren makes this point with reference to the Model Cities program. He identifies the multiple goals as easing the protest situation among the blacks in the ghettos; a step toward more effective participation in decision-making "on the part of a population largely shut out from the sources of power"; "a foot in the door toward block grants and revenue sharing." He notes further that it was seen as a program to strengthen the mayor's office by giving him "some leverage over such programs as education and urban renewal and housing, and also by helping him to build up competency in social planning." [29]

Other explanations include the complicated relations between local and state officials and the federal bureaucracy, political obstacles, rooted in the deadlock of entrenched interests, poor choice of strategies, and others.

Probably, the difficulties are a compound of many of these elements. None of the authorities cited has sought to ascribe the entire problem to any single factor. But in combination, they delineate the difficult process of translating social goals into reality.

I believe that the crucial problem is and has been rooted in assumptions about the causes of dependency and about the reasons why people apply for aid.

What one believes to be the cause of the condition of poverty is crucial to the strategy chosen to respond to it. Whether the cause is seen as within the person himself, as the product of individual failure, or as "structural" in nature, due to the malfunctioning or nonfunctioning of the mechanism of society, will influence the choice of methods to meet the problem.

William K. Tabb has identified three types of change in welfare which compete for priority. These include as possible strategies: "(1) increase the efficiency of the operation and level of payments under the present system, (2) modify it to give more individualized attention to client needs within programs of rehabilitation, and (3) change the institutions which work to create dependence." [30] The first calls for a "caretaker function," the second focuses on rehabilitation rather than "protective caretaking," and the third demands "structural reform of institutions that create dependency." [31]

There is evidence that the struggle more and more involves tension between the underclass of poor and the urban working class. The latter, as

Rainwater notes, has nearly doubled its income in the past twenty years. He perceives the future as a mixed picture. The working class has become increasingly hostile toward the underclass, politically more conservative, and opposed to welfare measures that would help those under them rise more rapidly. But there has been in the past several years, in the underclass, and especially among the minorities who make up a disproportionate number of its members, a political ferment "that set in motion processes that do promise possible political success for them— the bare beginnings of a mobilization toward making the basic changes necessary if America is no longer to *have* poor people." [32]

I shall close out this section with a quotation from John Romanyshyn, which briefly and eloquently summarizes the nature and purpose of our past and present welfare system:

> The central idea of welfare is humanitarian regard for our fellow-man. This can be expressed in the form of benevolence that seeks to reduce suffering without upsetting class inequality. In this case we have an exchange system that allows us to dole out benefits to the poor and disadvantaged provided they do not claim these as rights or question the legitimacy of the reward system. Such a system functions to maintain a status-oriented society in which our very sense of self-esteem may require the denigration and even the annihilation of the personality of others.[33]

Public Welfare Goals and Prospects

We may now be, as the columnist Harry Ashmore suggests, "at a tender moment in the progression away from the old puritan concept that alms should be doled out only when the donor can be sure that the object of charity is suffering due punishment for his sins." [34]

Unfortunately, I don't see much evidence that this is the case. The pressures for welfare reform are still largely from people who want it to emerge with its restrictive features intact and its liberalizing provisions eliminated. We are still looking for scapegoats in the welfare machinery and in the people who run it. We continue to blame the poor for their condition of poverty.

I see no disposition now to face up to the requirements of money and energy to deal with the hard questions of poor schools in the inner city, worsening slums, limited employment opportunities, and the whole host of social problems of which we became so painfully aware in the 1960's.

I see little evidence of the political leadership which must be exercised to move us toward decent goals for 1993. Nor is there much sign of public pressure to force more leadership, or of a disposition to support it as it emerges.

It is true that poverty and welfare have made the front pages of the newspapers, and are featured in magazines and on radio and television. Social scientists, politicians, civic groups, labor leaders, industrialists, are giving problems of poverty and inequality a lot of attention.

But their words are losing their impact. The crackling sounds of discontent in time are tuned out by the tired listener. The words of the social scientist become increasingly bland to people's tastes. But the problems persist.

It would, however, be wrong to extrapolate the future from the present. We can always hope for a moral breakthrough. Instead of perceiving social policy as an appendage to economic development, we can hope for a day when we shall see social services as a right rather than as a collection of benefits offered under severely limited conditions and restricted in their application.

This will require a combination of increased political power for the disadvantaged and dispossessed with greater willingness than the middle and upper classes have ever shown to sacrifice at least a part of their self-interests in the service of a greater measure of equality.

I can see a number of goals toward which we could reach if such a breakthrough should occur.[35]

We can eradicate hunger and malnutrition. People were shocked when they first learned of its existence in this land of plenty but showed their ability to put it out of their minds, as their Congressmen argued over who should get a few meager offerings of food stamps.

We can eliminate poverty. We can provide a guaranteed minimum level of income which would ensure a decent living for all people. We can begin by investing the $11.4 billions which it is estimated would be required to raise all incomes about the present officially defined poverty level.[36]

We can provide useful work for those who cannot find it now. There is plenty to be done to provide more and better hospitals, parks, playgrounds, cultural centers, and to improve our ecology. There are services which could be performed in day care centers, youth programs, homemaker services, services for our older people, and in many other social services.

We can provide this employment under conditions that protect and promote the dignity and self-respect of the worker. We do not need to degrade the labor or impugn the character of the laborer by making him work out his relief check.

We can avoid the danger of converting public jobs into segregated employment by articulating our public employment with job development, training and placement in the private sphere of the economy.

We can provide day care centers for all families which want and need them. We can provide facilities that are designed for the nurture of the personality of the child, rather than simply as parking places for the children of working mothers.

We can establish goals for life in the later years which will make the extension of life a continuation of living. We can devise programs which will work to that end.

We can provide better services for the disabled. It is possible to design a better system for the provision and distribution of health care and for income protection during periods of disability.

We can provide a better structure of protective services for the vulnerable old, young, the disabled, and the chronically ill.

We can provide family planning services, visiting nurse services, consumer protection, and legal aid. We can even conquer the apparently intransigent problem of housing.

Obviously, these are not just social welfare problems and aims. They are just as relevant to other systems of education, civil rights, manpower, health, and tax reform. In fact, it is important that these systems exist in a symbiotic relation. It is vital to the welfare system that this be the case, if welfare is not to be used as a meager recompense for people damaged or neglected by failures in the larger society. In all of the systems, the aim must be structural reform of our social, political and social institutions.

The problem is not so much an intellectual as a political one. Good planning requires a rational approach, of conscious decisions arrived at with forethought. Marris and Rein have written: "No other nation organizes its government as incoherently as the United States. . . . Its policies are set to run a legislative obstacle race that leaves most reforms sprawling hopelessly in a scrum of competing interests." [37]

Political decisions should be helped by a mechanism for national social planning which will set goals, recommend policies, monitor progress, and recommend changes.

The central goal should be one of establishing a right to live for all the people, for the racially, ethnically, educationally, occupationally, and geographically disadvantaged. Freedom of choice and of movement should be a universal goal.

The crucial element is the will to act. The resources are potentially there if we develop the capacity to make political decisions to achieve our goals.

2

Child Welfare Services Goals for 1993

FRED DELLIQUADRI

To predict invites a curiosity to crystal-gaze, but to crystal-gaze with some degree of substance and more than possible success. To prophesy and to set goals in Child Welfare Services for the future demands a reassessment of one's own experience and educational pursuits; it necessitates a continued reflective thought process that searches out those highlights that have brought about positive and beneficial changes to the lives of children and youth and to their families.

In over thirty years of experience and education devoted to child welfare services, I have been most fortunate to occupy crucial and strategic positions at the state, federal and international levels; as well as several educational positions in schools of social work. Interspersed with these working positions was a continual representation on local, state, national and international committee assignments that brought me into contact and work with outstanding leaders in the helping professions, legislators, program developers, citizens and consumer groups, international representatives and young people. All of these situations afforded a specific and analytical experience in viewing programs for Child Welfare Services both in our own country and many countries throughout the world.

Given the circumstances that have surrounded my professional life, what then would I venture to predict for Child Welfare Services for 1993? Prophesying brings criticism and dialogue as it should; it can also lead to more constructive thinking in directing change that will result in a better and more useful life for all children.

It is impossible to think in terms of what's ahead for Child Welfare Services without taking note of the changes that will be taking place in our economic, social and political life. The broad programs that fall into these categories will dictate the type of society we will live in. Other parts of this book undoubtedly will deal with these great problems and issues in more detail. May I, however, allude here in a general way to those problems that must be solved in the next two decades if services to children and youth are to be fully realized.

For example, in the economic field the question of money—its use, its sufficiency, and its distribution both domestically and internationally—must be solved in order to eradicate poverty. I am presuming that our agonizing experience in the 60's and 70's dealing with the question of poverty and racism will be solved. We will look forward to: full employment and an adequate wage; a guaranteed annual wage for all workers; minimum income maintenance for individuals and families; adequate social insurance coverage for all the physically and mentally handicapped as well as for the aged and survivors; manpower planning in government and private enterprises that will ensure training to meet each individual's capacity and career potential; safety programs that will eliminate hazardous employment conditions; a controlled economy in prices, wages, investments, profits; elimination of discrimination in race and nationality in employment opportunities.

Again, in the area of the major social conditions we face problems and issues in the health, education and welfare fields that must be resolved:

A population control policy that is effective not only on the domestic scene but also internationally is needed. Due to the disastrous results from the lack of planning and control of our environment throughout the world, important steps to preserve life on earth will have to be taken by the United Nations and the individual countries of the world. One very effective control will be in population stabilization. By the end of the century or shortly thereafter, the world must reach a zero population growth level.

A housing and environmental policy that will resolve segregated neighborhoods, ghettos, slums; and urban as well as rural renewal plans to ensure community participation and sufficient appropriations to realize a healthy and wholesome environment for families and children.

A consumer posture that would permit all persons to make optional use of consumer education and research in all goods, foods necessary to maintain life.

A leisure-time planning mechanism in government and nongovernmental groups to enable people to make constructive use of their leisure time as the work week diminishes.

An educational system from preschool through higher education; vocational and rehabilitation service to all children and youth. A program and curriculum that is flexible, adaptable and geared to individual and community needs and satisfactions; such a system that stresses and makes available continuing and adult education programs for retraining, appreciation of the arts and recreational outlets.

A system of health services and treatment that ensures a distribution of facilities and manpower to cover children, families and other adults both in urban and rural areas. A system of health insurance will have been accepted. Much stress will be placed on preventive medicine and a system of diagnostic and periodic examinations from prenatal care throughout the life-span. Extensive research programs will have revealed the causes of ill health and adoption of means to prevent them.

In the above paragraphs I have been discussing very briefly the broad issues in the economic and social welfare fields that will have a direct bearing on the extent and need of programs for children in what we term Child Welfare Services. A delay or an inability to solve those problems will have its bearing on the type of social service system affecting children and youth.

Before devoting the remaining portions of this paper to Child Welfare Services, I want to cite the third broad area of deep concern—*the political.* Reference is especially made to men and women who are elected to political office throughout our governmental system. In the next two decades one will find a much higher proportion of women and youth in elective positions and in appointive posts and high leadership positions of the administrative hierarchy. The minority groups, having won the struggle for recognition and the elimination of discriminaton, will find themselves well represented throughout our democratic system both in government and in business and industry. One of the basic questions that will arise in years ahead is whether the division of our country into fifty states and over 3,000 counties and countless local subdivisions is in need of reassessment. Our modern world with all its invention in communication, travel, mobility and computerization will lead us toward the consideration of a more efficient and responsible means of governing. A calling of a national constitutional convention to make such a reassessment may be one of the most far-reaching steps our country has taken since its birth in 1776.

Historical Background

One can point to many events and developments since the beginning of the twentieth century that have influenced Child Welfare Services programs. Perhaps of greatest importance was the establishment of the U.S. Children's Bureau in 1912. Its work in investigating the conditions of children, its reports to Congress and the people; its influence on legislation both national and state affecting lives of children; its sponsorship of White House Conferences for Children each decade; its leadership in behalf of children all over the world all made it a bureau that commanded respect and prestige in the United States and throughout the world. Through its strong and vigorous leaders and extensive community support it was able to maintain a status above political interference and pressure. This wholesome and desirable place in the sun came to a sad ending in 1969 when the Nixon Administration came into power. By executive order of the Secretary of Health, Education and Welfare and support from the White House, the Children's Bureau was dismantled with some of its functions being transferred to the Public Health Service, some to Community Service Division of the Social and Rehabilitation Service, and part of the research function and a few services to a newly created Office of Child Development.[1] A bureau created by legislative mandate in 1912 was allowed to slide into oblivion without too much protest from legislative, professional or community groups. The protests that were made were not in sufficient numbers or influence to deter the administration in its plan to create a new Office of Child Development by executive order. Because of insufficient funds this new office is not off to an auspicious beginning. Whether the years ahead will see it continue in its present status is an interesting question. A new administration in future years may use its own prerogatives in reordering, refining or reorganizing the Office of Child Development.

The status and development of Child Welfare Services throughout the country is closely tied to the Washington scene. The confusion, the morale problem, lack of sufficient appropriations, has had a detrimental effect on program development, leadership, training and research funding in the Child Welfare field during the past several years.

Signs on the horizon already begin to show a restiveness with the present situation. For example, at the White House Conference on Children held in December, 1970, in Washington, D.C., there was an overriding concern for a more rigorous, highly visible children's agency. Many referred to the conditions in our country that preceded the establishment of the Children's Bureau in 1912; that here in the 1970's we must recapture the spirit and fortitude of those early years and again demand that an agency serving children be granted higher status in government. If need be, a cabinet post for families and children should be created.

In the Congress, bills are being introduced to provide more money for comprehensive child care services, adoptions, foster care, day care services and neighborhood development programs. How these survive the legislative process remains to be seen.

Because the White House Conference of 1970 made advocacy for children one of its highest priorities, already a division in the Office of Child Development has been created to implement this recommendation. Senator Abraham Ribicoff of Connecticut introduced a bill on "Child Advocacy" that will create a new thrust in developing programs and services for children. This bill follows the suggestions made by the Joint Commission on Mental Health of Children in their report to Congress in 1969. After four years of study which included the thinking and suggestions of the most searching minds in our country, from all fields and disciplines pertaining to children, a courageous challenge was made. It now appears in the book entitled *Crisis in Child Mental Health, A Challenge for the 1970's: A Report of the Joint Commission on the Mental Health of Children.*

The report has excellent documentation of the general problems as well as specific issues that confront our children today. Although there seemed to be little evidence of its use at the White House Conference on Children in 1970, in my opinion it is the type of report that can be used as a basis for planning for many years ahead. It proposes a shift in strategy for human development in this nation—"one which will deploy our resources in the services of optimizing human development." To carry out this objective three major missions are proposed in the report: (1) comprehensive services which will ensure the maintenance of health and mental health of children and youth, (2) a broad range of remedial health services for seriously disturbed, juvenile delinquents, mentally retarded, and otherwise handicapped children and their families, and (3) the development of an advocacy system at every level of government to ensure the effective implementation of these desired goals.

The work is excellent in presenting in detail these three broad areas of concern. Space and time do not permit broad elaboration but some comment on the third mission is indicated. The development of a "Child Advocacy System" is most strategic at this point in history and can well lay the groundwork to resolving many of the problems that face our children today. The Commission Report discusses at length the manner in which the "Child Advocacy System" should be established, organized, administered and financed. It recommends that the President appoint an *Advisory Council on Children* similar to the Council of Economic Advisors; and the establishment of state and local Child Development Councils. These, of course, must be properly staffed to carry out such responsibilities and basic functions at the national level as:

1. To study the problems of children and youth in the United States and to provide long-range planning, policy making, and programming for both service and manpower.
2. To advise the President as to the allocation of money for children.

3. To provide information about how agencies are working together.
4. To assess and evaluate programs, budgets, et cetera, to avoid duplication and achieve better utilization of resources.
5. To assess the relationship and functioning of federal, state, local and voluntary efforts and do so under specific and concrete recommendations that would challenge professional organizations to exercise better their public trust; to advise the President and Congress with respect to any needed changes and reordering of federal programs and funding in order to realize a more efficient operation of state and local programs.
6. To act as the Advocate at the federal level for children and their families.

In a like manner state councils would carry out similar functions as outlined for the National Council. Many of the above proposals were incorporated in the so-called "Mondale Bill," the "Comprehensive Child Development Act of 1971" which was offered as an Amendment to the Economic Opportunity Act of 1964. This bill was adopted by the Congress but vetoed by President Nixon.

Even so, because of its importance and the prospect that it will eventually become law in some form or other, it is well to make reference to the Statement of Findings and Purpose of this Act (S.1512).

1. Millions of American children are suffering unnecessary harm from the lack of adequate child development services, particularly during early childhood years.
2. Comprehensive child development, including a full range of health, education and social services are essential to the achievement of the full potential of American children . . . regardless of economic, social, and family background.
3. Children with special needs must receive special consideration . . . pending the availability of such program for all children, priority must be given to pre-school children with greatest economic and social need.
4. While no mother may be forced to work outside the home as a condition for using child development programs, such programs are essential to allow many parents to undertake part-time employment, training or education.
5. It is essential that the planning and operation of such programs be undertaken as a partnership of parents, community, and local government.

The above "findings" clearly show the concern and attitude of our Congress toward children, placing their problems at the highest priority. This is further enunciated in the following words of the purpose of the Act:

to provide every child with a fair and full opportunity to reach his full potential by establishing and expanding comprehensive child development programs and services designed to assure the sound and coordinated development of these programs, to recognize and build on the experience and success gained through the Headstart program and similar efforts, to furnish child development services for those children who need them most . . . to provide that decisions on the nature and funding of such programs be made at the community level with the full involvement of parents and other individuals and organizations in the community interested in child development, and to establish the legislative framework for the future expansion of such programs to universally available child development services.

The findings and purpose of this Act were indeed far-reaching and highly commendable. It marked a long struggle by some Congressmen, professional child welfare groups, and citizens' organizations to bring about such sweeping and needed legislation in behalf of children. Its principles provide a strong and firm base to planning for children in the United States for the next several decades. Even had the Act been signed into law it must be recognized that there would still be much work to be done to realize the full potential of such a "Comprehensive Child Development Act." For example:

1. *Funding*—provision in the bill called for an appropriation of $2,000,000,000 for fiscal year ending June 30, 1973; $4,000,000,000 for fiscal year ending June 30, 1974; and $7,000,000,000 for fiscal year ending June 30, 1975. These, indeed, are vast sums and an excellent beginning compared to the money presently available to furnish services and aid as outlined in the bill. But to guarantee to all our children a high quality and standard of programs and services the appropriation after 1975 undoubtedly would need to go beyond the figures cited above, provided the interest expressed by Congress and the people did not diminish.

2. *Organization Structure*—There always will be debate on what is the most effective structure to administer the provisions of a bill such as the "Comprehensive Child Development Act." One of the overriding concerns of the delegates to the White House Conference on Children in 1970 was centered on this very problem. In fact, of the sixteen major concerns voted upon by the delegates, "the establishment immediately of a cabinet post of Children and Youth to meet needs of all children" was ranked fourth highest. In expressing this priority the delegates said:

We strongly recommend that the President and Congress immediately establish a Department of Children and Youth at Cabinet level, responsible directly to the President of the United States. This Department with heavy youth involvement at policy level, would encompass all Federal agencies and institutions dealing with children and youth; would present and protect the needs and rights of children and youth; and would set standards and monitor all federal, state and local programs serving the needs of children. This Department is needed because children have not received the attention due them in our society under the existing fragmented organizational structure.

I was one of the delegates to sponsor and support a Cabinet-level post for children and youth and I foresee such a department operating and functioning successfully by 1993.

The agency that administers a Comprehensive Child Development Act should be at the highest level of government where it is highly visible, prestigious and powerful. Lost, as it would be, in the Department of Health, Education and Welfare, it would not achieve its full effectiveness. The history of the Children's Bureau and now the Office of Child Development attests to the difficulty in accomplishing the goals for children if these offices are permitted to exist at sub-Cabinet level, as is now the case with their placement in Health, Education and Welfare.

The Child Advocacy concept which was highlighted at the White House Conference on Children, and to which I have referred previously in this chapter, is another illustration of the need to achieve Cabinet status for the federal office having responsibility for the affairs of children and youth in the United States. The delegates at the White House Conference voted the need for a child advocacy system as number eight in a list of sixteen top priority items. The Nixon Administration has already moved to implement this recommendation by restructuring the Office of Child Development and, as of July, 1971, a National Center of Child Advocacy was established in the Office of Child Development. It is commendable that this action has been taken as a means of implementing the recommendations and priorities of the White House Conference on Children. It will focus on three missions:

1. A Children's Concern Center which will accept inquiries and statements of concern from any parent, any citizen about matters concerning children.
2. A Secretariat which will draw together all available information about children and children's programs.
3. A Division of Vulnerable Children who "need continuing advocacy 365 days a year."

The Office of Child Development is located in the Office of the Assistant Secretary for Administration in the Department of Health, Education and Welfare. At such a sub-level Cabinet position, it does not have the freedom of operation, the high visibility, the budget that is absolutely essential to make it a strong advocate for children. As a result its potential effectiveness is greatly diminished. To remedy this weakness and pending the eventual establishment of a Cabinet-level Department for Children and Youth, a movement should take place to follow the recommendation of the Joint Commission Report on the Mental Health of Children by the establishment of a National Council on Child Development in the Office of the President.

Another influence on child welfare service is the proposed Family Assistance Program that has been discussed in Congress for the past two years. When enacted it will have accomplished the separation of income maintenance and social services, the need for which has plagued the present public welfare system for so many years. The income features of public welfare programs will be administered on a federal basis similar to the program now being administered by the Social Security system. The social service programs will be administered on a state and local basis under a variety of organizational patterns. In order to receive federal funding, state and local governing bodies will need to develop master plans that ensure social services for all children who need them.

The passage by Congress of some form of Family Assistance Plan has been delayed because of the inability to resolve some basic issues pertaining to the level of the guaranteed minimum income, work requirements for women and children, and administrative jurisdiction between the states and federal government. Because all segments of the population have expressed a serious desire for welfare reforms, Congress will act. Final action may not come until after the presidential election of 1972. Welfare reform will be one of the critical issues of the campaign and it is well that it should be. The lives of some fifteen million children who live in poverty or near poverty will be affected.

The eventual passage of both the Family Assistance Program, including social service provisions, and a Comprehensive Child Development Act will bring to a focus programs for children and youth at the local and neighborhood levels. Above all, it will mean coordinated planning by governmental, voluntary, citizen, youth, and consumer groups in the development and administration of programs.

The social service programs for children and youth will continue to stress preventive, protective, treatment, remedial and rehabilitative services. The years ahead will accelerate the emphasis on the preventive services that will aid in diminishing and eliminating the causes of dependency, neglect, delinquency and the emotional and physical factors which disadvantage a child. The latter can be more easily realized if sufficient funds become available for training and research to bring our higher educational facilities and program operations into closer and continuing harmonious relationship.

At this point a listing of the activities and services that constitute a comprehensive child welfare services program will give us the perspective we need to evaluate and project ahead: community coordinating and organizing services; advocacy services; family, marital and premarital services; emergency services; family planning; early detection of problems; services to unwed mothers; consumer education; legal services; parent education; safety campaign; recreation and leisure-time services; special services to the economically disadvantaged; special services to minority groups; specialized services for children with psychological and physical handicaps; school social services; vocational and educational counseling; day care; foster care and adoption; protective services; juvenile and family court services; probation and parole services; homemaker services; information, referral and communication services.

The writer does not intend to dwell on the analyses and details of each of the above-listed programs. All are of high priority and essential to every community. Whether or not they can be established and operating in the near future will depend on the outcome of some of the economic, political and social policy considerations that have been dealt with throughout this paper. To close this discussion I want to deal briefly with two additional factors: the manpower situation in social service and our international commitment to children throughout the world.

Personnel

A personnel policy that ensures an adequate supply of professional and nonprofessional workers is a key factor in operating and maintaining the numerous programs that constitute Child Welfare Services.

The painful struggles that characterized the attempt during the 60's and 70's to specify what are social services and who should deliver them will be resolved in the next two decades. Because child welfare services have depended and will continue to depend on a broad sweep of personnel, they will reap the benefits of a personnel system providing highly satisfactory services to people who need them. The professional worker, the paraprofessional worker, the volunteer and the consumer will all fit in a pattern of services delivery that will be understood and accepted by the community and the professions. Monies to ensure adequate and sufficient services will be assured. Most of it will come through various schemes developed under public auspices. *The guiding principle for children as well as other segments of our population will be that those who need services must receive them at the highest quality standards that have been developed.*

To achieve the goals that I have cited will demand that the helping professions, which include social work, develop a crash plan—a plan that will continue to assess the needs and conduct training programs that will ensure the skills needed to serve people. Social work will have resolved the types of training and development required in the social service career ladder (professional, subprofessional, volunteer and etc.).

The helping professions (social work, medicine, nursing, education) will have achieved a training program design that will make use of a common knowledge basis in both undergraduate and graduate training programs, as well as continuing educational programs.

The emphasis in meeting and encountering the social and economic problems that confront children and their families will need to move rapidly in the preventive areas. Treating the problems that hinder the child's development will of necessity be continued; but emphasis will shift at an accelerated rate to the prevention of problems and handicaps. Getting at the root of the problem—the causes and resolving them—will be the order of the day. The sophistication of our planning, research, evaluation in all the professional fields will enable us to realize the benefits of preventive programs.

Thus, education will greatly emphasize the preventive; but at the same time highly skillful personnel will continue to treat and remedy the ills that affect children and adults. In addition, personnel will be in sufficient supply to meet the research demands; the planning and management of social welfare activities.

It must be stressed that all of this implies the continued need for professional schools such as those of social work. Like many professional schools, schools of social work will become great research centers devoted to probing and investigating causes of society's ills; planning and demonstration centers. We will witness a much closer relationship between the social sciences and the physical and biological sciences that strive to understand man's problem and to alleviate the obstacles that delay or obstruct the achieving of a good life for all.

The manpower problem in delivering services to children and families will need the closest attention by management. The evidence is abundantly clear as to the range of personnel that is needed to man a given service. However, we have not satisfactorily come to grips or found solutions to the types of jobs or activities to be performed, the type of training programs demanded and the cost entailed in these total operations. Research, evaluation and demonstration by educational facilities and operating programs can provide the answers if sufficient funding is forthcoming from governmental and nongovernmental sources. In this regard the helping professions can and must provide a vigorous and continuing leadership.

World Planning for Children

At this juncture let me turn to the international situation. What we accomplish domestically for child welfare services must be reflected in world planning. It is my feeling that in the next two decades we will witness a more cooperative and realistic attention to world planning, if only for the sheer necessity of controlling wars and the environment in order for man to exist on this earth. The United Nations in its first decades of operation has been characterized as a forum and a deliberative body. The nations have shown a willingness to come together but lack the authority and strength of power to control and prevent wars and enforce its proclamations and findings. The United Nations' structure, its functions, power and authority must be reassessed in order to give the world body the strength, prestige and respect it needs to perform its basic function in keeping the peace and promoting human development.

Of the many facets of the United Nations, the agency that devotes its activities to children and youth is UNICEF (United Nations International Children's Emergency Fund). Because of its outstanding work in dealing with displaced, homeless children in the years following World War II, it became the permanent world agency for children. As the U.S. representative to this august body for eight years during the 60's, I was able to see at first hand amazing and constructive activities performed in over one hundred developing countries in the fields of nutrition, maternal and child health, disease control, social services, education, vocational training, and community development.

The UNICEF program has been so significant that it was awarded the Nobel Peace Prize in the year 1965. What is most unfortunate about UNICEF is the lack of sufficient funds to carry out its program on a broader scale so that developing countries can look to it for comprehensive planning and program implementation for children.

UNICEF has had a budget in the neighborhood of $54,000,000 for the past several years. Approximately 20 per cent of this money comes from voluntary contributions of nongovernmental sources such as trick-or-treat campaigns (e.g., U.S. Halloween activities) and Christmas card sales. The remaining 70 per cent is derived from one hundred governments throughout the world. The U.S. contribution for the last five years has been $13,000,000 annually.

A campaign is now under way to aspire to a goal of $100,000,000 by 1975. To double its budget in the next three years is most significant on the face of it. But in reality the sum is minuscule for world planning and program implementation in the developing countries.

As I keep implying throughout this paper, we must take giant steps in world planning. Nations, especially the United States, must in the decades ahead take more seriously an international commitment to the betterment of human life throughout the world. The most significant input can be made in behalf of children. UNICEF as the children's arm of United Nations should have an operating budget in terms of billions of dollars, not millions, as is the case today. An immediate step to be taken at this time would be the convening of a World Conference on Children. This might well begin by having the general assembly of the United Nations devote its entire agenda for its opening session to children. Such a commitment would necessarily say to the people of the world, our highest priority today is our children—their development and well-being. The resolution passed by the general assembly of the United Nations in November, 1959, called "The Declaration of the Rights of the Child" will then become a reality. It is important as I bring this paper to a close to do so by quoting the U.N. resolution as the goal we must achieve in in the next two decades.

1. The first of these needs is a name and a nationality, in other words, an equal civil status for every child at birth, regardless of the nature of the union between the parents.
2. Then comes the need for maternal protection, for love and understanding in the home. A child of tender years should not be separated from his mother.
3. A child has special needs with respect to health. From the time of conception, both mother and child should be protected against disease. A child that is sick should be treated.
4. Adequate food and shelter are basic needs. The child needs a diet that meets his specific requirements at different ages. He should live in a house that shelters him against the rigors of the climate.
5. Education is an essential need of the child, specifically the kind of education that will help him to develop the knowledge, judgment, and social and moral values to play his proper role in society when he has become an adult.
6. The child's need for play and recreation is explicitly recognized.
7. The child needs social protection if he is to enjoy the rights and liberties to which he is entitled without discrimination or distinction on account of race, color, creed, language, opinions, origin, or status.
8. The child needs to be protected from work at too early an age and from exploitation when he is old enough to work.
9. Finally, there are the special needs of physically, mentally, and socially handicapped children. Orphans, for example, must be placed under the protection of society, and other handicapped children must receive the special care and training they require.

3

Looking Backward From 1993: Services for Youth

HERBERT MILLMAN and ALVIN KOGUT

The planners were feeling mildly optimistic by the spring of 1993. In the face of the desperate nature of circumstances in the previous decades, partisan interests had been submerged and greater reliance had been placed on their skills. By 1993, signs of progress began to appear.

Fish were reappearing in Long Island Sound and in some of the inland waterways. The hospitalization rate for inhalation of noxious gases began to dip. Transportation technology advances were bringing greater sanity and comfort to air and ground traffic. The ability to mass-produce housing at low cost guaranteed the success of the "new towns." Perhaps most important of all, the birth rate had leveled off, somewhat downward from the average of the peaks and valleys of the previous decades.

Yes, by 1993, the country was entering a period of relative calm. It had weathered the turbulent storms of the late 70's and early 80's when personal existence was perilous and the question of survival itself was at issue. With the intervention of social and economic planners, called into service reluctantly and late, the country was beginning to move forward.

Generally speaking, the planners had been right in their feeling that society could manage the technical problems. By the last decades of the century, industry was no longer dependent on power lines, rail terminals, deep water harbors, or even heavy concentrations of workers as in the old cities. Decentralization, atomic fuel and cybernetic systems had come into general usage.

The progressive application of sophisticated scientific knowledge lifted the capacity for productivity to a point which required government intervention to protect against glutting of the market. Even sharply curtailed workdays and workweeks were insufficient steps to control overproduction. There was growing, if reluctant, recognition that only a limited number of skilled and motivated workers were required to operate the industries up to the level of need. By 1993, it was already necessary for local, state and national governmental units to cope with the reality that "full employment" as previously defined had become an anachronism, a realization that continues to unfold in all of its ramifications.

But even by 1993, efforts were being made to cope with this reality. A series of social welfare measures, including extensive social insurance coverage, family allowances and income guarantees, made it possible for those not engaged in production to live reasonably well. The recipient of social funds was viewed in a new light; the stigma that had been associated with government assistance for more than four hundred years had to a large extent disappeared.

The possibilities of greater individual choice about work and/or leisure, linked to an income floor based on entitlement, helped remove some of the distrust and anger between races and ethnic groups in the competition for resources and status. Intense ethnic parochialism, fed by discrimination and oppression, which in the late 1960's and early 1970's had expressed itself in separatist trends, tended to dissipate as successive layers of articulate middle-class leaders were incorporated into the establishment. In politics, integration tended to be the rule, while in the primary relationships—family and friendship groups—people generally preferred to remain within their own group. Thus, new expressions of cultural pluralism began to unfold as a result of the security floor which had been placed under all in respect to free choice and equality of treatment. Social psychologists specializing in intergroup relations who had puzzled over the phenomenon of persisting ethnicity over the years, began to accept this as a given by 1993.

Helpful as the planners were in the technical and economic sectors, they continually underestimated the difficulties involved in predicting human behavior. Theories that postulated rational response out of self-interest seemed to apply at certain times and not at others. For example, in 1993, as before and after, insufficient numbers reacted seriously to dire warnings about tobacco, alcohol and drugs. It was difficult, if not impossible, to identify the variables involved in the formulation of individual choices. Many pondered why, in the midst of affluence—in the midst of a society that offered hitherto unknown material comfort and care—there was a need for self-destruction. Could it be something inherent in the human condition?

Among the most stubborn problems were those associated with youth.

The vulnerability to changing conditions and the differential impact of societal contexts on that age group had led to a number of shifts in approach to services to youth by the year 1993.

Youth in the Social Context

The post-technological society that emerged in the 1980's tended to reduce pressure in some areas for youth but heightened it in others. On the negative side, observers cited the fact that the psychological and emotional needs of the young motivated them to struggle for identity and independence. The impersonalization that stemmed from technology— the increasing lack of intimate face-to-face relationships—worked in the opposite direction. Adolescents, more than ever, appeared to need closer ties with peer groups to overcome the isolation and loneliness felt as one moved away from parents spatially or emotionally. Yet, even by 1993 society offered little in the way of structured opportunities for satisfying the need for meaningful personal relationships.

From 1973 to 1993 and beyond, observers also noted that much of the population, and youth in particular, displayed many signs of irritation and anger, and engaged in irrational behavior in almost cyclical fashion. Neither the feeling tone nor the behavior could be traced to any identifiable cause. Researchers were gradually concluding that overcrowding and lack of privacy were connected, in some way, with these outbursts. Biologists theorized that the human organism was predisposed to tolerate crowding only up to a certain level. To what extent, asked the planners, could the level be raised by socialization and communication techniques?

Different locations in the social structure continued to engender different modes of coping. The division of youth into those who were born into or became part of the intellectual elite (or the "meritocratic" establishment as it had come to be known) and those that occupied roles of lesser status became a principal cleavage among the youth, rather than previous racial divisions which had been primary. The anti-meritocratic, anti-establishment movement became an important arena of activity for many deprived youth. Some were readily identifiable in the streets and elsewhere since they habitually shaved their heads and bodies (presumably to protest against hairy parents). Others sought to voice their protests through cultural outlets; music, drama, films and clothing carried the strong stamp of youthful protest.

Even though the contextual changes that had emerged between 1973 and 1993, as demonstrated above, were considerable, the family as an institution continued to reflect resiliency. In the main, it continued to perform its nurturing and supportive functions. Roles, however, to some degree were shifting. More and more female parents reacted to the progressive flexible male-female roles and, aided through the provision of day care centers and the availability of broader education and career opportunities, were able to choose between home and employment, either part-time or full-time. Cooperatives, communal dining rooms and "home helps" also facilitated the process.[1]

A few observers, partial to the "new" life-styles of the late 1960's and early 1970's, had somewhat prematurely speculated on the fact that other institutions, such as the communes, would soon replace the traditional family structure. The forecasts were not borne out; not only did the family prove tenacious, but the experimental communes of the twentieth century proved no more hardy than their predecessors of the nineteenth century. Despite the identifiable weaknesses of the monogamous structure, no workable alternative, one that could meet people's emotional, social and cultural needs, had developed. Rather, the basic tendency had been for supportive institutions and services to shore up family life. Thus, while at one point in time (approximately 1970–1973), some of the younger generation, reacting against the institutions and life-styles of the establishment, challenged the traditional family and bypassed the marriage relationship, eventually the overwhelming majority sought satisfaction in the traditional relationships. The experience of the U.S.S.R. revealed a similar cycle in its early years. Overly permissive behavior in regard to responsibility for child-rearing, the marriage relationship and divorce was found to be dysfunctional and abandoned.

This is not to suggest that behavior did not change. The perfection of birth control devices, the discovery of new drugs to combat venereal disease, the prevalence of sex education at an early age, and the more accepting atmosphere had more or less finished off the sex-as-sin syndrome by the 1990's. The youth felt much freer in this realm than previously and sexual behavior ceased to be a public issue. However, when attachments were strong, and when the rearing of children was contemplated, an inclination toward marriage and family asserted itself. Disproportionate divorce rates among the young did, however, remain a conspicuous problem.

While public anxiety over freer sexual behavior among young people continued to diminish over the years between 1973 and 1993, the problem of drug abuse was quite another matter. The actual extent and depth of the problem had never really been measured; reliable data simply didn't exist. The situation became increasingly serious, and though the government tried to cope with the situation in a number of ways, its efforts were futile. Law enforcement efforts accomplished little. Hard drugs continued to be readily available in the streets, while large numbers of students obtained marihuana with little effort. It was this inability to enforce the laws as much as any other reason that induced the legislators to alter these at last to the extent of classifying "addiction" as a medical problem.

Categorizing addiction and drug abuse as a medical problem enhanced the role of the Public Health Service in the drug area. The residential treatment centers, halfway houses and detoxification centers, private and public, were brought under its jurisdiction. And although the overwhelming majority of users of these services might be classified as "youth," the social welfare planners felt that services ought to be located in the health system because of the technical nature of some of the treatment programs. It had become painfully clear that to continue to concentrate on the treatment of the addict without any serious efforts toward primary prevention and toward protecting the community would be disastrous.

Government tried to cope with the situation in a number of ways. In line with the newly established medical approach, it made addictive drugs available without cost at local clinics and health stations under the supervision of physicians. The motivation seemed to have more to do with crime reduction than with treatment. Secondly, more elaborate attempts to arrest and prosecute pushers and addicts were inaugurated. Secret squads of narcotics agents, created outside of the regular law enforcement channels, attempted to penetrate the drug supplier networks. However, what turned out to be most helpful in the long run was the discovery of anti-opiate type drugs by the public health chemists in 1988. Within a few months after the use of these antagonists, which provided nonaddictive but euphoria-producing substitutions to opiates, methadone and other addictive chemicals, positive results became evident.

By this time, too, more and more young people, some ex-addicts, assumed responsibility for the operation of drug treatment and prevention programs. They functioned as board members, counselors, group leaders and aides. Addicts Anonymous succeeded under youth leadership in recruiting thousands of volunteers to work with the addicts along the same lines that Alcoholics Anonymous had used with alcoholics. Others, operating out of youth centers and settlements, emulated the older settlements and actually founded settlements in the midst of neighborhoods in trouble, to try to reverse the process of communal disorganization. In some instances they were successful in building youth cultures to counter the subcultures oriented to artificially induced mind-bending experiences that had an appeal for certain portions of the young population.

On the college campus fundamental changes had taken place during the twenty years prior to 1993. The vigorous protests by segments of college youth that had erupted during the late 1960's and which continued in sporadic and enfeebled form in the early 70's, seemed to evaporate entirely during the 1980's. An analysis of some of the key social factors that precipitated the student revolts sheds some light on why they ran the particular course that they did.

In the first place, they were not rooted in any balanced, realistic appraisal of the nature of society and the class forces involved. The lack of long-term perspective and the failure to develop any sustained ties with more stable forces outside the student movement precluded continuity and sustained effort. (After all, one was a student for a relatively short period of time.) Consequently, although some concessions were won, feelings of powerlessness and defeatism began to permeate the movement and activists began to abandon the struggle in favor of private concerns.

Actually, a number of objective changes—changes which by and large represented an extension of the welfare state into the 1970's and 1980's —tended to undermine the earlier militancy. At the same time, the schools had been made more democratic over the years: student participation in decision-making, greater freedom of choice with regard to curriculum, the elimination of marks, open admission, and the like. But, more important, by 1993 the connection between government, industry and education had changed.

The technological growth following World War II, accelerated by the launching of Sputnik by the U.S.S.R., altered the role of the university from preservation of social status or even as enabling social mobility to feeding the needs of a more complex societal system based on an advanced technology. Just as government and industry increasingly demanded a higher level of knowledge and research in the 1980's, so did the challenges of a more intellectualized society stimulate competition in cultural development.

Of more significance, achievement increasingly replaced ascribed status in the marketplace; the college years were no longer simply a *rite de passage*. The new meritocracy demanded talent and hard work.

At the same time, extension of the societal insurances and family allowances, discussed earlier, largely eliminated the barriers between work and education. Free tuition and the payment of a small salary for doing a student's work removed the adolescent dependence on the family and afforded public recognition that his work was important.

Student bodies became more diffused, as a variety of separate centers of learning developed. Students received their education at technical centers, at laboratories, at colleges under the auspices of private industry, as well as at traditional public and private universities. By 1993, then, one could move without too much difficulty between the world of work and the world of education; young people satiated with the student role accepted jobs, knowing they could return quite easily to their studies.

Thus, education became a never-ending process. People of all ages shuttled back and forth between employment and education.

Despite the fact that many of its citizens would have benefited greatly from a modern system of social services, no serious attempt at planning such a system was made in the United States until the late 70's. Somewhat earlier, a critic of the social services had pinpointed their deficiencies quite clearly: Many of the existing service agencies and network were the result of "historical accidents" rather than planning; they were created by groups of citizens who had evinced a special interest in a particular problem or category of people. (Many of these philanthropic endeavors were able to continue by shifting functions and altering goals over the ensuing years.) The services offered were fragmented, disconnected, understaffed, and often not related to the needs of the potential recipient. Where appropriate, they were generally in short supply. Mental hospitals, correctional systems and services connected to the public assistances carried stigma, while the nonstigmatic services, as represented by the Family Service and Child Welfare agencies in the voluntary sector, offered highly specialized services.[2]

The ordinary person could hardly negotiate the system in the sense of reaching the right place; no systematic way of channeling people to the appropriate service existed. To a very minor extent, the effort to cope with this was the development of about a thousand or so Neighborhood Service Centers that emerged under the aegis of the Economic Opportunity Act of 1964. (By contrast, the British and the French had institutionalized easy access to services much earlier.) [3]

Social Services for Youth

Looking backward to the 1970's, social services for youth were really the product of three separate, although overlapping, streams of development: the sectarian agencies, the settlements, and the government. By and large, all had come to recognize that "youth," designated as those between the ages of sixteen and twenty-five by the White House Conference on Children of 1970 and 1980, represented a particular stage of the life cycle and consequently had special developmental tasks. The Young Men's Christian Associations and the Young Men's Hebrew Associations and their female counterparts originated out of concern for what would happen to young people as they left their homes and responded to the opportunities for jobs in the growing urban centers. Would their characters be destroyed by new temptations? These "leisuretime" agencies offered socializing, educational and recreational types of activities aimed at building character and sectarian consciousness.

Looking even further back into history, the settlement movement, beginning in New York City in 1886, and in London a decade earlier, was part of the emerging reform stream of the time; it was a response to societal conflicts arising from industrialization and sharpened class conflict. The settlements pioneered in the use of the friendshp club, the small group experience, the functioning of the democratic community in microcosm. The education, recreation and play movements of the early 1900's influenced the settlement program. John Dewey and "progressive education" contributed to the understanding of the potential for developing social growth through personal interaction in guided group experiences.

Government efforts, on the other hand, did not focus on leisure-time activities but on more pressing matters. The Civilian Conservation Corps and the National Youth Administration of the 1930's provided some income for young people in the great depression, even though minimal. The Neighborhood Youth Corps and the Job Corps of the 1960's offered training of sorts along with the minimal income. Vista and the Peace Corps offered opportunities for more idealistic youth. Alarmed by the rise in street violence after World War II, governments at state and local levels created Youth Boards which sponsored street workers, recreational programs and other activities. In the 1960's, the President's Commission on Youth Crime and Delinquency funded more sophisticated anti-delinquency programs in sixteen cities, Mobilization for Youth among them.[4]

Toward a Clarification of Goals

An examination of agency programs and goal statements indicates that some of the trends that were discernible in the 1970's continued to gather momentum and were formally recognized in the Social Services legislation passed in 1983. Trends in youth services already expressed in the 1970's and earlier were clearly identified in the 1983 legislation as: (1) growing participation by the young people themselves in the decision-making process and in the delivery of the services, (2) greater acceptance by society generally of the right and ability of young people to engage in autonomous efforts, and (3) increased concern with the problems of the urban ghetto and minority groups.[5]

The deepening of these trends in the ensuing decade was accompanied and nourished by the clarification of goals:

1. To encourage youth to share and play a fuller role in the shaping of society.
2. To aid them in their self-development as influencers of social goals.
3. To improve environmental conditions affecting youth adversely.
4. To provide rehabilitative services where needed.

These were the shared aims of the youth-serving agencies whether under governmental or volunteer auspices.

The Social Services Act of 1983 established a network of universal services funded completely from federal general revenues. While the means test was not completely eliminated in the nation, its role became significantly circumscribed, and the test itself was simplified considerably. The first-line contact for most users of service and the nucleus of the system was the Neighborhood Services Center. The centers, established in all neighborhoods with a population of over 5,000 people, were intended to serve all classes in an informal atmosphere. Conceivably, one would use the center with the same ease with which one visited a library or a post office. Staffed by professionals, paraprofessionals, and volunteers, the centers offered information and advice, served as a link to other institutions and agencies, supplied advocates and made referrals to more specialized agencies when the situation warranted it. The services were comprehensive, and although the funding was federal, the centers themselves were administered locally. The act specified the mode of operation and the standards that would have to be complied with to make the locality eligible for funds.[6]

The Social Services Act established a parallel network of Neighborhood Youth Centers that performed similar functions for youth, but geared to the special needs of youth. Many communities debated as to whether or not the youth centers should be located in the same setting as the Neighborhood Service Centers, or be adjacent to them, or be separated completely. The issue has not yet been resolved and each community continues to make its own decision. Those in favor of separate locations argued that youth services ought to have an identity of their own while their opponents pointed to overlapping concerns (such as family problems and the need for close working relationships). By 1993, it was clearly demonstrated that young people themselves could staff the youth centers working closely with professionals and a board which reflected community composition. Youth organizations and youth movements served as a recruiting group for center personnel.

The relationship of the youth center to the community was a key factor in understanding its success. Decentralizing the service system while at the same time insisting on standards gave sufficient flexibility to the centers so that by and large they reflected community styles, and class and ethnic composition. The location of the centers, as well as their staffing patterns, encouraged neighborhood feelings of proprietary interest. It allowed the centers to draw not only on community resources in general, but, in many instances, on identifiable connections between consumers, their friends and their families for helping purposes. The centers provided a wide range of services and a "door on which to knock"; they also functioned as coordinators of youth services and filled "gaps in service."

On still another level, the relationship to community enhanced the ability of the centers to render assistance to the user of services. Hitherto, the concept of "treating" individuals had pervaded the helping professions to such an extent that patients were readily removed from their surroundings for helping purposes, thus destroying their ties with relatives, friends and others. Now, as the individual began to be defined somewhat differently as inseparable from his roles and relationships, new modes of helping developed. It was found that, for most, the closer one remained to the real world within which he ordinarily functioned, the more accessible he became to assistance; and at the same time others became involved in the process as well. In cases of serious impairment, the centers made use of the specialized and professional services available at the next level of the service hierarchy.

The centers provided direct asistance in a number of key social welfare areas: counseling, manpower and corrections services. Peer groups, found to be the most effective way of working with adolescents, became the mainstay of the counseling division, handling personal and family problems (e.g., problems of relationship, emotional difficulties of various types, drug abuse, etc.). Individual counseling supported the peer group experience and helped to monitor the service. Whenever deemed helpful, entire families were brought directly into the process by the youth center staff, while at other times liaison was maintained by arrangements with the adult center staff. The process, while only occasionally led directly by professionals, was periodically reviewed by the most skilled staff. Prolonged contact with individuals continued long after they left the group.

Centers maintained crisis intervention units and residential facilities and remained open twenty-four hours a day. There were options as to whether the consumer would live in on a full-time basis or remain for occasional evenings, days or weekends. Publicity and "reaching-out" campaigns constantly reminded the neighborhood of the services available. Schools, courts, police and other community institutions made referrals to the centers.

The manpower division of the youth centers maintained close contact with potential employers as well as with government agencies staffing public service jobs. If they so chose, users could utilize testing facilities and enlist in training programs to develop employment skills. Intensive follow-up programs helped the inexperienced through the early stages of employment. (The beginning weeks and months previously took a large toll because of the demands of an unaccustomed life-style, boredom, and the inability to envision any long-range satisfaction.) Somehow the manpower division, by having a number of job placements at its disposal, was able to overcome the ritual of training young people for non-existent jobs or equipping them with obsolete skills in the interest of industrial discipline.

By 1993, after more than half a century of experimentation with juvenile correctional systems, authorities began to recognize that there were agencies better suited to redirecting the conduct of delinquent youth than the juvenile court, or the traditional probation and parole systems. As far as possible, violators were worked with by nonjudicial agencies close to where they lived, and in a setting calculated to avoid stigma. It had been found that violators, after having internalized negative definitions of themselves, were far less susceptible to rehabilitative treatment.

Although police, courts and others referred violators to the centers on a voluntary basis, there was an authoritative ring about the arrangement that provoked considerable discussion, since the centers, if they deemed it advisable, had the power to refer back to the courts. The issue of how authority might be blended with voluntary rehabilitation was never resolved. The centers provided group and individual counseling, recreational activities and special educational programs for young people in trouble. They were also able to draw upon the job-training and job-placement services of the manpower division. And finally, the centers had supervised residences and foster home placements at their disposal.

While technology, particularly the computerized information and retrieval systems, improved the delivery of concrete services (as in health, housing, employment), the assistance it offered to those dealing with psychological and emotional problems turned out to be quite limited. It was not yet possible to type in symptoms at a remote terminal and then utilize the diagnosis that returned in a split second. Nor did the early expectations, that computerized predictions of potential family and individual breakdown would serve as a basis for programs of "primary prevention," come to fruition. Researchers pointed out that the computers could only reflect the existing level of knowledge, that a more refined conceptualization of the field was needed (which in this instance meant, among other things, a meaningful etiology of "mental illness," a stage not yet reached).

A breakdown of the frequency of utilization of services for 1992 indicated that the bulk of the users consisted of youth using centers and their extensive facilities for socializing and recreational purposes. Living in a post-technological society, if anything, highlighted the fact that basic human needs still had to be met. Consensus existed on the proposition that, more than ever, youth needed opportunities to develop friendships, to grow, to explore sex and to develop an identity of their own.

While overlapping existed in 1993 between the services offered by the voluntary youth agencies and the government-operated Neighborhood Youth Centers, the voluntary sector continued to emphasize the special purpose goals of their sponsors. The division of labor between the public and voluntary sectors could be described as follows: the public sector concentrated on the universal and more concrete type of service while the voluntary agencies stressed specialized programs—ethnic, cultural, problem-solving and/or special interest. Many took advantage of services and programs under both sectors. Again, aspects of cultural pluralism became possible within the framework of universal provision. Thus, youth agencies and programs provided under the auspices of ethnic and religious groups, as well as national youth organizations, augmented and filled out the services under public auspices with substantial interaction and communication.

The more interested and sophisticated youth were more likely to frequent the voluntary agencies, where they probed their origins and traditions, explored the meaning of life, participated in artistic endeavors and the performing arts, and generally tested themselves in relationships. Many of the agencies, striving to provide opportunities for youth to express their idealism and to pioneer, organized advanced versions of the Vista and Peace Corps programs of the late 1960's. Young men and women, living in a society that had overcome the problem of basic survival, saw a good portion of the world still struggling and desired to participate. (Actually, it was only the technically trained youth that the underdeveloped countries wanted.) Some of the adventurous joined training units designed to prepare volunteers to man one of the space stations.

Activities that, in some way, brought people closer to nature continued to grow in popularity. While many enjoyed camping and hiking, others, seeking a more prolonged and intense experience, would band together to form a cooperative or commune with the intent of spending a year or two in some remote area. Much staff time went into obtaining scarce unpopulated areas for settlements and in preparing the group for a totally unfamiliar experience. The idea of living off the land had a nostalgic and romantic appeal, but the difficulties involved were constantly underestimated by those hoping to escape from a complex society.

An unforeseen consequence of the establishment of youth services on a national scale was the emergence of youth agencies and organizations into an important pressure group in the body politic. The age group now had continuity of leadership and a national coordinating committee that enabled many diverse elements to coalesce around issues of importance. No longer were they dependent on students alone for leadership. The youth had become a sophisticated political force for the first time in history.

By 1993, the sixteen-year-old vote had become a reality.

4

The Future of Family Social Work

CLARK W. BLACKBURN and JANICE MARUCA *

Family social work has never been static. It constantly changes and adapts in response to the shifting needs of man and his society. In the United States, its development [1] is linked to the major economic and social transitions the country has undergone from the Industrial Revolution to our present-day emergence into a highly complex, mass, technological society.

The real beginnings of what is now the family service movement took place after the middle of the nineteenth century, and accompanied America's shift from a rural-agrarian to an urban-industrial society.[2] This period of rapid unrbanization and heavy immigration was marked by great poverty and all the attendant problems that we see even today—hunger and malutrition, bad housing, poor sanitation, sickness, child neglect, exploitation of both children and adults. The early voluntary relief societies, as they were known, were organized by private groups to try to alleviate the suffering of the poor who were crowded into the growing cities. These groups concentrated on providing direct emergency relief in the form of clothing, milk, fuel, ice, or vouchers for rent and

* Janice Maruca has done public relations and written for and about the social welfare field for ten years. I would also like to express my gratitude to Mrs. Ellen Manser, FSAA Consultant on Family Development, for reading and commenting on the manuscript, and Dorothy Fahs Beck, Ph.D., FSAA Director of Research, who provided the basis for much of the research, as well as many other staff members who, by their various contributions to the formulation of the new goals of the Family Service Association, have helped shape my thinking on the place and practice of family social work in the future of America.

food supplies. Economic assistance was provided mainly by local government units, and public funds were used to pay for medical care or institutionalization of the indigent.[3]

A major change in the focus of the private groups occurred in the latter part of the 1800's. The failure of subsistence assistance to eliminate poverty and its ills led to community concern over both the amount of public expenditures and fear that too-easily-obtained relief would demoralize the recipient or reward laziness.[4] New hope for the correction of poverty and poverty-related problems was placed in the social reform theories developed by a group of English philanthropists [5] and, in 1877, the first charity organization society was formed in Buffalo, New York. These societies grew rapidly in America, and by 1911 were active in more than sixty-two communities.[6]

The new charity organizations did not, at least at first, give any financial relief.[7] They attempted, instead, to reform unfavorable social conditions and to help families strengthen their capacity to cope with and solve their own problems. They went out into the community, into the homes of the poor, and tried to counsel and guide them, especially in economic matters.

This shift from relief to reform considerably advanced the social work movement. For it was study of the experiences of both the volunteer charity workers and the trained workers who followed them that led to the development of the social casework method and, later, to the adaptation of that technique for helping people with emotional and psychological as well as economic problems.

The next significant change occurred as a result of the Great Depression of 1929. For the first time in the nation's history the federal government, with the Social Security Act of 1935, assumed a responsibility for meeting some of the health and welfare needs of all the people.[8] The public sector had resources beyond that of any private agency, and the government, over the next decades, increased its commitment to providing both financial and counseling services to the poor.[9] As government involvement in this area grew, the family service agencies gradually turned their attention toward a new client group that desperately needed help—the financially self-supporting, but emotionally starving nuclear family. Increasingly, following World War II, family social workers became absorbed in helping struggling nuclear family units function and avoid breakdown in a rapidly changing society. And to meet the particular needs of this family form, professional family service workers developed the very personalized, highly individualized casework approach for which the profession is known today.

Then during the latter half of the 1950's and the early part of the 1960's, America began getting warning signals that all was not well with its society. At first family breakdown was blamed for the problems individuals were having. But as the extent of the problem became more understood, it became obvious that family breakdown was but a symptom of serious social breakdown. It was simply not true that the family was short-circuiting society; rather there was something wrong within our social system that was short-circuiting the family.

During the decade of the sixties the family service profession re-evaluated its focus and has come, in a manner of speaking, full circle. We have turned, once again, to community organization and broad social reform as a means of alleviating widespread human suffering.[10] Yet the shift in emphasis from case-back-to-cause is not really a return to an old way of doing business. Nor does it abandon the well-developed and sophisticated casework methods.

A new approach, in fact, is being forged today, one that will better meet the crisis and long-range needs of millions of modern individuals and families. This approach, called family advocacy, combines and broadens the concepts of social reform and casework into a new method of social service that will function both for the benefit of all families and for the single family unit.[11]

Family advocacy also differs radically from the past in both philosophy and intention. Historically family social workers have helped families adjust to the existing society. Today we realize that many families have been victimized by society, and we are allying ourselves with distressed families in an effort to adjust society.

Advocacy, then, is the beginning of the future of family service social work. But we are not the trailblazers; rather we, like the medics who follow the army into battle, must follow the path blazed by the family. And so, for a glimpse at the future of family social work we must turn to the family and see where it is going.

Can the Family Survive the Twenty-first Century?

A decade ago God was declared dead and now there are the Jesus people, the Hara Krishna people, and a whole potpourri of other new or revived religious groups. Apparently reports of His death, like Mark Twain's, were greatly exaggerated. Of course, the new god is a little different from the one most over-thirty Americans grew up with: he dresses differently, is more casual, he expresses his message in new-style words and rock lyrics. Yet, ironically, this new god speaks the same spiritual message as the other, older god of the ages. Love.

Today the nuclear family and, by implication, all family forms are declared dead. Yet the idea of a family is as old, at least, as is the idea of a god. Throughout history man has experimented with many family and many religious forms, changing each to suit his changing social and personal needs. Both institutions have played major roles in mankind's social history, as well as in each man's own, individual, personal history.

Something is definitely happening to the family today. But as we might have learned from witnessing the rebirth of religion, it is superficial to predict the demise of an idea or a need because one form has failed, or has failed for some. That is like saying that since a man has tired of green beans, he will cease altogether to eat vegetables.

The Family as a Social Institution

The importance of the family in the creation and successful development of the United States as a nation cannot be underestimated. Lone individuals and small family units (the earliest American nuclear family units) came from diverse foreign lands, settled, and re-created on these shores the family structures they had known in Europe, largely the extended family form. The movement west again involved the splitting of families into nuclear units, which grew again into extended families during the decades when the country was agraraian. The Industrial Revolution caused the third atomization of the extended family form and produced the modern nuclear family. However, this last splitting of the extended family, because of the success of industrialization and our consequent transformation into a mass, technological society, denied these nuclear units any opportunity to settle, put down roots, and expand as they had in the past. Instead, every generation was atomized, the cords cut, the bonds severed, the children scattered.

By constantly adapting in this manner, the family was, in reality, changing to meet the needs of the developing society. Families were, in fact, the backbone of progress, for they were strong and viable units that produced, generation after generation, creative, flexible, independent, self-reliant, secure individuals who aided and abetted social change and national growth.

Question: Why were American families and American individuals so willing to adapt and readapt to serve the changing social needs of the nation? Why were they agreeable to breaking tender bonds and setting out alone to fact unknown challenges? Because, until recent times, social change has always meant increased opportunity for the individual, a chance at a better life, social mobility, personal advancement, dignity.

Social Responsibilities of the Family

Since the earliest days of this country the family has carried certain social responsibilities, especially in regard to the bearing and raising of children, the provision of economic and emotional security, and the transmission of cultural and social values and mores. All these functions, insofar as society is concerned, are aimed at one result: the family's duty to produce healthy, mature, self-reliant adults who can participate responsibly in the development of American civilization. Unlike all our other institutions, the family receives no aid for its service to society, and no laws are directed toward its protection. However, the reality of these responsibilities is undeniable, since families who fail to perform these functions satisfactorily are morally condemned, and sometimes legally punished, by their communities.

Over the course of the nation's development the family turned over many of its original functions—in education, health care, job training, for example—to other societal institutions. By and large this help was welcomed, for technological change made these functions so complex and highly specialized that the family could not adequately perform them. Moreover, this trend is continuing, and in the future families will probably receive even more help from other institutions, especially in the area of child care and child development.

These changes, however, do not imply that the family has, or will, become less important as a social institution. For although its functions are being reduced in number, each has become increasingly more complex. Moreover, the specific responsibilities it retains are highly critical ones.

The family today continues to bear the financial as well as the social responsibility for reproducing, then nurturing and protecting the young and bringing them to a physically, intellectually, emotionally and psychologically healthy adulthood. This is no small task, even with help. Consider, for example, the family's complicated task in education. In earlier, simpler times a child could expect a good life if he learned how to farm well and he might well learn this by working at his father's side. Today a child needs twelve years of formal, full-time education if he wishes only to obtain the most menial, unsatisfying type of work. If he wishes a professional career, he must plan on a minimum of sixteen to twenty years, and even more if he wishes to specialize. Moreover, this is only one area of child care and development. All the attendant responsibilities—in mental and physical health care, clothing and shelter, community and social activities, provision of adequate cultural experiences, and so on—are equally complex, time-consuming and expensive.[12]

Much more importantly, however, the family continues to be the initial and primary socializing institution of the young. It is through the family unit that individuals acquire their most basic cultural and social values and mores, and form lifelong emotional and behavioral patterns. If one closely examines the implications of this influence, he will not be long in concluding that the family, despite its narrowed focus, actually retains the real key to social progress. For it is the family that prepares the child, physically, intellectually, emotionally and psychologically, to receive socialization by the other institutions. Thus the family has the power—by encouraging or discouraging its children, by supporting or denying support to an institution, by cooperating or refusing to cooperate with a teacher or other representative of an institution—radically to affect the entire socialization process.[13]

Furthermore, there is no evidence today to indicate that the family of tomorrow will have any fewer social responsibilities or that there will be any overt attempt to undermine its powerful influence on the young. The fact is, we are very reluctant as a society to tamper openly with the family, and there are strong economical, philosophical, social and psychological reasons for this.

First of all, despite our great wealth, it is not economically possible to create and sustain any other institution which could presume suitably to perform all the complex tasks of a family, especially in the areas of emotional and psychological need.

Philosophically, it is most improbable that the American public would even entrust the basic responsibility for the nurturing and raising of children to the state since this would necessitate a complete change in American social thinking. For such responsibility carries the implication that children (and by extension, all citizens) have become the property of the state and, therefore, exist to serve the ends of the state. This is contrary to all American social, cultural and legal traditions, which are based upon the concept of the "inalienable rights" of the individual, and especially his right to be protected from manipulation by the state. Such state authority is simply not consistent with the American-style democracy which is based not on the concept of a benign state, but on basic distrust of overly powerful government.

Socially speaking, it is difficult to imagine how America could, with any confidence, encourage further family breakdown and greater takeover of its functions by other societal institutions. Thus far, inroads into the family's domain have not led to increased social stability. Quite the contrary, our society's failure to recognize the relevance of healthy family life to social stability and to support it has, at least in part, led to a population composed of the most alienated, isolated, anxious, insecure and unstable individuals in our history.

Finally, and possibly most importantly, the family is becoming the private domain of the individual, and it is rapidly becoming his main source of emotional and psychological support.

The Family and the Individual

Today the individual in America is questioning the family, its traditions, its structure, its values. But he has also lost faith in nearly all his other social institutions as well. He expects government, business and industry, education, religion, the armed forces, to fail him, cheat him, lie to him, manipulate him, exploit him. That he should come to look askance at his own family is therefore quite natural. The family has, as has been pointed out, thus far served society with great devotion. Moreover, as of late, the family, at least the nuclear family, has not been adequately meeting the needs of all of its members. At the root of this disenchantment is every American's belief that, as an individual, he has an "inalienable right" to the pursuit of happiness, and his feeling that present-day society, including the family, blocks, rather than opens, opportunities through which he can pursue this quest.

There is another major cause behind the contemporary questioning of the traditional marriage and family life patterns, and that is a significant change in the definition of "happiness" and a shift in expectations and values. The family, like most other institutions, was originally an economic unit, and its traditions evolved out of its attempt to provide its members with financial security. In America today we no longer think of the family in these terms.

American individuals today are searching desperately for ways to improve the emotional and psychological quality of their daily lives. Significant change in large, complex institutions is painfully, heartbreakingly slow, since many are so brittle they break before they can be reformed or readjusted. But the family, small, simple, personal, human in scale, is highly responsive to human need, and the one institution wide open to direct, immediate change by the individual. If one is dissatisfied with his current family life, he or she need only find a willing partner, or group of partners, for a new experiment.

For many individuals the family has become the focus of this modern quest for happiness, largely because it is both so flexible and so accessible. Hundreds of thousands of Americans are now experimenting with new family forms that range from heterosexual communal living, with or without children, to homosexual marriage, also with or without children. Between the two poles are all manner of relationships, based on all varieties of human physical, psychological or philosophical needs.[14]

Studies of these experimental forms indicate that there is a general trend toward forming insecure and unstable relationships. Moreover, the experiments have not, thus far, been successful in bringing about a decrease in any of the psychological, emotional or practical problems that attend interpersonal relationships. The sexual revolution has not brought an end to sexual problems; mysticism and simple living have not effectively banished destructive personality conflicts; financial pressures have eroded the bonds of some of the most idealistic communes; liberated individuals who narcissistically declare they live only for themselves seek help because they find their lives empty and meaningless.[15]

Many point to the problems of the new families as further evidence of the bankruptcy of the family idea. Yet deeper analysis does not support this point of view. For one thing, there is no evidence that people are losing faith in the idea, or losing their need, of forming close human ties.[16] Moreover, those who fail to find satisfaction in one relationship do not withdraw into individual isolation, but seek new relationships, or experiment with new relationship patterns. For example, an individual who divorces tends to remarry, and, if several subsequent marriages prove unsatisfying, may then turn to a commune. There is, then, no indication of a decline in the basic human needs that motivate social union or family life, and those are the desires for intense interpersonal relationships, security, support, love.

The family form today is, however, undergoing significant transformation. Its functions are changing, both in relation to society and in relation to its individual members. The old forms, based as they were on economic and social realities that are not the realities of today, are passing from the scene. They are like old snake skins that must be shed because the living body has outgrown them, but they will be replaced with a new skin that better fits the needs of the owner. Viewed in this perspective, the unstable experimental family forms can be understood to be, not evidence of failure, but simply transitional forms.

The contemporary experimentalists are, in reality, grappling with the complex questions and issues that will determine the structure and functions of the family of the future. They are trying to invent a form that will equalize the role of the sexes, that will minimize legal, social and interpersonal restrictions upon human behavior, and that will provide the maximum number of opportunities for the growth and development and expression of the individual.

What this family (or, possibly, families, since it may be that individuals will be able to select from several workable models that which best suits his or her needs, or, even experience several models in a lifetime) of the future will look like is not yet discernible, for no framework has yet been found that adequately fulfills modern criteria. But it is, however, possible to begin to perceive what its function and importance will be to tomorrow's individual.

The family will most likely become the individual's primary source of emotional and psychological security. As the United States grows into an increasingly complex, mass society, the individual will need a special place where he can live his emotional life and experience the deepest, fullest emotional and intellectual intimacy with others. He will need a secure haven where he can find and experience love, and learn how to love. It may become that very personal sanctuary where, surrounded by others who share, confide and trust in one another and who are concerned and committed to one another's health and happiness, the individual can confidently seek and find his identity and personal meaning, and where he can freely and honestly explore and express himself to the fullest measure.[17]

Is Technology Destiny?

Forecasters of the future often view the potential of the sciences and then project their effects upon our daily lives. They look at advances in reproductive biology and genetics, for example, expound upon the possibilities of laboratory-grown babies or the implications of presetting the eye and hair color, I.Q. and character traits, and suggest how this will change human attitudes toward motherhood, child-rearing and the purposes of marriage. They study the increasing pace of change, the rising mobility demands of industry, and suggest how these will affect marriage and child-rearing patterns. They examine the capacity of a technological system to create the most open, free and diverse society man has ever imagined, and they describe how people will be able to enjoy more, do more, think more, be more than ever before.[18]

The implicit assumption held by most forecasters is that technological advance is synonymous with progress and healthy change. It is seen as a sort of omnipotent, irresistible force that acts upon man, changing him with or without his consent. Man, it would seem, will jump on the technology merry-go-round and hold on tight, and those who don't will fall by the wayside and blight the social landscape like throw-away cans. It is important to realize that the implication of this point of view is that adaptaton, or lack of it, will prove the measure of the individual man or woman, as if to say that those who do not keep up are somehow less worthy as human beings than those who do.

Technology certainly has brought many changes that have radically improved the quality of our daily lives. Advances in medicine have made it possible to cure many previously fatal conditions, to increase our lifespan, reduce pain and suffering from illness and disease, and to control the birth rate safely and efficiently. Advances in agriculture have eliminated fear or famine as a threat to human life in the United States. Indeed, our capacity to produce food is such that we could, with little extra effort, feed the world. Industrial technology has eliminated need for all serious concern over the availability of clothing, shelter, or other material goods. In this area, too, we could provide for the world's population, were we so inclined. Moreover, we double our knowledge of the physical world every ten years, which should make it easier and easier for us to meet human needs.

Ironically, these advances and changes have not fulfilled their promise, at least in America. Although we have made greater strides in medicine than any other nation, our infant mortality rate is higher than twenty-two other countries. We are the world's masters of production, over-supplying the nation's market with toothpastes, detergents, television sets, automobiles and flip-top cans, yet our hospitals are undersupplied with life-saving equipment. We have the money and the know-how to feed the world, yet millions of Americans go hungry every year. We have the highest per capita income of any people in the world, yet 23 million people live in poverty. We are a nation whose principles are based on equal opportunity and equal justice for all, yet millions are denied access to education and jobs, and nearly everyone regards the legal system as more prosecutor than protector.

So one might well question the assumption that technology marches hand in hand with social progress. For America today is the richest and most technologically advanced nation that the world has ever known, yet has prevented neither social chaos, human misery, nor widespread public rejection of our way of life. We are, in fact, at this moment a highly unstable society, teetering on the verge of total social breakdown. One might well ask what good are our treasures and our skills if we cannot avoid the human pitfalls that have caused other great civilizations to decay and collapse?

Indeed, many Americans are wondering today if we have not had to pay too high a price for even the good things of technology. Are we not concerned that, as a society, we have become so dependent upon technological advance for economic security that we cannot stop polluting our environment even though it condemns future generations to certain death? Do we not often feel that, somehow, scientific progress in America has proven a Pandora's box, and that in loosening its whirlwindlike advance we innocently and inadvertently surrendered control of our destinies?

What is so unique about modern American technology that causes it to act as such an *un*stabilizing force? Why does it contribute to family breakdown when families in other societies that have experienced periods of technological development have remained intact and vital? [19] Is it, as many say, the unnerving effects of our particularly rapid pace of change? Or the depersonalizing effects of overpopulation and urbanization? Is it that individuals and families simply can't cope with the demands and diversions of a highly complex, mass, technological society?

In other words, are present-day social problems merely the public agonies of those individuals and families who are unable, whether physically, intellectually, psychologically or emotionally, to adapt to the technological society? Or possibly, might there not be some other, larger cause?

The failure of American leadership to recognize and correct the growing negative effects of our technological system resulted in the alienation and isolation of the early sixties and, later, the general public feeling that the "establishment" was the enemy of the people. Many Americans came to believe, not without reason, that the American system no longer belonged to them, that it no longer offered opportunities for individual growth and expression, and that, instead of freeing them, it had enslaved them.

Today hundreds of thousands of people are in open rebellion against the "system." And many millions more, not engaged in open hostilities, fantasize and wish for radical change. Moreover, it is important to realize that the discontent is not restricted to the poor, the young and the reactionary. Millions of middle-aged and older Americans still participating in the "system" are distressed, cynical and unhappy. Anger and resentment run deep everywhere, and it is rooted in the general awareness that real human needs are simply not being met—either for those participating in the social system, or for those revolting against it.

Technology, as it turns out, is not the measure of a society. The real measure is the use, or misuse, a people make of their technology. For, as the American experiment is proving today, although men may live in a world where technology reigns supreme, they need not enjoy it. And although human beings have, over the course of history, proven themselves perfectly capable of miraculous adaptation,[20] they may not choose to adapt. People may be encouraged and invited to join a social system, but that is no guarantee that they will participate constructively in it. Indeed, they may even choose to destroy it.

Thus, the future of America cannot be divined by imagining how technology can change the details of daily life. The future lies in the relationship yet to be forged between the American individual and his social institutions. The question, then, that forecasters should be concerned with—and which the family social work profession is now and will continue to be concerned with—is: How can, and how well, will America succeed in adapting her technology, humanizing it, to make it better serve the needs of her people? Or will she, blindly caught in her own whirlwind, drift toward, not Orwell's 1984, but chaos and social disintegration?

Today's Need and Tomorrow's Challenge

Modern society might well be compared to the human body. It is a highly complex, highly interdependent network of systems, each function dependent upon the successful operation of every other function. If one of the systems fails to operate properly, or becomes "sick," the entire network is thrown out of kilter; the body goes into a turmoil, sending out signals of distress and marshaling all its energies to repair, or reform, the malfunctioning parts. If the effort to heal is successful, the body regains its health and vitality; if it fails, total breakdown or death often results.

Today many systems in America are not functioning well and these systems failures have resulted in an imbalance in our society similar to that created when a vital body function—or a series of functions—goes awry. In effect, society's mutual support system, upon which stability and vitality depend, has broken down. America today, like a sick body, is frantically sending out warning signals and struggling to regain its balance, repair its malfunctioning parts, restore harmony and health.

The repair, or reform, of these malfunctioning systems is the great challenge that faces the social work professional today. We must help focus the goals of society and reshape our institutions so that, once again, they are responsive to the real needs of the American people. As was noted earlier, the family social work field is already beginning to work toward this objective.

What must we do to make our social system more humane?

First, we must find the means of drawing into our society those millions of poor who have been disenfranchised because of racism or discrimination, and the young, who have abandoned society.

Second, we must improve communication—between one individual and another; between different neighborhoods; between people and their institutions; between different institutions—so that single individuals, families, groups of families, whole communities, all voices, can be heard and play an effective role in determining the social and economic policies that affect their lives.

Third, we must alter our social and economic policies so that they complement, not conflict with one another. More importantly, both should be based upon real human needs, not simply business and economic needs.

Moreover, while we work toward the larger goal of humanizing society, family social workers will also continue to work at the important task of helping people humanize their daily lives.

There is today great need for sympathetic counseling on a wide range of human problems. Parents need help in understanding their children's behavior and attitudes and in coping with new types of intergenerational relationships. The young, the old, the poor, all need assistance in dealing with an antagonistic culture. Many wish for help with problems of marriage and growth, communication and marriage enrichment generally. others need guidance on the practical problems of birth control, or abortion counseling, or with adoption problems.

But what happens when, and if, America succeeds in humanizing her social system? How will this change the role of the family social worker? How will the profession fit into a society that is geared to meet human needs? What jobs are left to be done? What kinds of help, if any, will people still need?

Even if adequate system change occurs and America becomes a more unified and fully integrated society, there will nonetheless be many social and human needs that will challenge the family social work field. These challenges will arise from the very complex nature of our technological society, combined with the additional problem-producing factors of overpopulation and urbanization.

For example, many people will continue to need assistance with the oftentimes difficult task of effectively communicating with huge institutions. This kind of help will be needed even if our institutions are willing to listen, because large organizations must have procedure simply to function, and procedures have a way of becoming barriers to communications. (This is especially true when individuals are not familiar with an institution and its operations, and in tomorrow's world individuals cannot hope to be fully cognizant of all the institutions that hey must, at one time or another, deal with.) Family social workers will play an important bridging role here, facilitating communications and helping improve relations between individuals, families, and the institutions.

Also, large complex institutions can easily drift off the track, even when they are possessed by the best of intentions. That is to say, it is simpler for a large organization to develop policies and procedures that make operations easy for itself, whereas it is difficult to remain flexible, open to frequent change and modification, and sympathetic and responsive to the diverse and changing needs of millions of people. Yet this flexibility is the quality our institutions must develop and retain. In this area, the role of the family social work field will be, as it is becoming today, to search and discover when and how institutions fail, and to help them to readjust to better serve the needs of people.

Moreover, the family social work field will also be challenged by a growing demand for both preventive and remedial counseling services. There will, first of all, be increased need for the full array of counseling services that are today provided. But by 1993 we can expect to see, in addition, several new types. One potential area of service might be called "choice counseling," and it would focus on helping people learn how to make the complicated decisions that will be a difficult part of life in the future. For as the United States becomes more diverse, more mass, more complex, the range of choices open to the individual and family in all areas of life will be staggering, bewildering, and, for many, confusing and frustrating.[21] Hundreds of thousands of people will want and demand professional help in closely examining their needs, evaluating alternatives and analyzing the implications of various possibilities, so that they might choose wisely and avoid costly emotional, psychological and economic mistakes. Choice counseling will have both preventive and remedial dimensions, the latter focusing on helping people find ways to correct the unsatisfying results of poor judgment and poor decision-making. It is quite possible that this form of counseling will become a major family social work service in future decades, although it is not likely to be so by 1993.

But for a closer look at the future directions of family social work, let's turn to an examination of the individual family social worker and the family social work agency as they might be in 1993.

The Family Social Work Professional of the Future

The exact role of the family social worker in 1993 will be determined by the progress America has made in integrating social, institutional and human needs. If, for example, individuals and families remain in conflict with the large institutions, then the family social work professional will be similar to his present-day counterpart. That is to say, he will be an advocate and will seek to bend the institutions which are jeopardizing individuals and families. On the other hand, if our social system and individuals have become more reconciled, then the family social worker may be considerably different. In this latter case, truly the preferable alternative, the family social worker will have become himself an integral part of a mutually supporting system. Instead of helping people stay afloat in a stormy, turbulent, hostile social environment, the professional will concentrate on helping individuals and families get the most out of life.[22]

Regardless, the family social worker will, in 1993, share three basic concerns with his 1973 counterpart. First, he will try to strengthen the effectiveness of individual, or groups of, families in dealing with other social institutions, and in exercising their potential to influence the goals and priorities of society.

A second, but equally important, area will be the worker's efforts to help individual families function better internally. Here, for example, a worker might assist a family in developing a more efficient or more satisfying pattern of internal operation that better meets the needs of all its members.

The family social worker will also be concerned with helping the individual find greater personal fulfillment within his family. Here the emphasis might be on helping a person discover ways to strengthen, enrich and deepen relationships through mutual growth, communication, sharing, and caring. If serial marriages indeed become a reality, as some predict, the professional would no doubt be concerned with helping individuals try to get the most out of each relationship. Or, if an individual was not getting satisfaction from a relationship, or from a series of relationships, the worker would try to help him discover and remedy the problem so that satisfaction could be found in the future.

However, although he may be recognizably related to the family social worker of 1973, the professional twenty years hence will be nonetheless considerably different.

What differences can we expect to see in tomorrow's family social work professional? What will be his, or her, daily concerns? Day-to-day activities? How will he approach and deal with the problems he will encounter in the world of 1993?

One of the most striking differences will be the diversity of settings in which we can expect to find a professional family social worker. For it is quite conceivable that within the next decades all, or nearly all, of our institutions will become involved in providing some level of family social work service. Thus the family social work professional may well be employed by a factory, a hospital, a school, a government agency, a union, or a baseball team.

Another dramatic change will be the increasing diversity of both new people and new professions that will have become involved in providing service to families over the next twenty years. It is certain, for example, that professionals from such important related fields as housing, health care, jurisprudence, and education will be brought into the family social work forum, either as employees of social agencies or as consultants to social workers.

There will also be many more paraprofessionals involved, such as homemakers, case aides, and child care technicians. There will be increased participation of many other nonprofessionals who are, nonetheless, experts. These will be people with special understanding of a problem, such as ex-addicts, ex-alcoholics, unemployed or unskilled job seekers, veterans, welfare recipients, senior citizens, and they will bring to the field of social work a highly specialized brand of expertise never before utilized. Ghetto-street educated, or otherwise deprived of their human needs or rights, they will provide firsthand knowledge of the social and human problems of America's most distressed, pressured, disabled and jeopardized families and will work alongside social work professionals toward the solution of these problems.[23]

Moreover, the family social work professional himself is much more likely to be a member of a minority group. This change, already noticeable in 1973, will no doubt continue to alter both the public image and the social effectiveness of the field. For it brings new people, new talent, and new points of view to bear upon our social problems, and will result in many innovations in service and in many new approaches to social and family problem-solving.

In addition to these changes in setting and personnel, we will also see important differences in the attitudes of the professional family social worker toward himself, his job, and his clients.

In contrast to the social worker of the nineteen-fifties, tomorrow's professional will no longer see himself as an independent specialist working within the small, tight, rather closed framework of a social agency. He will see himself as a part of a working team, a highly interdependent network of skilled people, any number of whom might be called upon to help resolve a family, or social, problem. Moreover, he will be working within a much enlarged, very open framework—society. He will be much more accessible to people in trouble, because he will go out into the streets, into the housing development, the schools, the churches, the storefronts, and offer his help to anyone in need.

The professional will approach the work with a considerably expanded definition of the word "family." For several decades in the United States, "family" has been culturally defined as a legally married man and woman with children. But this definition is not workable in a society where individuals are searching for new family forms and where past cultural traditions are unable to meet modern needs. Thus the family social work profession today is beginning to think of the family in functional, rather than legalistic, terms. This means that professionals are now free to deal effectively and sympathetically with the problems eroding the base of any form, whether it be a family composed of a single parent with children, a childless commune, a homosexual couple with children, and so.[24]

Over the next twenty years this functional point of view will serve the professional well in his efforts to ally himself with struggling and experimental family groups. For it will tend to help erase, over time, the stigma many family social workers have encountered in their recent attempts to reach out to jeopardized, especially poor, families. And that is the feeling on the part of many distressed families, and contemporary experimental groups, that social workers are representatives of the "establishment." Tomorrow's family social worker will neither morally endorse, nor morally condemn, any family form, and families will think of him as a resource to whom they can turn for help with any kind of social or personal problem.

Furthermore, the family social worker of the future will also have a much-expanded definition of his job. In other words, whereas in the past family social workers could generally be divided into caseworkers and administrators, the professional of 1993 will, in fact, be many things to many people. He will be a provider, supplying those in need with emergency food, clothing and shelter. He will be an advocate, acting on behalf of the inarticulate, the distressed and the oppressed. He will be an organizer, helping families band together to obtain for themselves the services they need. He will be a mobilizer, pulling together defenders to act on behalf of those who are being denied their rights. He will be a reformer, taking issue with those institutions that have destructive or inhumane policies, procedures or intentions, and working to bring about constructive change.

Casework counseling will continue to be a major activity, although professionals will, as has been indicated earlier, provide a much wider range of services. Indeed, the scope of counseling services that may be required suggests that family social work professionals, like medical doctors and engineers, may come to specialize in one or two areas. In the area of marriage counseling, for example, family social workers may find themselves specializing in the problems of a particular type of family form (such as the nuclear or the single parent family, multilateral or homosexual families or communes). These specialities may either include or be further subdivided into both preventive and remedial forms of counseling. That is to say, one professional may well be consulted by a group that wishes to, say, set up a commune and be asked to help them study their individual needs and desires and help devise a structure that will be both functional and need-satisfying. If this same commune begins having relationship differences, its members may then consult another professional, possibly in consultation or cooperation with the first professional, who will help them explore and understand how destructive patterns developed so that they might remedy the problem or avoid similar problems in subsequent relationships.

But more important than the wide range of services that professionals will offer in the future is the new approach they will use in family and social problem-solving. This new perspective, called the family-centered or environmental approach, is today being developed in the field and is based upon the interdependent relationship that exists between individuals, families and institutions in modern society. It is an approach which operates on the premise that individuals and families function in a mutually affecting social context, and that the individual's problems are both the result of, and contribute to, family problems; and that individual and family problems are both the result of, and contribute to, social problems.

By 1993 the family or environmental approach will dominate the family social work field. What this will mean in casework practice is that the professional will always view the individual client in the context of his total pattern of family relationships as well as his total social environment. Similarly, individual families in counseling will be viewed, not as solitary, isolated units, but as part of and interacting with, society. In serving these individuals and families the social worker will help them marshal their own resources to deal with destructive social or environmental problems, while assisting them in forming more functional and need-satisfying patterns of internal operation.[25]

Finally, the professional of 1993 can expect to have a much greater array of tools and technology to help him provide service to more people, more efficiently and more effectively. Increasing scientific knowledge of humans, human behavior and the human psyche will contribute to the development of many new and more sophisticated social work skills and methods. But also the field will, over the course of the next twenty years, begin to benefit from the technological advances that will transform much of advanced scientific knowledge into usable social work tools.

The Family Social Work Agency of the Future

Today the great area of consumer need is in the health and welfare field, and in the future we will see enormous development of those institutions and organizations that specialize in real services to people. Moreover, this shift will not destroy our economy, but will breathe new life into it. Businessmen and industrial leaders will have learned what the medical and social work professions have long known: in the area of human physical, emotional and psychological needs, the supply has never exceeded the demand, and these types of goods and services experience no difficulty in the marketplace.[26]

What his responsibility means, specifically, to the family social work agency is—growth. In the course of the next twenty years agencies will expand rapidly and, in doing so, they will become far more diverse and complex than they are today.

Agencies, for one thing, will provide many more services than they do today. By 1993 it is possible that many agencies will have well-developed departments that specialize in, at least, advocacy, family life education, information and referral, consultation, family and individual counseling, casework and research. Furthermore, each department may well have several subdivisions and provide an array of services.

Advocacy, for example, may include such functions as community organization, legal counsel and legislative research, among others.

Family life education might, hypothetically, include a speakers bureau, a mobile unit that travels from neighborhood to neighborhood providing free information, showing films or filmstrips, or person-to-person conversations on birth control, child development, human relations, marriage enrichment. This department also might well have specialists in conducting family life education courses suitable for elementary and high school students, college students, women's groups, and so on. Additionally, a production subdivision will no doubt create radio and television and printed materials for use by the mass media and geared to help the general public get more out of their family life.

Family and individual counseling will make available highly personalized, specialized, in-depth professional help with a wide variety of serious personal emotional, social or psychological problems. Moreover, types of counseling may be offered, such as sensitivity and T-group experience, marathons, confrontations, as well as individual, private sessions.

Consultation services might range from providing assistance to a business or industry that wishes to establish a family counseling service for its own employees, to advise on how a public or private facility could reshape its policies or procedures to make them more relevant to the needs of consumers and less depersonalizing and bureaucratic. This department might also conduct training courses and workshops in human needs and behavior for planners and policy makers.

The research department will act, primarily, as a system monitor. It will study the effects of our social and various institutional systems upon family life, pinpoint destructive or negative elements, and help develop methods of humanizing these systems. It will analyze the programs and service delivery systems of the family social work agency, testing for efficiency and effectiveness. This department might study developing trends in family living patterns, locate gaps in service and help develop new techniques and service programs to meet emerging needs. It might also conduct tests to determine when and whether the pace of change or social demands are exceeding tolerable limits for proper human adaptation, and thus act as a sort of social weather vane.

Along with services, the staffs of future agencies will be more diversified. In addition to the professional family social worker, we will see people possessing many different skills and specialties including the ability to communicate effectively with various cultural subdivisions and the expertise of analyzing the most complex research data. Moreover, the staffs will more accurately reflect the diverse nature of our society, and will be composed of representatives of all economic, social and cultural groups.

This trend toward consumer representation and participation, already evident in many social agencies in 1973, will be carried even further. Tomorrow's agency boards of directors and other governing bodies will include a cross section of service users, as well as service planners and providers. Perhaps most importantly, the voice of the consumer will not only be heard, but heeded, since the boards will be structured so that he can effectively influence agency policy and planning.

This, is generally, a picture of what the agency of 1993 will look like. But how does it fit into the community, or society, as a whole?

As in the case of the professional family social worker, the social role of tomorrow's family service agency will be determined by the progress America has made toward developing a system that truly meets the needs of both modern man and modern society. Thus it is possible to say that the agency of 1993 can be one of two things: It may be, as it is becoming today, a gadfly to society and a defender of the individual and the family in conflict with society's institutions; or it may become a welcome partner in an integrated society whose institutions desire its monitoring and people-oriented services.

Which of these two alternatives actually becomes the reality of the agency of 1993 depends, in large measure, on the progress the family social work field makes over the next twenty years on four main fronts:

First, institutional change. Agencies will work with all other societal institutions, as well as with other social agencies, (a) to make and keep them aware of the relationship of healthy family life to a healthy, productive, secure, stable society; (b) to make them understand the ways in which their policies and procedures or goals may be inhibiting, or curtailing, or destroying family life; and (c) to help them change.

Second, public education. Agencies will strive to (a) make individuals and individual families more aware of their place and importance in society; (b) increase understanding of family problems and encourage the seeking of help for these problems; and (c) provide families with information relevant to their everyday lives, such as on birth control, child development, interpersonal relationships, etc.

Third, statutory recognition of the family. Agencies will seek true societal recognition of the relevance of the family to national life through passage by the United States Congress of a national family policy that will guarantee to all families the rights of adequate income, medical and rehabilitative services, decent housing and a voice in determining the economic and social policies that affect their lives.[27]

Fourth, direct service to families. Agencies will provide the full range of services required to (a) help families function better both for their own members and for society; (b) prevent family breakdown and human suffering while institutions are being humanized; (c) provide support for families who are jeopardized by neglect, racism, persecution, or other destructive social force; and (d) help individuals attain fuller, richer lives through their family life.

Beyond 1993

The 1973 problems of American families may well not be fully solved by 1993, although certainly we shall have made progress. But even so, the pace of change and growth of our population will have by then created new problems, all of which are not foreseeable, and to which attention must be paid, imagination applied and solutions developed.

Certainly the challenge facing the family social work profession and the family service agency is a formidable one. The job of meeting the complex service needs of our large population, and of constantly monitoring a mass society and keeping it in turn responsive to human need is a never-ending task. It is a Sisyphean labor that will be finished only if and when America ceases to be a large, diverse, mass complex, technological society—in other words, it will last as long as this civilization stands. Yet this challenge is being, and will continue to be, accepted with courage and hope, for it is the major contribution that the family social work profession can make to the improvement and preservation of American life.

5

Services for the Aged

BERNARD E. NASH

Who would have predicted in the 1940's that man would walk on the moon within little more than twenty years? It is no less difficult today to predict with any great certainty what our society will be like in 1993. But those of us who are concerned about the welfare of our people and our nation must try.

The federal government Administration on Aging has estimated that there will be 33 to 38 million Americans over the age of sixty-five by the year 2,000 (compared to 20 million in 1970). Dr. Philip Hauser of the University of Chicago predicts an even greater increase—55 million by the year 2011. The proportion of older persons in our total population is also expected to increase substantially during the remaining years of this century. As medical advances allow people to live longer and birth control practices reduce the number of births, the percentage of persons in the older age categories will rise. Thus, the age profile of our society in 1993 will be markedly different from what it is today.

The social, economic and political implications of this are enormous; yet decision makers seem oblivious to the trend. A similar, albeit far less serious, mistake was made in the United States about twenty-five years ago. At that time, administrators were well aware that the so-called "baby boom" of the 1940's would substantially increase the number of children enrolling in the public schools. But virtually nothing was done about it until the children actually arrived. Only then were steps taken to provide the necessary facilities, manpower and financial resources.

Have we learned from our mistakes? Perhaps not. Opportunities and services for today's older Americans are woefully inadequate and we are doing little or nothing to prepare for twice their number in the next thirty years. If we fail to act, we will sentence future generations of the elderly to lives of poverty, loneliness, frustration and fear.

Still, I am optimistic. I believe that this, the richest and most compassionate nation on earth, can bring independence, dignity and purpose to the lives of its older citizens. If we are to help this nation undertake such a formidable task, however, we must begin now.

In the following pages, I attempt to describe the plight of the elderly in our society in the early 1970's, the changes which I hope will have taken place in twenty years, and the steps which we must take in order to bring about these changes.

Social welfare is a frustrating field of endeavor, and those who practice it are often equally frustrated, for their idealism—their recognition of America's unparalleled potential for human service—is invariably tempered by the disappointing realities of our past and present performance. Thus, my hopeful expectations about aging in 1993, idealistic as they may be, are tempered by the realization that they cannot be achieved without a fundamental change in our national attitude.

We must attempt in the next twenty years to change the meaning of growing old in America. The problems of the elderly are not unsolvable. We have always had the resources, but never the will to solve them. Our programs have been ineffective, our concern sporadic, our priorities confused, our promises unmatched by our performance. What is needed is a national commitment on aging—a continuing effort in every area of our national life to improve the lot of older Americans.

To bridge the gap between promise and performance will not be easy. We should not expect miracles. But we can and should expect substantial progress by 1993.

Here then, as I see them, are the grim realities of the present, my hopes for the future, and the challenges which lie ahead.

Income

The Present

Perhaps our greatest priority in the next two decades must be the creation of an equitable, realistic, adequate income maintenance system which reflects both the needs of the elderly and their contributions to our society.

Today, ten million Americans over the age of sixty-five do not share in the nation's abundance. At a time when the gross national product has passed the $1,00,000,000,000 mark, five million Americans over sixty-five (one-fourth of that age group) are living below the poverty level; one in two retired workers are "poor" for the first time in their lives. Millions of other retired Americans are forced to reduce substantially their standard of living.

Despite several recent increases, it is obvious that Social Security benefits remain an inadequate source of retirement income. Many workers are also discovering that they may never receive a cent in return for their investments in private pension plans because of the strict requirements of certain plans. Add to this the increasing cost of most goods and services, and it is not difficult to understand why retirement is a time of financial hardship and worry instead of leisure and enjoyment for too many older Americans.

The Future

By 1993, no older American should have to live in poverty. He should have ample opportunity to obtain an adequate income during his later years, and if he cannot, his income should be supplemented—not as a handout or a "dole" but as a reward for past services; the economy should be considered a common enterprise, with those who have contributed to its growth entitled to a share in its abundance.

The Challenge

In order to alleviate the economic problems of retirement, we must first recognize some pertinent facts: The present Social Security system was never designed to be the primary source of retirement income; the benefits are obviously too low; the present system is inequitable for several reasons: (1) Benefits do not always reflect contributions. For instance, a married woman who worked is entitled to no greater benefit than a married woman who did not work. (2) The Social Security tax base places a disproportionate share of the burden on low and middle-income workers. (3) The present system penalizes through the earnings limitation those who are in the greatest need of full benefits—those who are forced to work beyond age sixty-five in order to subsist. (4) Benefits for men are computed on a different basis than those for women. Automatic increases in Social Security benefits to match increases in the cost of living were established in order to prevent undue delays in increasing benefits—delays which were traditional when Congress had to approve each increase. Nonetheless, this provision does nothing to solve the real problem of inadequate benefits. Consider the following: (a) the cost of living increases by 5 per cent; (b) an individual's benefit is automatically increased from $100 to $105 (for example); but (c) the individual is really no better off than he was before. If $100 was inadequate prior to the increase in the cost of living, $105 will still be inadequate following the increase. By recognizing the faults inherent in the present system, we can more readily determine what needs to be done in the next twenty years.

I would like to see a restructuring of the Social Security system to include the following features: an "adequacy of income" standard which would provide benefits, equal to 50 per cent of the individual's average earnings during the years immediately prior to retirement (with specified minimum and maximum benefit levels); elimination of the Social Security Tax base so that all persons, regardless of income, will pay a specific percentage of their *total* income as their contribution to Social Security (with the present tax base, a person earning $10,000 per year pays the same amount of Social Security tax as does a person earning $50,000 per year); use of general revenue to help finance Social Security; automatic increases in benefits to match increases in productivity (as reflected by the gross national product), so that those who have contributed to our nation's economic growth may share in its continued prosperity; greater benefits for those who work beyond age sixty-five and an allowance for a greater amount of earned income without reduction in benefits; minimum benefits for all persons age seventy and over who would not otherwise be eligible for cash benefits under Social Security; more equity in terms of computation of benefits and the ratio of contributions to benefits. These features would greatly enhance a comprehensive income maintenance program for older Americans.

There is also a need to improve our system of public and private pension plans, for more and more Americans are turning to these plans as a source of retirement income—at least 30 million men and women have invested over $130 billion in more than 35,000 private plans. Because of their growing importance, some form of administrative regulation is both necessary and desirable. I would suggest the following: adoption of a national policy of (a) the transferability of public and private retirement credits, (b) five-year or earlier vesting of retirement benefits, and (c) adequate funding; establishment of a national pension fund corporation permitting persons to belong voluntarily to one central pension system; establishment of a federal insurance program to guarantee benefits from all pension funds, both public and private (many workers have lost their entire pension investment because their employers went out of business before their pension plan was fully funded); creation of minimum vesting standards for pension plans so that an employee with a certain number of years of service would have a nonforfeitable right to a certain percentage of any pension benefits earned up to that time; inclusion of automatic cost-of-living benefit adjustment provisions in all private and public pension plans. With these improvements in our pension system and the suggested changes in Social Security, I am confident that most Americans would be able to obtain real financial security for their later years.

The Present

The mistaken tendency of management to equate youth with productivity, combined with labor's "recession psychology"—the belief that older people must retire to make room for younger people in a limited job market—has spread the concept of compulsory retirement throughout industry. In addition, the provision in the Social Security Act which reduces benefits for those who earn more than a certain amount per year discourages and penalizes older persons who work. A tremendous proportion of older Americans are thus forced to retire and can no longer contribute to the economy or share in its productivity. Besides causing financial hardship and contributing to mental and emotional deterioration, this concept robs our society of the services of knowledgeable, experienced and dedicated men and women—a truly valuable resource.

The Future

By 1993 an individual's opportunity for gainful employment for as long as he wishes should be limited only by his abilities and desire, not by his age. His skills, knowledge and experience should be valued by business and industry and recognized as an asset to society.

The Challenge

Particularly as advances in medical science make it possible for people to stay healthier longer, our nation must reconsider its cruel, short-sighted, self-defeating policy which forces millions of potentially productive citizens out of the mainstream of American life.

Those who favor compulsory retirement usually contend that people must retire at a certain age in order to make room for younger workers in the job market; and older persons are unemployable because of loss of ability or lack of job skills. These contentions may have had some validity at some time, but they are certainly not valid today. Many vital services are not being provided today simply because of manpower *deficiencies*. The accomplishments of thousands of older Americans in government, business, and the performing arts, among other fields, discount the theory that people lose their abilities as they grow older. The claim has always been made that a certain number of Americans are "unemployable" because of age, illiteracy, physical handicaps, or other reasons. Yet, during World War II, thousands of these so-called "unemployables" were put to work, and the unemployment rate fell below one per cent. There is something terribly wrong with the manpower policies of government and the private sector when services cannot be provided because of lack of manpower while people cannot work because of lack of jobs (I discuss services in more detail in the section on "Employment").

This nation must develop a well-defined policy which will create more job opportunities for the old as well as the young. "Full employment" must become more than a political phrase; it must become a national goal. Furthermore, our national leaders must recognize the fact that discrimination based upon age is no less evil and dangerous than racial or religious discrimination. The Age Discrimination in Employment Act of 1967 was a declaration by Congress that such discrimination is contrary to the national interest, yet, because of business hostility and apathetic enforcement, this law has never been effective. It is of paramount importance to older Americans and to the nation itself that this law be vigorously and effectively enforced, and that its provisions be extended to cover all older workers with no age limitation.

Progress in this field in the next twenty years will hopefully put an end to forced retirement at an arbitrary age will definitely benefit the nation and its older citizens.

Employment

The Present

Dramatic technological advances in recent years have been a mixed blessing for many older Americans who are faced with two conflicting trends: They are healthier longer, but their skills are becoming obsolete sooner. An older person who loses a job because of technological advances has little chance of obtaining another one in competition with a younger person. Besides being victimized by blatant age discrimination in employment, the older worker has little opportunity to be retrained; the limited amount of job training resources in this country are directed primarily toward the young. He is trapped, in effect, in a society which places a premium on productivity (which it mistakenly equates with youth) and technology (which eliminates jobs). He is suddenly in a position in which he cannot help himself—creating for him and his family a severe financial and emotional burden.

The Future

By 1993, I foresee a marked change in the concept of work in America. As automation increases, as technological advances reduce the need for man as a producer of *goods,* I believe that the need for man as a provider of *services* will be more clearly recognized. I expect to see a substantial number of new, service-oriented job opportunities developing in the next twenty years. And who will be better suited for many of these positions than knowledgeable, compassionate and dedicated older Americans?

The Challenge

We are already moving toward what might be termed a "service-oriented" society.

By 1975, according to the U.S. Department of Labor, nearly one out of seven American workers will be employed in some level of government service—federal, state or local. We are confronted by an acute shortage of doctors, nurses, paramedical personnel, social workers and others in fields of human service. As more programs are developed in these fields during the next twenty years, more personnel will be needed. Therefore, we must expand and develop our manpower training and retraining resources in order to provide opportunities for older Americans to fill some of these positions.

Let me stress that I am not speaking merely about gainful employment, for I expect a far greater emphasis in the next two decades on voluntary service—ideal for many older persons who do not need or want salaried positions but still wish to remain active and involved. In day care centers, hospitals and clinics, schools, social and recreation centers, orphanages, and elsewhere, many opportunities for service are, or should be, available. Throughout the community, older citizens can assist in such programs as homemaker services, visiting and telephone reassurance, transportation services, meals-on-wheels, employment counseling, and information and referral services. Among the many examples of successful volunteer programs now conducted by older Americans are three sponsored by the National Retired Teachers Association and American Association of Retired Persons: The Tax-Aide Program (Income Tax Help by the Elderly for the Elderly) in which Internal Revenue Service-trained volunteers provide assistance to other older persons in need of income tax counseling. A Defensive Driving Course specifically designed for older persons and taught by volunteers trained by the National Safety Council. A Consumer Information Desk Program in which local volunteers provide free consumer information and referral service to other older persons in their communities. These, again, are only examples of the many ways in which older Americans can help themselves by helping others.

Whether we are speaking of paid or voluntary service, full or part-time, we must put an end to the unfair classification of many service jobs as "menial." Such service should be recognized as a valuable contribution to our society.

Above all, we must remember one basic fact: Inactivity is the elderly's greatest enemy. And whether the producing of goods or the providing of services is our objective, the elderly can and must play a role, both for their own well-being and for the benefit of the nation. Our leadership at all levels of society must provide them the opportunity to do so.

Housing

The Present

More than 65 per cent of Americans over age sixty-five own their homes. But many face the prospect of losing them because of the steady increase in property taxes and maintenance costs. The rising cost of public services financed through property taxes has placed an ever-increasing burden on older Americans, particularly those who live on fixed incomes. This has created, in some communities, a bitter and divisive conflict between those residents who benefit from certain services—primarily elementary and secondary education—and those who do not. The growing hostility expressed by many citizens over school budgets is testimony to that fact.

It is also most difficult for an older person to purchase a house. In FHA's largest program for home ownership, only one per cent of the mortgagors from 1960 to 1968—about 37,000 out of 3,500,000—were age sixty or over. Despite the fact that the average mortgage is kept by one person for *less than five years,* lending institutions are still reluctant to enter into mortgage agreements with person fifty-five or older.

For those who do not own their homes, the situation is equally deplorable. Rents have risen tremendously. Progress made in providing low-cost housing units for the elderly is pathetic when measured against the need. What is worse, many of the units which have been built or are being planned are little more than "geriatric ghettos" which tend to further isolate the elderly from the rest of the community.

The Future

By 1993, all Americans should be able to live where they choose. Older homeowners should no longer have to fear losing their homesteads because of circumstances beyond their control. Older tenants will have a wide range of housing to choose from, including, but not restricted to, retirement communities, with the built-in features so necessary to their comfort, mobility and security.

The Challenge

The Older Americans Act of 1965 stated as a national policy that "the older people of our nation are entitled to suitable housing." We must make substantial progress in the next twenty years if we are to fulfill that commitment. As I see it, we are making several mistakes in our present housing policy for the elderly. Despite the fact that the majority of older Americans own their homes, virtually none of the federal or state housing programs for the elderly directly affect the homeowner. Increasing property tax rates and maintenance costs are compounding the already serious shortage of housing for the elderly by forcing thousands of older Americans to sell their homes; yet little or nothing is being done to provide relief. Housing programs, generally designed to serve all low-income persons, neglect the special design and availability needs of older Americans. New housing for the elderly is becoming increasingly segregated, thus depriving them of the freedom to choose their surroundings.

An important step in alleviating the housing crisis for older Americans must be relief for those whose fixed incomes cannot keep pace with increasing property taxes and maintenance costs. The landmark decision of the California Supreme Court in 1971 that use of property taxes to finance elementary and secondary education is unconstitutional may result in a great breakthrough in this area. By excluding the property tax as a source of revenue for education, it may be possible, for the first time in years, to stabilize and control the tax rate, thus easing the pressure on older homeowners (and perhaps ending the bitter community conflicts which I discussed previously). As a further remedy, however, I would suggest strongly that homesteads or persons over sixty-five years of age whose family income falls below a certain level be exempt from property taxation. For those who meet these criteria while renting, a state income tax credit would afford equivalent relief.

As far as maintenance costs are concerned, I envision a program of special low-cost home improvement loans and, in certain cases, grants for older homeowners. In addition, some of the surplus building material not being used by federal, state or local governments could be utilized for this purpose.

I also advocate the establishment of an effective, government-supported mortgage guarantee program so that all Americans, regardless of age, will have the opportunity to purchase a home if they can afford to do so.

In addition to aiding the elderly homeowner, we must provide thousands of new and renovated rental units to meet the needs of older Americans who do not own their homes. The federal government and the states must expand their programs of low- and moderate-rent housing for the elderly, keeping in mind their special needs. These units should be located so as to insure that their tenants will not be isolated from needed services and community activities.

The construction of so-called "retirement communities" and "senior citizen housing projects" throughout the nation in recent years resulted, in part, from the desire of many older Americans to live with persons of similar age and with similar interests. We should not, however, make what is desirable for some mandatory for all; yet, the continued construction of segregated housing for the elderly leaves older Americans with fewer and fewer alternatives. Whatever the type of housing, therefore, freedom of choice for the elderly must be our goal. And the design and scope of all housing should recognize the peculiar needs of the elderly.

Transportation

The Present

A major factor contributing to the isolation of many older Americans is the lack of adequate transportation. Except in large metropolitan areas where commuters use it, public transportation is basically used most by people who can least afford to operate their own vehicles—the student, the handicapped person, the older person. Unfortunately, many of the new public transportation systems being designed today do not take into account the physical impairments of the elderly or the handicapped (for instance, the proposed Metro subway system in Washington, D.C., was originally designed with only one elevator in the entire system). This disregard for physical handicaps is also evident in the construction of many homes, office buildings, and public facilities.

If mass transportation for the elderly has been neglected, local intra-community or intra-neighborhood transportation for them has all but been ignored. Thus, many older Americans are cut off from other parts of town or even, in some cases, from parts of their own neighborhood, making access to necessary services increasingly difficult. When we hear tragic stories about men and women who spend years alone in their rooms, we must remember that many such tragedies occur not because these people have nowhere to go, but rather because they have no way to get there.

The Future

By 1993, no American should have to fear isolation. Door-to-door public transportation should be available; all public conveyances and facilities as well as homes and apartments should be designed to provide maximum mobility and access, regardless of the individual's physical condition. For those unable to leave home, a wide range of community services should be available in the home.

The Challenge

When applied to the elderly, the word transportation is actually a misnomer. Most of us tend to think of transportation in terms of mass transit, of traffic jams, late trains, crowded airports. To the elderly, however, the problems are more severe. For many of them, walking down the street, negotiating a flight of stairs and getting through a revolving door are of more immediate concern. When discussing the need for improvements, we must not limit ourselves to public transportation; we must concern ourselves with the over-all mobility of the elderly.

This is not to say that mass transportation is not important to older Americans; as I stated previously, the lack of such transportation contributes to their isolation. Furthermore, the improvements which have been made in this nation's transportation systems have, more often than not, ignored the specific needs of the elderly. Our present systems are designed for those who can walk through huge airports, endure crowded trains, stand for long periods at bus stops, and carry their own luggage. Those who cannot are, all too often, unable to use the larger planes, the faster trains, the more efficient buses with which technology has provided us. Our transportation planners must ensure, through such improvements as the redesigning of buses to provide lower steps and the use of more porters and baggage-handling equipment, that older Americans can effectively use our mass transit systems.

But what of the older American who does not need this type of transportation as much as he needs transportation to and from the market, the doctor's office, the church or elsewhere in the immediate vicinity of his home? It is this area of transportation in which we have most seriously failed and in which the elderly are in the greatest need of assistance. In the years to come, we must provide such assistance through proper transportation planning at the state and local levels. This might include minibus service, more convenient bus routes, subsidized car pools, reduced-fare taxi service (with Medicare cards used as identification), and other methods of transportation specially designed for the elderly. At the same time, we must expand programs such as Meals-on-Wheels so that the elderly will have access to necessary services even if they do not have access to local transportation.

Finally, we must realize that the very act of walking is painful, if not impossible, for thousands of elderly and handicapped Americans, and we must make it easier for them to move about in homes and buildings. Wider doors and ramps for wheelchairs, elevators and escalators instead of stairs, automatic doors, safety railings—all of these may seem insignificant to those of us who are able to move about without difficulty, but they are of vital concern to thousands of those who cannot. Particularly in the construction of public places, the inclusion of such safety and comfort features should be mandatory.

When we consider transportation for the elderly, we are actually considering barriers to mobility—barriers which make it difficult for them to climb stairs or go to the corner store, let alone go downtown or travel across the country. And as long as these barriers exist, we can never create a truly comprehensive system of transportation to serve all our citizens.

Health Care

The Present

The United States, a leader in medical science, is lagging far behind other nations in the delivery of health care, particularly to its older citizens. For some it is too expensive; the tremendous increase in medical costs hits hardest at those who lived on fixed incomes. For others it is simply not available. Whatever the reason, the failure of this nation's health care system is undermining the basic security of all Americans.

Although changes in our health care system have been advocated for years—for instance, a Commission on the Cost of Health Care was established in 1929—the fact is that far too little has been done. It took years to establish the Medicare program, and a substantial portion of the millions of dollars appropriated for that program has been spent on increased prices instead of increased service. The high cost of out-of-hospital drugs—so necessary for the treatment of the chronically ill—is not even covered by Medicare. Hospitals are overcrowded and costs are skyrocketing; they rose five times as fast as the cost of living between 1960 and 1970. Nursing home conditions are disgraceful. While many provide excellent care, some, as President Nixon said in 1971, are little more than "dumping grounds for the dying" and "warehouses for the unwanted." We are faced with a shortage of physicians and other medical personnel at a time when our medical schools and other training facilities are in serious financial difficulty. All in all, the health care picture in this country, particularly for the elderly, is indeed bleak.

The Future

By 1993, all Americans should be able to afford and have access to adequate health care. Paramedical personnel, social workers, homemakers, and others should make it possible for many older Americans to recuperate at home, thus alleviating overcrowded conditions in our health facilities. For those needing extended care, nursing homes which have passed strict federal tests for operation and safety should be available. In addition to continuing the fight against cancer and heart disease, medical science should make it possible for many older Americans to live more rewarding lives free from the pain of arthritis and similar disabling afflictions.

The Challenge

Many older Americans are living in fear—fear of catastrophic illness, fear of medical neglect, fear of their inability to afford adequate health care. Despite the fact that the United States leads the world in medical science and technology and despite the fact that America's expenditures for health care have tripled since 1960 (to over $70 billion per year), many of these men and women have every reason to be fearful, for this nation's health care system is simply not working as it should.

There are four major problems contributing to the health care crisis in America today: rising costs; geographic maldistribution of service; low quality and unresponsiveness of care; and inadequate emphasis on preventive medicine.

These problems invariably affect our older population more than other age groups. The elderly have more difficulty paying for the increased costs of medical care because many of them are living on limited, fixed incomes. They have more difficulty traveling long distances to obtain medical care if it is not available to them where they live. They have a greater need for prompt, effective care. Their greater susceptibility to illness makes preventive medicine more important for them than for other groups.

In making changes and improvements in our health care system, therefore, we must address ourselves to all of these problems. Simply providing a system of benefits is not the answer, for any solution must recognize the relationship of price, cost effectiveness, manpower, distribution of services, organization, and research to the total health care picture.

There are several steps which must be taken if we are to improve appreciably this nation's health care system:

A National Health Plan which would guarantee the availability of comprehensive, quality health care to all Americans, regardless of age or the ability to pay, should be enacted. Comprehensive care should include preventive, curative, therapeutic, rehabilitative and long-term care.

This health plan should provide full coverage for physician care, inpatient care, services of specialists such as optometrists and podiatrists, payments for eyeglasses, hearing aids and similar health equipment, at least 120 days of skilled nursing care, inpatient and outpatient drugs furnished by hospitals, and all drugs for certain chronic illnesses.

The concept of prepaid group medical practices (often referred to as health maintenance organizations or HMO's) should be expanded. Such practices can centralize and make more efficient health care delivery and can ensure, through competition, higher standards of health care at less expense.

The federal government must increase significantly its expenditures for medical research, facilities, and manpower programs. Construction of research facilities, hospitals, medical schools, custodial and long-term care facilities should be given a high priority. Grants and loans should be provided to increase substantially the number of educational programs and individuals training to become physicians, nurses and paramedical personnel, such as physician's assistants and lab technicians.

Special hospital and community centers should be established to provide comprehensive care for the elderly. These centers should receive financial assistance from federal, state and local governments and should provide outpatient social services, including homemaking service, in order to allow elderly patients to live at home rather than become institutionalized.

More stringent federal regulations requiring more frequent, thorough and unannounced inspections of the operation and physical facilities of nursing homes should be enacted at once. Federal assistance to states for the purpose of carrying out these recommendations should be substantially increased.

All drugs purchased under federally aided programs should be prescribed and dispensed by generic rather than brand name, whenever possible.

In addition to continuing research to cure or control cancer, heart disease, and other terminal illnesses, a greater effort must be made to find cures for debilitating illnesses, such as arthritis, which cause great pain and limit the ability and mobility of many older Americans.

By adopting these proposals, America will reaffirm for all its citizens the basic doctrine that good health is a right, not a privilege.

Life-Style Options

The Present

The problems of income, retirement, employment, housing, transportation and health care underscore a greater concern—too many older Americans have lost their freedom to choose their own life-styles.

After contributing to our society throughout their working years, many of these men and women find themselves: penalized by the government for attempting to earn an adequate income (Social Security earnings limitation); forced to retire; victimized by technology-induced unemployment and age discrimination; in danger of losing their homes because of increasing taxes for services which they do not receive; un-

able to purchase homes regardless of their financial status; isolated because of physical impairments, inability to afford or use an automobile,
lack of public transportation, and lack of in-home community serivces;
in need of adequate medical attention but unable to obtain it; forced to
live in substandard conditions in their own homes or certain institutions, or forced to live in segregated housing. Is it any wonder, then, that
many older Americans are frustrated, fearful, lonely, and, in some cases,
resentful? They do not seek special treatment; they merely want the same
opportunities, the same options, the same choices that other Americans
enjoy. Yet, in almost every area of national life in the 1970's, they are
denied their freedom of choice.

The Future

By 1993, the older American should be a first-class citizen in every
sense. He should have the freedom to choose his own life-styles, his own
associates, his own pursuits. And he should be respected by our society
as never before, not because of his age, but rather because of his wisdom,
dedication, and achievements.

The Challenge

To provide new opportunities and new options for millions of older
Americans will be a monumental task. Yet the adoption of all the specific
programs and policies I have suggested will be meaningless unless it is
accompanied by a change in national attitudes toward the elderly.

In 1973, too many of our older citizens are being deprived of the
basic rights of life, liberty, and the pursuit of happiness; scorned and
neglected because of age; denied the freedom to live as they want to live.
We must change these conditions in the next twenty years, and we must
give real meaning to those rights which have been denied older Americans for too long. We should be guided in our efforts by the "Declaration
of Aging Rights," a document prepared by our Associations for the
1971 White House Conference on Aging:

> . . . As love and nourishment are due the infant, as education and guid-
> ance are due the child, as freedom to work and build and lead are due the
> grown man and woman, so also are certain conditions of justice due our
> older or retired citizens. Among these we declare to be: 1. The right to
> live with sufficient means for decency and self-respect; 2. The right to move
> about freely, reasonably and conveniently; 3. The right to pursue a career
> or interest regardless of age; 4. The right to be heard on all matters of gen-
> eral public interest; 5. The right to maintain health and well-being through
> preventive care and education; 6. The right to receive assistance in time
> of illness or need; 7. The right to peace and privacy as well as participa-
> tion; 8. The right to protection and safety; 9. The right to seek collectively
> redress of grievances; and 10. The right to live fully and with honor.

The Elderly in 1993—A Prognosis

In terms of their numbers alone, older Americans will have a far greater impact on our society in 1993 than they do today.

It is quite likely, for instance, that more Americans will be living for longer periods on fixed incomes by 1993. Such a development will have a profound effect on our entire economy: It will create a greater economic stability by providing a steadier, more certain amount of purchasing power through guaranteed benefit payments (for instance, one of the reasons for the great depression of 1929, according to some economists, was the fact that very few financial commitments were made to individuals; very few unemployed or retired workers received monthly benefits since Social Security, unemployment insurance and pension plans were all but unheard of). Because of its effect on the tax base, it will result in the need for new sources of tax revenue. Such revenue may be found, hopefully, through the closing of so-called "loopholes" and other steps which will make our system of taxation more efficient and equitable. It will increase pressure for a reordering of budgetary priorities; more funds will be needed for Social Security, health care and similar services, particularly since Social Security benefits will have to be increased to a more realistic level.

Much of the increased pressure for a meaningful reordering of priorities may be brought by the elderly themselves (already there is evidence of a major attitudinal change taking place in our society, both in the self-image of the elderly and in the nation's image of them—the stereotype of "the poor old needy" is being replaced with a much more positive concept). In the past, older Americans have seldom voted on a large scale as a bloc in order to protect their own interests or bring about governmental change; the few examples of such voting patterns have been, for the most part, negative (for instance, the defeat of school budgets by the elderly and others as a reaction to increased property taxes). I expect this to change by 1993. Greater numbers of older Americans, many with more political awareness and expertise than ever before, voting more frequently than those in other age groups, will bring about a change in the balance of political power in America, particularly if they vote as a bloc on such key issues as Social Security and health insurance. And this new political power will be duly noted, I am sure, by our state and national political leaders, who will, in turn, make a greater effort to provide the programs and services needed by our elderly population.

This development will also have a marked impact on politics and government at the local level. All too often in the past, the needs of the elderly have been downgraded or ignored in community planning, and community growth has been fostered at the expense of older citizens. Furthermore, certain public officials in areas where large numbers of retirees live have attempted to force or keep retirees out of the community instead of "planning them in." With greater political power, however, older Americans will be able to maintain their rightful place in the community while contributing to its growth. At the same time, local leaders and planners will have to reassess their concept of community design—both in terms of land use and community organization—in order to ensure the elderly their rightful place in the community.

We may also see in the next twenty years a change in the political philosophy of the elderly. For some time it has been widely held that older Americans are extremely conservative in their political outlook. Recently, however, I have detected a more activist feeling among many older citizens—a belief that they are going to have to act in their own behalf if they are to obtain happiness and security in their retirement lives. Older Americans are becoming highly informed about governmental programs which affect them and the extent to which they are, or are not, being implemented. I expect this trend to continue; in fact, I foresee more and more retired Americans playing an active role in political campaigns, political research and pressure group activities during the next twenty years. Thus, by 1993, no astute politician will be able to take the so-called "elderly vote" for granted.

Another area in which older Americans will increase their power during the next twenty years is in the marketplace, for the fact is that the elderly will own, by 1993, a greater percentage of savings and investments than they do today. With a greater emphasis on retirement education and preretirement planning, older Americans will be encouraged to save more for their retirement years; with the savings creating, in turn, the investment through which our economy can continue to grow and prosper. And the fact that the elderly will control a greater share of the nation's purchasing power by 1993—constituting a change in economic distribution—will not be lost on business and industry, with the result that more products and services and more advertising will be directed at our older population than ever before.

Finally, this newly acquired economic and political power will hasten the day when older Americans will have true freedom of choice in their lives. For such power will stimulate government, business and private social service agencies to do more to help the elderly help themselves. By 1993, our older citizens should have the freedom to choose their life-style, the freedom to participate in our society individually and as a group, the freedom to select their own options and to help determine America's.

Conclusion

In 1973, it is indeed ironic that poverty exists amid plenty, that illiteracy is permitted in a society of unexcelled intellectual achievement, that discrimination stains the record of a land which proclaims that all men are created equal. Perhaps the most tragic irony of all, however, is the fact that millions of older Americans who toiled so long to provide comfort and security for all of us are today being deprived of comfort and security in the twilight of their lives. These men and women have sought no special privilege or treatment; they wish to be partners in progress, not wards of the state. Yet, in almost every area of national life in the early 1970's, they have not been given that opportunity.

We are now in a position to end this injustice, for America stands at a crossroads today. Behind us are decades of indifference and hostility to social progress. To our right and left are the paths of status quo, upon which we have made too little progress in terms of human needs. Ahead is a path of promise where human life is the ultimate priority. Which do we choose?

My hopes for 1993, which may seem fanciful and unrealistic at this time, can be achieved if only America will choose the right path. We may not perform miracles in the next twenty years, but we can chart a course which will lead this nation from a past of apathy and neglect to a future of human dignity, compassion and understanding. Or we can sit back and do nothing while the legitimate needs of millions of Americans go unmet. Which do we choose?

It is clear that our nation's older citizens, who have contributed so much to our society, deserve better treatment from it. For their sake and for our own, do we attempt in the next two decades to right the wrongs, heal the wounds, correct the mistakes? Or do we bequeath to future generations of older Americans the same frustration, fear, loneliness and misery endured by many of our older citizens today?

The choice is simple, but the time is short and the task is great. So let us learn from the past and act in the present, lest we forfeit the future.

6

Corrections in 1993

MILTON G. RECTOR

In projecting a view of what will exist in the field of corrections a number of years ahead we have a choice of being pessimistic or optimistic. A pessimistic view is fully justified, with the end of the human race being projected by some scientists for not more than decades ahead; and with what all must acknowledge to be terribly acute problems of living, just breathing and avoiding automobile injuries, in society today.

There is justification, however, for an optimistic view. It must be one as pragmatic as the pessimistic view. That is, conditions and methods must be noted by which corrections by 1993 could be transformed from the bleak, cruel system it is today to one that is humane and helpful in improving behavior and reducing crime. They do exist.

A spin-off of the civil rights movement in the 1960's was a greater acceptance that offenders against the law were also a minority deprived of civil rights. Segregation as practiced in schools and institutions for the correction of offenders was attacked with the demand for racial integration of other public schools and institutions. Whereas institution riots of the previous decades brought little permanent change for the better, riots in the early 1970's found a public conditioned and more sympathetic to the need for protection of rights of prisoners and supportive of change in the inhumane conditions common to correctional institutions. The militant demand of minorities for equal rights was being echoed in the prisons.

During the 1970's sentencing still selected a majority of committed offenders from the ranks of the economically, educationally and culturally deprived, and the courts at long last were taking cognizance of the fact that they too shared responsibility for detaining and confining prisoners in destructive and inhumane jails and prisons. Judges were ordering that institutions unable to rehabilitate offenders at least should meet minimum standards for physical health and personal safety. Legal services and ombudsmen were increasingly available to the prisoner although correctional administration still viewed litigation producing regained rights for prisoners as devastating setbacks for the autonomy of corrections. One could predict that the day was near when the statutes would more clearly define that the intent of corrections is to re-educate and redirect attitudes and behavior. Such statutory intent bolstered the appropriation requests of administrators whose systems were staffed and equipped for little more than custody and surveillance. Such intent also served as a handle for litigation and change through the courts where the legislative and executive branches of government were reluctant to lead.

There was an articulated trend toward community-based corrections. This unfortunately in the early 1970's meant new kinds of institutions, somewhat smaller and located nearer to communities which offered a variety of resources. The silver lining of economic inflation yielded political support for a moratorium on institution construction in favor of maximized staffing and fulfillment of community-based noninstitutional corrections.

The role of the lay volunteer in corrections was rediscovered. The optimism the writer holds for corrections in 1993 assumes that fear of competitiveness from the volunteer has subsided as the security and professionalism of the career correctional worker increases. The voice and action of informed volunteers in changing public attitudes and in influencing and supporting essential systems changes had been multiplied manifold.

The training and utilizing of experienced and skilled offenders and ex-offenders in correctional programs progressed from a potentially limited and short-term fad to an important place in corrections personnel policy. Programming for systematic feedback from the victims, witnesses and families of offenders as direct and indirect users of correctional services was finally developed as a guide for the improvement of those services.

Concomitant with the emergence of an active, aggressive civil rights movement, the same spirit and activity emerged in prisons. Contrary to what appeared to the public—through the press and television—the civil rights movement in prisons was not riotous. Starting with the pressure for religious rights by black Muslims, the emphasis extended to complaints, backed by legal action, against the brutality and dehumanization of whipping (abolished by one United States court), solitary confinement (restricted by some courts), censorship, etc.

It was only when these methods appeared to have no impact that demonstrations and riots occurred, but no more than in earlier decades. The killings at Attica aroused worldwide attention, whereas the killings at North Carolina State Prison only three years earlier caused not a ripple of public concern.

A change also occurred in the correctional establishment. Administrators at their conferences had turned to self-criticism, an almost unavoidable change, in the face of what courts were acknowledging, as well as other exposures. Unfortunately, the self-criticism still lagged behind, and remained not more than an echo. Administrators continued to defend, in court and elsewhere, their right to deal with prisoners as they saw fit.

But more recognition than that was needed. Some old standby ideas were subjected to examination. Was individualization serving as a cover for discrimination? Was even the concept of treatment serving as a cover for unnecessary confinement and brutal discipline? Even the indeterminate sentence was called into question. It has resulted in long minimum terms before parole eligibility. Also, parole was too restrictive, and the statutes were part of that pattern. They facilitated long maximum terms. A means was needed not to keep terms long or lengthen them but to shorten them.

There was at last wide acceptance that prisons were a failure. What had been invented to isolate wrongdoers as sinners requiring solitude to do penance had evolved into penitentiaries that caged the poor, the unskilled, the undereducated and the minorities. The means of transforming prisons by proof that offenders could be changed within the community, existed and had to be used. Several states established subsidies for community services to help reduce state prison commitments and increased the use of probation which had been started in 1840 by a volunteer seeking to save men from criminal lives and imprisonment.

With all of these things occurring in the 1970's, what can we find existing in 1993?

1993—Prisons Are Empty

Any utopian would think first of projecting a system of corrections that abolished prisons. Even the lesser utopian, the mere optimist, had to see prisons of the future as being limited to dealing with the most dangerous offenders only. Otherwise they should be, *and have been,* abolished. They were abolished much more realistically than doctors could project the abolition of hospitals. The difference is that hospitals have been needed for intensive care of sick people; and by and large they achieve the goal. But prisons did not serve an equivalent purpose.

Prisons did not protect the community, any more than capital punishment did. The recidivism rate of people leaving prisons always was notoriously high; and it contrasted with the no worse—usually better—record of those placed on probation. Studies showed that equivalent offenders, that is, those committed for equivalent crimes and with equivalent backgrounds, did at least as well on probation as in prison.

The best one could say was that prisons retained the criminal acts of prisoners within the prisons, at least as long as they were locked up. This "protection" of the "outside" community was statistically so minor as to be trivial. The volume of crimes when imprisonment was used extensively was such that the crimes prevented by keeping people locked up was statistically insignificant.

It was more significant that offenders came out worse criminals than when they went into prison, more than compensating for the "protection" of having kept them locked up for a while. A report of the Pennsylvania Board of Parole, reporting on convicted parole violators returned to prison over a ten-year period, noted that 3,424 parolees had been returned for new crimes. Eighteen of them had been orginally committed as drug and narcotic offenders. While eleven of the eighteen were returned to prison for new drug crimes, 103 others were also returned for drug offenses. Had prison experience helped them to learn the new crime? Another example: Thirteen of the parolees had been originally convicted for carrying weapons, but 101 of those returned were returned for this crime. "Where did the parolees acquire this habit of carrying weapons, or were they smarter in that they 'beat the rap' for a more serious crime?" asked the author of that report.

The same question may be asked for nine of the parolees who had originally been sentenced for receiving stolen goods who did not repeat this crime on parole, but fifty-one others of the parolees did.

A large number of crimes were committed *in the prisons,* both by administration and by prisoners. Rampant and violent homosexuality alone, endemic in all prisons, was a considerable crime factor. In fact, government promoted homosexuality in preference to heterosexuality in the prison systems.

If prisons did not protect, did they rehabilitate? Few people could claim that they did so.

What purpose did they serve? Why was institutionalization the dominant and underlying philosophy of corrections for so long a period? Even when 80 per cent of the country's convicted offenders were serving their sentences on probation or parole, these and other community-based services were promoted as "alternatives to institutionalization." It was not until the 1980's that institutions were perceived as "alternatives to community corrections."

One practical approach to the protection that incarceration could provide and which led to the demise of prisons and large congregate care institutions was to sentence only truly dangerous offenders to prison. Then it was found that most seriously assaultive offenders were mentally ill, and should be taken care of in mental hospitals where they could be treated, as they could not be in prisons. The Model Sentencing Act first published by the National Council on Crime and Delinquency in 1963 introduced the definitions of dangerousness in sentencing statutes and provided for extended terms of incarceration for dangerous offenders.

The Model Sentencing Act first established two classes of commitments, one for the dangerous offender, who was carefully defined in the Act. He could be sentenced to up to thirty years, but a substantial procedure was required before such a sentence could be imposed. Besides a presentence investigation, referral to a diagnostic center was required. There was a full hearing, with the defendant having access to all of the reports submitted to the court. If the judge sentenced the defendant as a dangerous offender, he was required to make findings and give his reasons for the sentence. With full record and the requirement of findings and reasons, the sentence and the entire proceedings were thus reviewable by an appellate court.

By the year 1971 only the first state (Oregon) had adopted this act. In the following twenty years many more states adopted the concept of requiring proof of dangerousness before permitting any period of institutional confinement beyond two years. The concept stimulated the first significant state and federal research into the problems of behavioral deviancy related to violent and assaultive crimes. With the clear determination that, with few exceptions, the sicker the crime, the sicker the criminal, the majority of persons committing violent crimes became charges of mental health rather than correctional systems. Thus the way was paved for the abolishment of maximum security prisons by 1990 in favor of security hospitals staffed as mental health treatment and research centers. Coupled with the development of community psychiatry, hopeful progress has been made in concert with the anti-poverty programs to reduce the community conditions and influences which for decades produced cultures of violence in our society.

The opposite of dangerousness is nondangerousness. By carefully defining dangerous offenders, the first Model Sentencing Act and its subsequent revisions also defines the rest of the offenders as nondangerous. By the very definitions of the dangerous and nondangerous offenders in the statutes the courts were encouraged to sentence the nondangerous offenders to one or another form of community treatment rather than imprisonment. With the release of the large staffs and capital funding required for custodial care, appropriations were transferred to community corrections. For the repetitive thief, for other repeated offenders who did not threaten violence against other persons, and white-collar criminals for whom fines proved to be no deterrent, commitment of up to two years with periods of trial release to community-based centers or institutions has been found more effective than the long sentences to large prisons of the past. The damaging effect of confinement has been reduced by a one-month leave following each period of six months spent in the institution. Prisoner conduct during the period of leave can reduce the length of sentence.

The abolishment of long-term prisons and the establishment of the one-hundred-bed as maximum size for the present community correctional institution and smaller residential centers have permitted the abolishment of parole boards. Definite sentences by the courts with maximum of two years, with required leave every six months and administrative discretion for interim periods of leave for training, employment, education, special therapy or family requirements no longer require quasi-judicial boards to deal with the disparity and unfairness of sentences so common in the past.

Extended periods of commitment to mental health authorities for dangerous offenders require a review by the court at least annually. The review record requires documentation of treatment and subsequent diagnoses. All records are reviewable by the defendant's counsel whose presence is required at the review hearings. Periods of trial release under mental health supervision and final discharge are authorized by the court upon recommendation by the Mental Health Authority.

The model correctional codes of 1993 enlarge the power of judges to use a variety of dispositions allowing the defendent to remain in the community; for example, suspended sentence without probation and deferred conviction with voluntary supervision. Under deferred conviction, controls equal to probation are obtained, but the defendant avoids a conviction if he successfully completes the voluntary probation term.

Other forms of sentence that avoid a great deal of institutionalization with great deterrent effect are the fine and financial restitution to the victim. In the past these sentences were used too sparingly. In cases of organized crime, embezzlement, fraud and other crimes where victims have lost large sums of money, restitution orders equal to the losses, even to millions of dollars, have proved more effective as well as satisfying to victims than did former prison terms. Installment payment of both fines and restitution over extended terms have made such sentences realistic.

Prison Industry

An unexpected assist to prison reform and the subsequent abandonment of prisons came from business and labor leadership. By the year 1940 private contractors had been excluded from the use of prison labor in most states. The exposure of scandalous exploitation of prisoners at slave wages during the 1930's and financial kickbacks to wardens and other officials by contractors brought demands for reform. Reform through federal and state legislation resulted primarily because open market sale of products produced by cheap prison labor was allegedly unfair competition for business and labor.

State and federal prison systems then set about developing industry systems wherein the products were purchased entirely for governmental use. Such state use of inmate-produced goods, it was claimed, did not compete with business and labor. In time a few states invited advisory committees of persons representing business and labor to help improve the relevancy and efficiency of prison industry. In general, however, the system retained the evils of idleness and negative motivation of the old contract labor system. Prisons were equipped with machinery which became antiquated long before it could be changed. Several prisoners would be assigned to tasks requiring but one. Training was substandard and seldom related to the employment potential for released inmates. Prisoner pay often was even lower than under the contract labor system. Studies of the better state and federal prison industry systems showed the production costs to be excessive, inmate production to be low and few prisoners were released with training required for the employment market. Some job opportunities and trades such as taxi driver and barber were excluded by law. Government agencies which exhorted the employment needs of ex-offenders were among the worst for excluding ex-offenders from the government services.

The recognition of individual rights as an essential concomitant of positive corrections caused a re-examination of prison industry in the 1970's. Business and labor were made aware that their involvement in direct operation of prison industry rather than indirect advisory roles was essential. They saw for the first time that the $165,000,000 in prisoner-produced goods purchased by state and federal government in one year would have been purchased otherwise from private business. The goods also would have been produced by labor paid at union wage rates. Government was indeed competing with private enterprise and was doing so by exploiting prison labor in much the same ways as the former contract labor system. Texas as late as 1972 was found to be using state and federal grant funds to pay substandard wages to prison labor to build a huge criminal justice education center at a state college.

Experimentation with the involvement of business and labor directly in the training of prison inmates was followed by the direct operation of business and industry within closed prisons. Organized labor was found eager to cooperate in inmate training and opened up opportunities for union apprenticeship and membership for prisoners. Products were sold on the open market and prisoner were paid union wages. The U.S. Department of Labor helped accelerate the development by providing incentive grants to business and industry to equip prison factories and service training centers. Subsidies were provided to pay inmates during the early and nonproductive training periods.

Problems were manifold and often the resourcefulness of organized business and labor surpassed that of corrections in resolving them. Corrections budgets had to be increased to permit union wages for inmates employed in work essential to institution operation and maintenance. Personnel conflicts arose when full work training and employment required heavy rescheduling of professional treatment services during evening hours. The changes, however, forced the development of accredited education systems in the prisons with choices between full-time work or education and part-time work and part-time education. Treatment services learned to adapt to the scheduling required by work, training and education within the walls as they do within normal communities.

The first organized union of prison inmates at Greenhaven Prison in New York State in 1972 to negotiate wages for prisoners was a shocking but forward-looking development for corrections administration. The same year the National Council on Crime and Delinquency published the first model statute for the protection of rights of prisoners and convened a group of national experts from labor-management arbitration and negotiation to initiate development of comparable guidelines and skills to help correctional management take a quantum leap toward recognition of prisoners' rights as basic to correction and toward the use of developed knowledge and skill in dealing with conflict rather than by force and firearms.

Correctional management had to learn and use the skills required in negotiating and resolving labor-management conflicts. Governmental officials at first generally resisted the concept of union organization within the prisons and for the same reason many progressive corrections leaders at first opposed the new partnership offered by business and labor. There were escapes, injuries and violations of contraband regulations while corrections learned to adapt and redesign its security rules and practices. Business and labor learned to understand the institution subcultures and related pressures which caused some differences between the hard-core unemployed inside and those outside the prison walls.

The benefits were many, however, and the involvement of organized business and labor undoubtedly contributed as much as any other factor to the demise of the prison in American corrections.

The use of arbitration techniques gave corrections a vital new skill in resolving other conflict issues and eventually led to the disappearance of riots as a means of bringing unfair and inhumane conditions to public attention. Business and labor leaders and their outside personnel assigned to prison industry became a significant and informed force in influencing corrections to abandon the overreliance on security. Where professional and technical corrections staff concerned with rehabilitation functions accounted for only 5 per cent of all institution personnel in 1970, they outnumbered custodial staff in number and in functions by 1980. The escalation of institution costs and comparable institution and community corrections cost effectiveness studies confirmed the need to phase out prisons.

Business and labor having observed firsthand that most prisoners were both rational and trainable human beings, joined corrections in pressing legislative bodies for a number of transitional changes until community-based corrections became reality. They attained dramatic increases in the use of releases and furloughs for work, training and education. They raised for public debate and change the system's tolerance of the disparity and destructive length of sentences, and the uneven parole practices which proved more destructive than positively punishing and rehabilitating. They succeeded in their insistence that new prisons built during the 1970's as a gesture to demands for prison reform be smaller, located near industrial centers and redesigned to permit training, education and employment functions without interfering with security requirements. At long last and many new prisons later they raised for ultimate solution the need to transfer the few dangerous and unmanageable offenders to research-treatment centers under mental health auspices. This permitted the abandonment of the traditional large, isolated prisons as well as the newer 300- to 500-bed correctional institutions. Thus many correctional institutions unnecessarily built at great expense during the 1975–1990 period are being converted into public facilities for vocational education centers and community colleges.

Institutions for Juveniles

The demise of large, congregate care institutions for children in trouble preceded the abandonment of adult prisons by almost a decade. These institutions, like those for adults, went through a number of transitional stages before the correctional and child welfare officials could accept that the general public expected better than destructive institutional care for children.

First called reform schools, then training schools and later juvenile correctional centers, the search for new names was replaced in the 1970's by a search for new approaches. The forerunner of change had been first through forestry camps and ranch-type facilities which demonstrated that smaller, open-type facilities with less idleness and shorter commitments were as effective, less destructive and less costly than were longer-term institutions which often housed several hundred children. The most lasting impact of the camp and small institution era, however, was an acceleration in the institutionalization of children. The heightened expectations for new successes resulted in commitments of thousands of children who otherwise would have been placed on probation. The same results had been noted in the introduction of group homes and residential-type commitment facilities within a few cities.

Appellate court decisions in the mid-1970's struck a telling and permanent blow to the practice of institutionalizing children. The first such decision forbade the common practice whereby correctional and child welfare authorities transferred juvenile court committed children from training schools to correctional institutions for felony offenders. The defense for this practice acknowledged that such transfers were by administrative discretion without court review or representation by counsel, and placed children in institutions to which they only could have been sentenced originally for felony convictions. The children, however, had become so obstreperous and resistive of rehabilitation efforts in the training schools that the more secure confines and program of the adult correctional institution were deemed necessary.

After striking down the transfer practice the Chief Justice of the United States expressed personal dismay in 1975 in a unanimous decision removing from the jurisdiction of juvenile and family courts those children who had not committed an act which would be a crime if committed by an adult. For the first time the U.S. Supreme Court had had evidence presented to the effect that under provisions of dependency, neglect, and persons in need of supervision the juvenile courts were assuming jurisdiction over the lives of tens of thousands of children who had committed no crime. The juvenile courts sought to retain this jurisdiction until required to admit to a Chief Justice of the United States that the juvenile and family courts could do little to correct the conditions creating truancy, disrespect for parental authority, dependency and neglect. While more appropriate services were in short supply from other agencies the Supreme Court found there was little justification for retaining jurisdiction in the juvenile court where the children were detained and committed as though they were delinquent. Indeed, it was stated, such retention of jurisdiction under the pretense of meeting the needs of nondelinquent children could retard the allocation of funds for needed services through child welfare, mental health, education and other such agencies. Thus in 1993 children in need of special help as indicated by deviant behavior are helped through a consortium of community services. No child, however, can be arrested and processed through the court unless he has committed what would be a crime if he were an adult. The measure of help received therefrom has been found to be far less than the harm which was done under the former child protection statutes. These changes in jurisdiction of the juvenile court resulted in dramatic reductions in both probation case loads and institution populations. Not only was the trend accelerated toward community-based corrections, but for the first time it was recognized in public policy that all services for all children can best be provided, funded and programmed within the local community.

New Roles for State and Federal Government

Traditionally state government prior to the 1960's was content to provide correctional institutions without questioning more appropriate dispositions for every person committed by local juvenile and criminal courts. For those offenders who violated a federal law rather than state law the federal government had established a separate correctional institution and probation parole system to receive federal court sentences. During the late 1950's and early1960's a few states adopted the practice of subsidizing local probation services with state funds. While the allocations were nominal in every state the immediate result was a reduction in institution commitments.

It wasn't until 1964, when California enacted a subsidy plan of sufficient amount to reimburse counties which reduced commitments substantially and adopted innovative probation programs, that a new concept for state correctional leadership was established. Ironically, California was the state where forestry camp subsidies prior to probation subsidies produced the country's and perhaps the world's greatest per capita institution population for youthful offenders. The concept had been introduced earlier for state mental health and retarded children's services. It was found that the most effective as well as most economic role for state government was to invest state funds in community-based services. Backed by state expertise in the form of innovative program guidelines, research and technical assistance, the new state role added another significant blow to the abandonment of prisons and large isolated training schools. The first five years of the California plan eliminated nearly 200 million dollars in new institution construction and operating costs with an investment of about 60 million dollars in state subsidy to the counties. Four state training schools and two state prisons were closed by the end of 1972. The state's reliance on institution confinement, however, was not reduced until later. Study of state subsidy effectiveness revealed a sharp increase in the use of local county institution commitments for children and county jail sentences for adults.

Correctional reform as an essential part of the country's drive to upgrade juvenile and criminal justice services was highlighted in the 1967 Report of the President's Commission on Law Enforcement and the Administration of Justice. An Omnibus Crime Bill adopted by Congress introduced the concept of returning federal funds to state and local governments on a shared revenue basis to help improve criminal justice systems. Correctional reform and community-based corrections received priority after the first few years of the Act which also established the Law Enforcement Assistance Administration in the Justice Department. Unfortunately, the new initiative for correctional reform and community-based corrections was to hasten the building of new 200- to 500-cell prisons and smaller residential-type institutions located near population centers. It was not until 1976 when several hundred million dollars had been spent in new institution construction with a concomitant increase in prison population that the federal leadership role became more clearly defined, and federal-state guidelines required proof of maximized non-institutional services before permitting shared revenue funds to be spent on construction.

As early as 1956 it was perceived that the role of the federal government must change in the administration of correctional services for juvenile offenders. The need was to strengthen the local juvenile courts and community services for delinquents to justify the remand jurisdiction of all juvenile offenders from the federal to the local juvenile courts. At least twenty years after such remand had been authorized in the federal statutes the Federal Bureau of Prisons was still opening and operating institutions for juvenile offenders.

The issue was sharpened in 1970 when the Federal Bureau of Prisons was instructed by the Attorney General to plan itself as a model correctional system which could be replicated by the states. The mandate in time became an obvious non sequitur. While it had as a national goal the promotion of community-based corrections through the LEAA grants to the states and cities, it made no sense to pursue a conflicting goal within the same federal agency which would result in the transfer of offenders great distances from their home communities.

In 1971 the NCCD testified before the Congress on the need to disestablish the Federal Bureau of Prisons as an operating agency for institution administration. It was suggested that in its place there should be a Federal Corrections Administration to give technical assistance and leadership to the states to help them design and establish innovative community corrections, to help them in program research and assessment, and the training of personnel. It was suggested that such technical assistance and leadership should be separated from the agency administering the federal grants to assure maximum objectivity in program recommendations and development. The plan called for federal funds to help strengthen state corrections systems to maximize community services, and for the federal government to contract with the state systems for all services for federal offenders.

The matter was brought to a head in 1972 when California was acclaimed for having initiated community corrections which were emptying the juvenile and adult institutions. The Federal Bureau of Prisons' budget for the 1972–73 financial year called for the planning and ultimate construction of new federal youth institutions on the West Coast—at least two in California. California and federal officials conferred on the advantages of contracting with the state for care of federal prisoners and the new concept was tested. By 1975 all federal institutions except four regional research institutions for special offenders were offered for sale to the states. By 1985 all of the former federal prisons were closed as the state systems had developed a gradation of community services in which the small, short-term local institution or residential center was the predominant institution.

Today—in 1993—the federal leadership role is still ill-defined. Crime and delinquency are recognized basically as problems of deviant behavior requiring maximum research and treatment knowledge from the behavioral sciences. Therefore, there is considerable support for transferring the Federal Corrections Administration (Bureau of Prisons) and its complex of research, information and technical assistance services from the Justice Department to the Department of Human Resources. However, because the Department of Human Resources' predecessor Health, Education and Welfare, had traditionally shown no interest or leadership in the field of criminal behavior and very little in juvenile delinquency it is difficult to get Congressional support for the transfer. The solid linkage the Law Enforcement Assistance Administration has developed for criminal justice planning in concert with other federal agencies whose services relate to crime causation adds strong support for both LEAA and the Federal Correctional Administration to remain within the Department of Justice. This Department is itself being studied for possible changes into a more comprehensive administration of justice service to include federal public defender services, a consolidation of all federal criminal law enforcement services and comprehensive criminal justice reporting and research services. It might be best for the behavioral and social sciences to maintain their linkage and influence with law enforcement and legal services through LEAA and the Federal Correctional Administration as part of the Department of Justice.

With the abandoning of federal institutions the federal parole board and the federal probation and parole services were also phased out. All such services are now a part of the state correctional systems.

Parole as an Interim Step

As those versed in the history of American penology will know, parole was developed as a response to the unfair and inaccurate sentencing of the courts and to the exceedingly long sentences so long regarded as a deterrent to criminal behavior. First, as a ticket-of-leave to release on a trial basis prisoners with unnecessarily long sentences, parole later evolved as a procedure to select the most appropriate time to release rehabilitated prisoners and as a service to continue rehabilitation efforts within the community.

An unattained goal of parole was someday to develop scientific criteria for selecting prisoners for parole release at the optimum time. At the very least, parole boards were to have become expert in equalizing the disparity in sentencing resulting from illogical definitions of crimes and maximum terms fixed by state legislators and Congress, and wide ranges in sentences within those terms reflecting biases and emotions of judges inexperienced in criminal law. With few exceptions, however, the professonalism of parole boards was impeded by patronage appointments and efforts to apply scientifically tested criteria to parole decisions were again and again overruled by political criteria or more often by no criteria.

Parole boards had discretion to reduce the disparity in sentencing and the destructiveness of long sentences long before the courts responded to sentencing institutes, research showing the counterproductivity of long sentences and the potential gains in public safety and rehabilitation from community corrections. However, even when a few states placed with paroling authorities the power to fix the length of sentences for imprisonment, the sentencing boards did not rise to the challenge. The period of time served in prison was invariably longer than when maximum sentences were fixed by the courts.

By the middle and late 1970's parole systems were experimenting with the use of professional staff based within the institutions for case analysis and recommendations as to parole release dates. The parole boards themselves became smaller in size and limited their functions primarily to reviewing recommendations of staff and legal counsel of prisoners. The provision for legal counsel helped sharpen the criteria for release and reduced the secrecy which had long clouded parole decisions to release from prison and to return parole violators to prison. However, few boards proved to be willing to accept the responsiblity and risk of paroling all prisoners to the advantages of supervision at least a short time before the termination of sentence.

Several states during the 1970's adopted the American Law Institute concept of a parole term fixed by statute as a part of every prison term. The intent was to give every released prisoner a period of helpful supervision when parole boards refused to parole prior to the end of the sentence fixed by the court. The result, however, was an increase in length of time served by prisoners as politically sensitive parole authorities became even less willing to experiment and to submit their decisions to assessment and research for more accurate releasing criteria.

During the 1980 decade the research which proved beyond doubt the values in shorter terms, and the readiness of the public to phase out large and small prisons also pointed up the incongruity of parole boards. Thus the power to fix sentences at any period up to a two-year maximum in 1993 lies with the courts. The month of leave with supervision required for every six months of incarceration and the requirement that the community corrections agency make its employment, housing and social services available to every discharged prisoner finally made the need for a separate parole service unnecessary.

For several years after all the states adopted the concept of committing dangerous offenders for indefinite periods to the mental health departments there was a trend to maintain parole boards for those mental health institutions housing dangerous offenders. Professional mental health personnel were troubled about their capability to determine when an offender was no longer dangerous. Many, uncertain about their professional expertise, supported the retention of the power to release by independent parole authorities. Others, however, questioned whether such decisions should be made by boards whose orientations were more political than professional.

Acceptance by all correctional and mental health institutions of the principle of the right to treatment after a series of appellate court decisions in the 1970's brought the debate to an end. Judges indicated to legislative bodies their determination to see that the intent behind the commitment of dangerous persons for study and rehabilitation was carried out in practice. The legislative requirement of an annual court review, whenever possible by the committing judge, with the offender represented by counsel, was first resented and resisted by mental health authorities. In time, however, the requirement of legal counsel and court review induced such doubt and concern about the criteria for determining dangerousness, treatment, and recovery from the condition of dangerousness that more public funds than ever before were allocated for research into the problems and treatment of deviant behavior.

Thus, the bonds of partnership between the legal and behavioral science disciplines were enhanced. Also the state of knowledge about the causation and treatment of violent and repetitive criminal behavior in 1993 is at least a century beyond what might have been predicted in the law-and-order periods of the 1960's and 1970's. Parole had served an important interim period of search for alternatives to severe sentences and to an era of harsh, destructive penology. The refusal of parole authorities to submit to rigorous assessment and research may have even accelerated the demands for research and change in the criminal laws, courts, the mental health and the correctional fields. That parole could not be made to work more effectively was an important factor in the elimination of prisons.

Community Corrections

Out of that research and change came 1993 community corrections based on the concept that the wrongdoer can best be disciplined, and behaviorally re-educated and redirected within his community. In city after city and state after state it was necessary to confirm repeatedly that centuries of reliance upon length of commitment and caged confinement produced more problems than they solved. Persons normally responsive to punishment for purposeful misconduct had seldom been confined. Persons who were the least responsive and whose disregard for the rights and property of others stemmed from a culture of violence, alienation, or various kinds of societal deprivations and isolation, received incarceration in disproportionate amounts. Experiments with shorter periods of confinement and increased services through community correction always demonstrated at least as much if not more reduction in delinquent behavior.

The greatest impediments to change came from criminal justice leaders rather than from the public. Law enforcement leaders had great difficulty in accepting research findings and repeatedly highlighted heinous crimes by former offenders to prove that the decline of prisons was a tragic error. Many prosecutors and judges, proclaiming their responsibilities to protect the public, demanded long periods of confinement for a select few whose crimes received most publicity. Correctional leaders themselves during the 1970's found it difficult to accept as an argument against building smaller prisons the fact that corrections had long been dealing with the majority of offenders on probation and parole with but minor portions of correctional manpower and money. Even as assessment of correctional programs gave repeated assurance that the greatest return for the correctional dollar would come from community corrections, the early trend through 1970 and 1980 was to build smaller and newly designed prisons near urban centers. Only after the expenditure of several hundred million dollars for such "community-based institutions" and the findings that they were no more successful than larger, more isolated institutions did a majority of the leaders of corrections departments join in support of priority allocations to maximize noninstitutional community corrections.

Probation, long underused and understaffed, came into its own during the 1980's. In some states where political domination and patronage had delayed the expansion and change of probation, state correctional departments appointed correctional specialists to work innovatively and directly in the community with offenders sentenced to the care of the corrections department. Some state corrections agencies induced change in local probation services by legislation authorizing state administration of probation, and others allocated state funds directly to local probation agencies for expansion of community corrections with technical assistance and standards to improve the quality of local services.

The most successful probation programs in 1993 are those in the states where corrections has been linked structurally at state and community levels with other human resource services including health, mental health, social welfare, education, employment and community planning and development. The trend now indicates that within a few more years the terms probation and probation officer will no longer be used. The practice is increasingly for the courts to commit offenders to the corrections department of the human resource agency for supervision and rehabilititation in the community corrections programs. The probation functions of presentence investigation, of supervision in view of detention and of community supervision for the duration of sentence, are also the functions of community correction officers.

Probation officers and their counterparts, community corrections officers, have become less concerned with a long-considered need to offer offenders intensive casework. Their primary function now is to serve as counselors and advocates for offenders to see that they receive priority for the training, treatment or other assistance required from one or more of the consortium of human resource services available in every community. Offenders, ex-offenders and victims of crimes are recruited and trained both as volunteers and as employees for correctional programs. Experience has shown that having offenders work to pay restitution to their victims and to know personally of the losses and suffering of their victims has had a positive twofold effect. Victims' fears of future victimization are lessened as they see firsthand that corrections is drawing on every community resource to help reduce conditions which are conducive to crime and is placing responsibility on the delinquents and criminal offenders for the development of inner resources and self-help; offenders develop a greater sense of personal responsibility for having hurt others from the experience of helping repair that damage with the help of community rsources and often with help from the victims themselves. This process helps reduce alienation and greatly enhances the ability of offenders and their families to utilize community resources.

The use of security detention for both children and adults pending court disposition has been reduced to about one per cent of arrests by the development of volunteer and paraprofessional community correctional aides within the neighborhoods where arrested persons reside. Some of the aides take arrested persons into their own homes or apartments when closer custody is necessary to avoid jail detention. Other persons are charged to remain within their own residences during time not spent in school, work, job training or visits to such resources as the community mental health center for diagnostic studies. The majority are released on summons without supervision. Predisposition detention and sentences are also served in apartments and residential centers which have been located for the corrections agency by neighborhood aides and volunteers.

In a substantial majority of cases the courts permit both criminals and delinquents voluntarily to accept the status of probation in lieu of a conviction or finding of delinquency. Restitution to the victim and fines are also paid voluntarily in such cases. When the offender is no longer considered by the court to be in need of correctional assistance the case is dismissed without an official record.

Several departments of community planning and development as divisions of the human resource agencies have built public housing in sections of metropolitan and suburban areas to which offenders requiring more rigid controls are restricted but may live with their families. These neighborhoods are open to other families including ex-offenders who may come and go as they wish. The offenders are permitted only to leave for work, or other corrections program requirement. All offenders not otherwise employed or undergoing special training are employed in public service at regular wages and thereby support themselves and their families. Many are retained in public service positions when their sentence or commitments terminate.

Near the large urban areas small confinement instiutions are still required and range from 50 to 100 capacity. While few prisoners serve an entire sentence of up to two years in one of these correctional centers, some do. Therefore, a few of the centers offer a range of education training and job opportunities within their confines. Others permit daytime release for work, training or education. Full wages are received for all work within the institutions, and confined inmates are expected to support themselves and their families as well as make restitution payments to their victims. In every community citizen committees have been organized to visit the institutions regularly to see that they don't deteriorate into small closed prisons.

The elimination of separate institutions for misdemeanant and felony offenders came about as large institutions were phased out and dangerous offenders were committed to the care of mental health departments. During the 1970's a ground swell of public support resulted in the decriminalization of much behavior which was primarily a problem of morals or health rather than crime. Thus, relieved of the huge volume of drunks, alcoholics, vagrants, addicts, drug users, readers of material classified as pornographic, and persons involved in consenual sexual behavior, the differentiation between misdemeanor and felony became less important to law enforcement and the courts. The dramatic reduction in the overload on police, prosecution and courts permitted funds destined for the criminal justice system to be allocated to departments within the human resources agencies. Court reorganization equalized the criminal courts into one trial court and the six-week trial rule long ago was found feasible and effective for adjudicating all but a few criminal cases. Had these changes not occurred it is doubtful that America in 1993 would have made the progress it has in developing a community corrections system which complements rather than denigrates a free and democratic society.

Reduction in all crimes of more than 50 per cent and in violent crimes of more than 70 per cent have occurred between 1973 and 1993 —not because of a more effective and humane criminal justice system, but because as a people we stopped pretending that more police, more courts and more corrections as a comprehensive but isolated system could either control or reduce crime.

PART II

NEW WAY TO MEET NEEDS: GOALS FOR THE FUTURE

7

Social Casework

CAREL B. GERMAIN

Fifty years ago Clarence Day wrote an engaging essay [1] in which he suggested what man might have been had be descended from an ancestor of the great cats, say, instead of from an ancestor of the great apes. There would have been great differences in the physical and psychological attributes of human beings. Similarly, feline patterns of social organization, uses of language, value systems and other cultural artifacts would have been amusingly different from those derived from a monkey heritage.

Speculating about the practice of social casework twenty years into the future might, too, be an engaging fantasy in which the imagination plays freely over the likely impact of social change on ways of viewing and handling phenomena in the casework domain and on the value system and other cultural artifacts of social casework. For his speculations, Day utilized an actual past represented by aeons of evolutionary time to construct an imagined outcome as replacement for the known outcome. For our speculations, we can postulate an imagined possible outcome on the basis of an actual and palpable present. Such a casework utopia will inevitably contain ideological elements since it is influenced by preferences concerning the goals and methods of casework's future practice. It is as if a selection were being made among alternative futures.

In assuming the speculative task, some might declare with gloom that the future of social casework is already a thing of the past. Others might assert with optimism that casework's future will be assured when its practitioners embrace the demands of science, on the one hand, or those of a newly awakened humanism on the other. In this paper, a projection of future practice will be made on the premise that social casework can achieve greater social significance by the 1990's as it reaches toward a vital balance between its scientific and humanistic components. First, however, attention will be given to how casework evolved out of its past since interaction with its socio-historical environment produced its present characteristics and will yield its future features.

During the 1880's a beginning conviction about the usefulness of science in handling the problems of charities and corrections crystallized in the commitment to scientific method known as scientific philanthropy. The charity organization movement saw its inchoate processes of social diagnosis and social treatment culminate in Richmond's 1917 conceptualization.[2] Over succeeding decades social casework strengthened its scientific commitment by absorbing knowledge from the behavioral and social sciences, developing a method based on the logical principles of scientific inquiry, and adopting scientific attitudes of objectivity and open-mindedness. In these same years social casework, as an art, developed its system of values and its sense of humanistic concern. Despite its long adherence to the values of science and humanism, however, social casework reached the 1970's at a low point of self-regard and a high point of externally based criticism. Elsewhere I have suggested that the fault may have lain in the cultural lag in casework's scientific point of view.[3]

Even more importantly, however, casework implemented its scientific orientation by adopting a model for practice derived from the medical-disease metaphor of study, diagnosis, treatment. The model advanced professional status and offered a practice base transmittable through professional education. Enriched by the hypotheses and insights from psychoanalysis and the social sciences, it also offered a method of helping individuals and families within a philosophical context that emphasized the worth of the individual and the interdependence of society. Yet the metaphor of study-diagnosis-treatment constructed by Richmond from the ideas of earlier thinkers was, after all, only a metaphor and not the reality of the practice domain.[4]

A metaphor is a legitimate device used by scientists and poets alike to extend or deepen understanding. It is a kind of make-believe that retains its usefulness only to the degree that its make-believeness is recognized. When the metaphor is mistakenly assumed to be the "real thing," confusion can result. Richmond and others used the analogy of diagnosis and of treatment quite legitimately to explain, clarify, and illustrate their ideas. Yet the terms "clinical," "patient," "curative treatment" belonging to the medical idiom were inappropriately applied to the casework idiom without sufficient awareness, by some, of their make-believe aspect. The medical-disease idiom intensified the focus on individual processes and led to an implication of sickness and of the ascribed dependency and passivity of the sick role.[5] For those who accepted the make-believe as literal, thereby mistaking the metaphor for reality, social casework became the same kind of "thing" as medical practice—it diagnosed and treated something that was wrong inside a "patient." This confusion of medical ideas with casework ideas apparently occurred because the sharing of the same terms supported the mistaken belief that the two sets of ideas were identical. Spokesmen did not always make clear that they were using an analogy and that the two sets of ideas were actually very different. Yet even when the analogy was specified as such —and occasionally it was—there was still a natural tendency to transfer properties belonging to one idea to the other idea long associated with it because association of the two ideas had theoretical and practical benefits for social casework.[6]

An effective metaphor, such as this one was, tends over time to be taken more and more literally and, in the process, distorts the very reality it seeks to illuminate. Despite Hamilton's conceptualization of the psychosocial, person-situation configuration of modern social casework,[7] the medical metaphor as practice-based obscured social processes and led to an almost exclusive concern with individual internal processes. Most interventions then took place largely at the individual, intrapsychic level,[8] and knowledge and skills that were developed pertained largely to that level. The distortion of a fragment of reality—the human phenomena to which casework attends—contributed, in part, to the crisis state of social casework in the 1960's and 1970's.[9] Distortion that occurs through metaphor often tends to continue until it is corrected through the construction of a new metaphor when a new era uncovers the falsification of reality that the old metaphor engendered.

Clarence Day's delightful fantasy depended for its effect on the fixity of human nature as biologically determined over evolutionary time. Because the characteristic features of any species are imprinted in its genes and are relatively unchanging, Day's humor derived from man's being locked into certain monkeyish traits while barred from developing certain other traits related to other species. Casework, however, is not similarly constrained by evolutionary determinants. We are free, within the limits of historical accidents, to invent its future if we can but unlock ourselves from a conception of social casework based on the medical-disease metaphor.

If the practice and theory of casework in the 1990's depends in part on plans and decisions to be made in the 1970's, it is important to specify alternate choices out of an understanding of contemporary life and its significant trends. One of the greatest developments in realm of values has been the great push forward by people everywhere toward more autonomy and control over their own destinies and toward more active social responsibility. This is seen in the peace and civil rights movements and in the activity on their own behalf of minority groups, students, women, clients, consumers, and citizens at all levels. Perhaps the greatest contemporary development in the realm of thought has been the emergence of an ecological perspective in our world view. By the April, 1970, celebration of Earth Day, sizable numbers of people were coming to realize that the old dichotomies of person-environment and subject-object in Western philosophy and the old notion of man's centrality on earth and his dominance in the web of life must give way. These old conceptions are yielding to new ideas of man's being by nature inseparable from the rest of nature. Many are coming to understand that man's relationship to his physical and social milieus is a delicate and continually adjusting equilibrium requiring the application of compassionate concern, knowledge and wisdom just for survival, let alone for achieving and maintaining the greatest possible potential for human freedom and autonomy. These conceptions are both scientific and humanistic, for science will have to help us develop control over the very problems science has helped to create: technological pollution, overpopulation, and dangerous new sources of energy and power. But such a science must be informed by a sense of human values and social purpose so that scientific solutions do not generate new problems.

The ecological view is both scientific and humanistic. With its emphasis on adaptation—the mutual fit of organism and environment—and its emphasis on growth, development, and the interdependence of organic systems, the ecological perspective suggests one way in which social casework might develop a socially significant practice. Though an "individualizing service" to people, social casework can help urbanized mass society overcome the social pollution of our times. Man has himself created social environments that violate common human needs and inhibit freedom and autonomous functioning: slum milieus that perpetuate poverty, and systems of justice, education, health care, welfare, and urban services that are no longer able to achieve their avowed objectives. Instead, they dehumanize human beings through the social pollution of racism, scorn for the poor and the deviant, and clogged institutional channels blocking access to essential resources. If both science and humanism are necessary in dealing with the technological pollution of our national environment then surely both are essential in dealing with the social pollution of our social and man-made environments. Yet today when science is viewed as a negative exemplar of modern life and humanism as a positive exemplar it has been easy to slip into the so-called conflict of two cultures in which the ideas of science and the images of the humanities are viewed as oppositional instead of complementary.[10]

The pseudo-conflict between science and humanism has a particular pertinence for social casework. The dialectic between knowledge, reason, and science on the one hand, and feeling, concern, and compassion on the other hand is reflected in the long ideological controversy in social work between cause and function and in the accusation that social casework has been more concerned with method and process than with the crusades for social improvement that social work leaders in the Progressive Era began so brilliantly. Modern caseworkers are urged to relinquish their long preoccupation with scientifically oriented function and to pick up on their sense of humanitarian social purpose. They are exhorted to move out of the arena of rehabilitative services, skills, and functions and into the arena of social action and social change. Yet what may be needed to prepare for the 1990's is both more science and a clearer sense of social purpose, a dynamic synthesis of the two points of view previously seen antithetically.

It is possible to envision a social casework conceptualized on an ecological metaphor and rooted in a commitment to the science and humanism inherent in an ecological perspective. It does not matter whether by 1993 casework continues to be called by that term or whether all individualizing social work services to people—as individuals, families, groups—will be called by some other term. An individualizing service to people will be concerned with the transacting forces in the man-environment ecosystem within an adaptational, evolutionary frame of reference. Adaptational refers not only to that form of adaptation in which the organism and environmental niche develop a mutual fit, but also to the more creative forms in which the organism seeks out new environments or creates and re-creates a changing environment to which it then adapts.[11] By evolutionary is meant the associated ideas of growth and development, differentiation and elaboration, unforeseeable properties and novel emergents.

The ideology that developed over the years to justify the preference for the medical-disease model of practice obstructed change and closed off exploration of new and variant streams of knowledge and new themes in science and culture. In that sense, the medical metaphor and its ideology inhibited the potential adaptability of casework to achieve a "fit" with the new conditions of contemporary life. The ecological metaphor is closer to casework's domain or fragment of reality and thus has potential for remaining open to change as the conditions of life change. This is because casework practiced on an ecological model will depend upon natural life processes as helping media of action in a life space, while casework practiced on a medical-disease model tended to depend upon contrived clinical processes as treatment media in an artificially created setting.

Nineteenth-century scientific ideas of discrete objects, irreducible entities, and the certainty of cause and effect continue to work with limited classes of phenomena but have been found to be inadequate in describing organic events and processes.[12] In the biological sciences, for example, an atomistic view of the cell has given way to notions of organized complexity at all levels. Ideas of organic systems and subsystems in transaction to maintain moving steady states have come to the foreground of attention. To be in harmony with new perspectives in the life sciences social casework must seek theoretic concepts that will enable it to understand phenomena in terms of growth, action, potentiality, uncertainty, and systems in transaction. It must, at the same time, seek action concepts which will permit engagement with adaptive and coping capacities, progressive forces, autonomous ego functions, and purposive activity in human beings, and with social supports and natural processes in the milieu.

The theoretic science to underlie casework activity is emerging in the work of a few social work thinkers. It builds on the advanced thought of Gordon Hamilton who first led the way toward a positive engagement with modern thought in the sciences and the humanities.[13] It encompasses Gordon Hearn's work in general systems theory,[14] which lay a long time fallow, and it has reached its clearest expression in the work of William Gordon.[15] While Gordon is addressing the whole of social work, his work suggests a possible direction for theory development through which social casework can achieve a socially significant practice. Gordon suggests that the unique locus of social work—in both its theory and its practice—lies at the interface of the person-environment system. Here the phenomena of concern are the transactions between the subsystems to which is given the term "social functioning." Desired transactional outcomes, both from a value stance and a theoretical position, are those which promote natural growth in the individual and are also ameliorative to the environment. In this conception, the objective of professional action is a matching between the coping behavior on the person side of the ecosystem and the qualities of the impinging milieu on the environment side, in order to assure positive feedback to both through appropriate exchange. Actual interventions would be directed either to the coping behavior, the environmental qualities, or both.

Gordon's work contains the outline of both theoretic and action concepts on which to build a social work science congruent with social work's humanistic concerns. At the level of service, casework based on an ecological metaphor will encompass the whole human being within his fluid real-life situation. It will utilize the healing potential and the growth potential in the individual's adaptive and coping capacities, and the social supports in his real world. It will search for ways to provide experiences in a social context that will promote growth and maturation in those being helped. In the medical model, environmental modification, for example, had been narrowly conceived as the provision of concrete services such as child placement, financial aid, institutional care, and as the manipulation of human objects in the environment including relatives, landlords, teachers, health personnel, etc. In the ecological model the environment will be viewed very differently. It will change from a passive noun to an active one. The word ecology derives from the Greek *oikos* meaning house, and housekeeping is a very active process. The ecological caseworker and his client will be actively engaged in modifying, restoring and "keeping" the environment. Indeed, the milieu itself will be utilized as "activity" for the client.

An ecological casework utilizing life processes has its antecedents in ideas of treatment advanced some years ago by Lucille N. Austin.[16] At that stage in its development, casework was moving rapidly toward an intrapsychic, psychotherapeutic focus. It is all the more significant that Austin underscored environmental activity not only as the substance of social therapy but, where indicated, as an important element in all methods of psychotherapy as well. Still more remarkably, for 1948, Austin called attention to the importance of stimulating growth experiences in the social reality. "Supportive" treatment was said to result in actual change because the alleviation of anxiety often gives the ego strength to handle immediate situations successfully; this in itself becomes a growth process. "Experiential" treatment was described as offering positive experience in the transference and in life situations. Its objective was to promote growth through increased satisfactions in living.

In developing her ideas of dynamic work in the environment to provide for positive experiences in actual life situations, Mrs. Austin drew on the work of Franz Alexander,[17] and to some extent on Grete Bibring's[18] ideas of manipulation. By manipulation, Dr. Bibring meant offering suggestions for better coping (manipulation through attitudes) and activity in the environment (manipulation through experiences). She felt that manipulation so defined offered new experiences to the client which could result in attitudinal changes just as experiences in real life influence attitudes.

After this early beginning, interest in the life situation and its use in treatment waned until the work in the 1950's of Redl and Wineman[19] which drew on the earlier life-space notions of Kurt Lewin,[20] and concepts of the therapeutic milieu.[21] The concept of life space offered a view of inner and outer phenomena that reduced the dichotomy of subject-object. Adopting this concept for institutionalized settings, Redl and Wineman presented techniques for direct intervention into critical incidents occurring in the immediate real-life situation of clients. These supplanted the delayed "after-the-fact" discussions in the clinical situation of psychotherapy.

Notions of therapeutic milieu had arisen from the observed effect of administrative structure and institutional culture, peer and staff expectations and interactions upon the course of psychiatric illness. By the 1960's, the Cummings [22] had developed a theory and practice of environmental therapy designed to bring about behavioral change and specific changes in the personality structure of schizophrenic patients. Building on Erikson's idea of ego growth through crisis resolution [23] the Cummings developed crisis resolution, a life process, as a therapeutic tool in which growth toward effective living and competence in social roles is fostered through a series of graded crises under circumstances supportive of resolution. Milieu therapy taking place through graded tasks or problems presented to the patient is considered by the Cummings to be more lifelike and more easily generalized to the total life situation than is dydadic therapy. In effect, milieu therapy is practice for the competent role behavior that will be demanded of the patient when he returns to society.

The work of Gladwin and his colleagues [24] suggests that additional, potential milieu instruments can be found in a variety of social systems such as schools and other total institutions viewed as ecological units where help can be offered in developing and enhancing personal competence in social life. He defines the ecological unit along a wide range of contexts involving the person and his immediate social environment, and suggests that social competence can best be achieved through intervention at the level of the ecological unit where the ineffective person can learn more successful modes of behavior. The experiencineg of greater competence contributes to the development of greater coping capacity available for use in future life-space events.

For the organizational arrangements of casework services now existent or still to be designed, some of the milieu concepts have been applied or will become applicable through a new metaphor of practice. The importance of the physical environment of the setting itself has been commented upon by Seabury.[25] The uses of indigenous helpers and of client peer groups represent natural life processes soundly based in ecological concepts of mutual aid. The designing of organizational roles for client-consumers whether at policy, planning, or direct service levels emphasizes activity, self-determination, and autonomy as desired behaviors and offers real-life practice to enhance social competence which is then generalizable to other life situations. All of these techniques contribute to the improved fit between the individual and his environment as well as its adaptation to his requirements. The important difference is that milieu concepts are concerned with restructuring the social environment to induce individual growth and development while psychotherapy on the medical model is concerned with restructuring the individual's personality largely for reconstitutive purposes.

Still another development in the use of life processes as a model for practice is the interrelated work of Bernard Bandler,[26] Louise Bandler,[27] and Eunice Allan.[28] Despite the casting of Bandler's ideas in the mold of the traditional medical-disease metaphor, they are distinctive, innovative departures from the metaphor's constraints and easily generalizable to the larger helping arena posed by the ecological metaphor. In contrasting the conservative aims of restitution with progressive aims of growth and change, within ego-supportive psychotherapy, Bandler uses as a model the natural events and processes of growth and development that occur over the life cycle. He suggests that we extract treatment principles from the parenting provided by successful fathers and mothers in raising well-adapted children rather than relying on what the physician does to treat the ill.

By extending Bandler's ideas we may be able to extract additional techniques through studying and observing the processes of spontaneous recovery within the perspective that even "normal" life is essentially problematic and conflicted. Helping procedures might be developed out of the successful methods used by many in solving life-cycle and situational crises, achieving goals, surmounting problems, or resolving conflicts without professional help or regressive decompensation. More needs to be known, for example, about how changes in attitudes and values, self-concept, role performance, and coping styles take place when "effective" people asume new roles, tasks, and responsibilities; and how they thus achieve a mutual fit with the qualities of their social milieu through adaptation to it or creative, meliorative modification of the milieu. From this knowledge, helping techniques could be devised much as the Cummings developed the technique of graded tasks out of the understanding of the relationship of crisis resolution to growth. Study of the association between competence in role performance and particular types of environments and styles of coping may also yield additional helping principles related to re-education and resocialization, to be especially useful for adults having psychosocial disabilities.[29]

Allan's work on the superego and Louise Bandler's work on sublimation, neutralized energy, and secondarily autonomous ego functions, indicate ways the caseworker can engage the progressive forces in the personality and avoid stimulating the regressive needs. The similarity of the goals and procedures in these approaches to the natural life processes of child rearing and socialization is striking. Further evidence of their usefulness is found in the experimental work of Pavenstedt and her colleagues.[30]

All of the formulations alluded to draw on Robert White's work on competence.[31] White postulates an inborn ego drive toward effectance. This is a need to have an effect on the environment that is not conflict-born and that is manifest in an ego interest in exploration and mastery of the environment. Demanding of satisfaction that leads to a feeling of efficacy and to "fit" with the environment, this is a primary motivation having survival value to the species. Thus White builds on Hartmann's ideas that the human infant is innately equipped with autonomous ego functions guaranteeing potential adaptation to the average expectable environment. White goes beyond Hartmann, however, in suggesting that these ego capacities have their own psychic energy and do not depend upon neutralized libidinal and aggressive energy. The importance of these ideas lies in the availability—though not necessarily the immediate accessbility—of these interests and energies without the need for prior psychotherapeutic work in conflicted areas. Life processes, not medical-disease processes, are at issue.

Crisis intervention as developed for caseworkers by Rapoport [32] and by Parad [33] delineates techniques for restructuring of the cognitive field, for placing irrational feelings in a rational context, and for stimulating and mobilizing interpersonal and institutional resources in the milieu. These techniques also highlight the centrality of the primary and secondary autonomous ego functions in growth and mastery. Earlier they had been considered to be of lesser importance in helping procedures than were the functions born of conflict. The relationship of the concepts in this approach to Erikson's conception of the growth occurring through the resolution of the crises of role transitions and age-related tasks over the life cycle will be of paramount importance in the further development of an ecological practice. For example, the psychosocial phases of ego development including basic trust, autonomy, initiative, industry, identity, etc., as functions of the transactions between the ego and its social and cultural environment are highly suggestive of possible targets and vehicles of change in elements of the ecosystem. When these ideas are considered with Erikson's other ideas of the cogwheeling of the generations, of the mutuality of their adaptive tasks, and of their reciprocal creation of environments, one for the other, within an evolutionary, adaptational point of view, his theoretical framework is seen to be congenial with an ecological metaphor for casework practice.

Other currents of thought have equal significance and promise for the further development of the ecological metaphor as a base for practice and theory in social casework. They refer to ideas of autonomy, task, activity—life processes of unquestionable pertinence to the human condition and the social milieu. Autonomy in a psychosocial sense refers to man's ability to govern himself out of an inner sense of self-regulation, purpose, and satisfaction congruent with societal needs.[34] In the more technical psychoanalytic sense it refers to the relative freedom from bondage to the demands of both outer reality and inner drives and needs.[35] Autonomy contributes to and emerges from a sense of identity and individuality, and is associated with that freedom and spontaneous activity which arises out of awareness of one's own needs and the reciprocal needs of others in the social milieu. In the impersonal, bureaucratically organized, mass society, man's ability to achieve personal autonomy and freedom is threatened by the seductiveness of passivity and conformity. His sense of autonomy recedes in the face of greater and greater relinquishment of decision-making and control over his own destiny, interest, and individuality of life-style. Merton has suggested that the pressures of contemporary life that demand adaptation beyond biologically—and psychologically—evolved limits lead to rebellion, alienation, retreatism, and apathy or conformity.[36] These are four deviant responses to the social structure, while an adaptive response might well lie in assuming a position of activity vis-à-vis the self and the milieu.

Ecological casework services to strengthen coping patterns of people and to meliorate the qualities of environments will emphasize the client's assumption of activity and decision-making on his own behalf. At first glance, this appears to be only another way of expressing the traditional commitment to client self-determination and active participation in the casework process. More often than not, however, the worker's professional goals rather than the client's goals have influenced the process while the client's active participation has been measured by his verbal activity, his willingness to reveal his subjective state and to describe his objective situation, and his continuation in treatment. Some "doing" may be expected of him such as obtaining documents, talking to a caretaker, applying for a job. Autonomy, in the sense of an ego quality associated with a feeling of efficacy on the self arising from competent, purposive activity in the milieu, requires for its maintenance or acquisition something more than the vagueness of self-determination and haphazard participation. For some it will require the planned restructuring of situations, to provide successful experiences of mastery in the environment for ego growth. Services to supplement the adaptive capacities of many others may include means to stimulate activity and decision-making at the personal, neighborhood, community and other levels, and to counter the trends toward passivity and conformity in urbanized society. It is in this conception of autonomy that the notion of task as developed by Studt has merit.[37]

In a correctional setting, Studt designed task-oriented work groups of staff and clients. The goals were the clients' goals. The client had primary responsibility in the work of achieving his goal in which certain tasks were delineated as his. The worker had the secondary responsibility of creating the conditions under which the client might pursue his tasks with some assurance of success. Goals and tasks were arrived at jointly after the problem or the need was defined. Since staff comprised all methods, it was possible to select the method of helping after the problem was defined and the goals and tasks specified rather than the method's determining the way the problem is defined and influencing the choice of goals and process as in ordinary practice.

There was success enough with this ordinarily resistive client group to suggest the usefulness of the approach in areas other than the "total institution" setting. On theoretical grounds alone, its promise for other fields of practice seems clear. Its implications for generalist practice and for multimethod team approaches are beyond the scope of this paper, but also seem clear.

All of the approaches described support the potential usefulness of an ecological metaphor and life model in developing a new type of social casework for the future. Obviously any "alternative future" for casework assumes a milieu characterized by social justice and economic security for all citizens. In addition, it requires of social casework that it design new organizational arrangements for service which will be flexibly responsive to continually emerging needs in a rapidly changing world. Using Alfred Kahn's elaboration of the institutional-residual conception of social welfare, Carol H. Meyer has constructed a scheme for casework practice in urban society.[38] In her view, casework would move away from an overemphasis on its residual function of picking up the pieces left in the wake of dehumanizing social institutions It would move instead toward an increasingly important focus on its institutional function as part of the usual, normal arrangements of society. All citizens in a superurban industrialized society are subject to tasks beyond the coping capacities of human beings whose biological and psychological evolution has not kept pace with socially and culturally induced environmental changes. Ecological casework as an essential individualizing service in a mass society is designed, then, (1) to help all individuals and family members supplement their adaptive capacities and develop their potential for satisfying living, autonomy, and goal achievement, and (2) to support and foster the environmental conditions necessary for attaining these objectives. Such a view may require the substitution of the medical-disease metaphor by the ecological metaphor, for Professor Meyer's casework would place its practitioners in social and natural environments where social roles and ego tasks intersect with institutional sites at various points in the life cycle.

During the 1960's and 1970's many caseworkers have been turning away from the diagnosis-treatment dimensions of the disease metaphor, and are searching for terms more expressive of an ecosystems perspective. This is not merely a semantic matter, but further refinement at the conceptual level will be required in order to incorporate such elements of the casework process as: (a) engagement, response to need, and study or analysis; (b) definition of problem, specification of goals, planning for action and prediction of consequences; (c) purposive action, task management, and monitoring of feedback; (d) evaluation of outcomes. Some of these elements may be sequential, others are more pervasive throughout the helping process. All are characterized, however, by the mutuality of client and worker. Continued work is needed on developing the principles and procedures within such a framework and connected to social purpose; on specifying emerging roles of the caseworker; and on utilizing newer dimensions of the client-worker relationship including authenticity, congruence, and social system aspects.

The ecological metaphor for practice in a new age can replace the older medical metaphor of an earlier age, for it touches the scientific and humanistic concerns of social casework in new ways. Ecology is science, and casework must continue its commitment to a scientific orientation in defining needs, planning and taking action, and assessing outcomes. Ecology is humanistic as well. In the essay alluded to earlier, Clarence Day observed that every living thing on this earth grows and develops, and it tends toward splendor. Casework must continue its humanistic concern for the potential splendor of man and his milieu.

8

Social Group Work

RUBY B. PERNELL

An attempt at projection into the future is a risky task at any time, but especially so at a point in history when so many structural elements of our society are in a state of change or under siege to change. One is tempted to take the way out as did ancient cartographers, who, having charted their known world, simply labeled the realms beyond, "Here Be Dragons," and let it go at that.*

Faced with the necessity, however, of naming the "dragons," one turns almost instinctively to an effort to predict the future on the basis of trend lines extending into time and space, rooted in the past; juxtaposing social trends with a developmental line of social group work.

There has been a continuing chorus of voices all through the last decade and into the present telling us that we are in a time of change which has portent for reshaping our society in its social, political and economic dimensions, resulting in new power equations, new national priorities and new life-styles. Precisely what these will be is too hazardous to project because of the unpredictable occurrence of events and crises which change the course of history. Nevertheless, there are trends which only cataclysmic events are likely to deflect. These trends seem to be in the areas of technological changes, increasing leisure, changes in social structure, changes in ideologies, intensification of life's developmental

* I am indebted to the anonymous author of a United Nations pamphlet for this bit of interesting cartographic history.

138

crisis periods (adolescence, parenthood, career, etc.), changing institutions, life-styles, and changes in the pace of change itself.

Among the increasing volume of forecast literature, I have found Alan Toffler's *Future Shock* [1] especialy stimulating, both for his wide sociological view of the forces of change which are propelling us forward and his imaginative projections of man's needs and ways of meeting these. I want to use some of his ideas about the future as the backdrop against which to identify social group work's potential utility in the world of tomorrow.

Toffler calls attention to the fact that in any society a vast number of streams of change occur simultaneously, at differing speeds, difficult to measure, but that there is widespread agreement that many social processes are speeding up in striking, even spectatcular ways. He points out how technological innovations, while suggesting and compelling changes in machines and techniques, also suggest novel solutions to social, philosophical, even personal problems, altering man's total intellectual environment.

Toffler identifies three characteristics of the changes we are caught up in today: transience, novelty, and diversity. He speaks of the effect of the acceleration of change on the individual's ability to cope with life, forcing him to "live faster." He postulates that the people of the future will live in "a condition in which the duration of relationships is cut short. . . . In their lives, things, places, people, ideas and organizational structures all get 'used up' more quickly." [2] In interpersonal relationships, duration and depth become increasingly limited and "much of the social activity today can be described as search behavior—a relentless process of social discovery in which one seeks out new friends to replace those who are either no longer present or who no longer share the same interests." [3]

We are faced increasingly by a bewildering situation of "overchoice" and a freedom which is somehow terrifying. "The individual searching for a sense of belonging, looking for the kind of social connection that confers some sense of identity, moves through a blurry environment in which the possible targets of affiliation are all in high-speed motion. He must choose from among a growing number of moving targets. . . ." [4]

Accompanying this is a bewildering diversity of values, with fast turnover, and no stabilizing consensus of "core" American values. "Subcults" proliferate and attract adherents through the universal need of individuals to "belong." The techno-societies in their size and complexity force the individual to find some such group in order to maintain some sense of identity and contact with the whole.

In considering novelty as a key to understanding the new society,

Toffler points out that we are living in the midst of a revolution, which implies novelty.

> It sends a flood of newness into the lives of countless individuals, confronting them with unfamiliar institutions and first-time situations. Reaching deep into our personal lives, the enormous changes ahead will transform traditional family structures and sexual attitudes. They will smash conventional relationships between old and young. They will overthrow our values with respect to money and success. They will alter work, play and education beyond recognition. And they will do all this in a context of spectacular, elegant, yet frightening scientific advance.[5]

Against this description of the growth and development of dragons let us examine one small professional effort: social group work. Is there any vitality in the concept and practice of social group work to carry it forward into the brave new world, or is it destined to disappear as an identifiable activity? What are its dynamic and enduring elements which should be nurtured for their utility and meaning in the new society? What service designs shall carry its content to which sets of "new society" problems? And how are we to conceptualize it for purposes of identifying its place in social work education, in order to sustain it in practice?

Alfred Kahn pointed out in a future-oriented paper in 1959 that as social workers we had tended to narrow our horizons to what could be conceptualized. "The institution of social work, as depicted through the resultant efforts in the major social work methods of group work and casework is narrower in responsibility, potentiality and scope than what is possible, desirable, or actually observable!" [6] So far as group work is concerned, the narrowing process was a gradual one in which historic circumstances, crucial decisions by the professional association, definition and status needs of social group work within the profession and of the social work profession itself, and the ebb and flow of currents of thought and practice in the field all played a part. It is this fact of a narrowing of scope which has marked the present and more recent past that impels me to move backward in time to search for a better take-off point for moving ahead into the future. In Henry David's words, "strong roots and a sense of history are major sources of a profession's strength. . . . But what matters enormously is *the purposefulness and intensity of its forward glance*." [7] It is this connection between the roots of social group work and future-directed growth that I wish to examine.

Social group work, as Clara Kaiser has pointed out, has no exact birth date, "nor is there full agreement of its progenitors." [8] It evolved out of the recognition of common interests and concerns of a number of persons who were working with groups in a variety of educational, recreational and social service agencies, and was shaped significantly by a number of philosophical and scientific systems of thought.

Throughout its history its practitioners have been defining and redefining it,[9] and in both definition and practice have tended toward narrowing and specializing its scope. It started out as a method firmly committed to the growth and development of healthy individuals through interaction wth others around program interests and activities within a group and agency context in which social responsibility and democratic participation were valued and actively promoted. In 1928 Margaretha Williamson wrote:

> Workers are seeking the development of the individual to his fullest capacity and encouraging more satisfactory relations between the individual and his environment. . . . Group work concerns itself with services toward individuals in a group, brought together through common interests and guided by means of suitable and congenial activities toward a well rounded life for the individual; and for the group, a cooperative spirit and acceptance of social responsibility.[10]

As Hartford [11] points out, in the 1920's and 1930's three major strands of emphasis were repeating in the various definitions being attempted:

1. Individual growth and adjustment through the group;
2. Group development toward specified ends;
3. Social action, social change, or change of society through group experience.

Through the ensuing years, each of these elements was reworked and reworded in various ways but with a discernible trend toward an increasing focus on the malfunctioning individual and decreasing emphasis on the social action, social change, and education for citizenship component. In the 1950's social group workers made a historical decision about their identification and affiliation with social work and let go the identifiable bonds with recreation and informal education. The problem orientation grew, especially as social workers moved in increasing numbers into problem-oriented settings and away from the earlier "leisure-time" services.

Between 1959 and 1963 the National Group Work Practice Committee of the National Association of Social Workers formulated a "Frame of Reference for Social Group Work" which listed five purposes for which the social group work method was used: corrective purposes, preventive purposes, facilitating normal social growth, personal enhancement and citizenship responsibility and participation. In the ensuing discussion across the country strong voices were heard for letting go the "personal enhancement" and "citizenship participation" purposes, and there was some doubt that "normal social growth" was an appropriate target for professional services which were in scarce supply. Many variations of the definition of purposes, the relative priorities and emphases, or the comprehensiveness of the definition were offered then and later, but the fact was that the weight had shifted toward the therapeutic or corrective purposes due to a number of historical circumstances, including the search for status within the social work profession itself. The subsequent narrowing of focus and lessened attention to the purposes of development of citizenship participation and social responsibility and to the place of program content other than problem-focused discussion was reflective of the general interest and milieu of the period.

In 1962, commenting on this shift of attention, I wrote, ". . . Our present practice developed out of the formulations of concepts about the experiences of normal groups, rather than around the abnormal; and while other professions are moving in the direction of understanding the meaning of health, and directing services and resources towards its maintenance, we may be moving away from identification with such concerns." And regarding services to normal groups, ". . . There are growth needs among members of some of these so-called 'adequate' groups which we are still fumbling in our efforts to skillfully effect. The loss or confusion of meaningful values, the denial of rights to others, the anxieties and strivings for relatedness to others are some of the needs which persist." [12] Interestingly enough, the social changes and federally funded programs of the 1960's brought about a renewed activity in the area of citizenship participation and social responsibility and something called "community group work" began to appear in the literature, reflecting a reawakening of professional interest in this area.

David [13] has reminded us of the words of the White Queen in *Through the Looking Glass,* "It's a poor sort of memory that only works backwards." Thus the purpose of this backward look is only to indicate the roots and shoots of social group work which carry the genes for significant growth into the future. It is analogous to dropping back a few paces to gather the impetus to carry us over the hurdles ahead.

A number of powerful and distinctive concepts derive from the early development of social group work which seem to have important potential for today and tomorrow and which were different from the more common concepts of the dominant social casework of the earlier period. These are "member" versus "client"; doing with versus doing for; doing versus talking about doing; activity and others as primary agents in the helping process versus worker alone as agent; personal and social development and social contribution as legitimate professional foci versus remedial, palliative and rescue purposes; health and strength versus sickness and breakdown.

The key words of the earlier period were "democracy" (as a way of life, not just a political concept), "responsible citizenship," "social growth" and "character development." The agency context and the worker's purpose were value-laden, and the individual was viewed within his society and in interaction with it; and, though "social adjustment" may have meant conformity to some, to the leading group workers of the period it was closer in meaning to Grace Coyle's comprehensive definition as "training in cooperative relations for common ends, increasing capacity for social contacts, development and enrichment of personality through activity, and training for world responsibility." [14] The fact that the interlocking socialization institutions of the period presented little of the value discontinuities so prevalent today gave the concept a quality of conformity. However, the concepts themselves are equally adaptable and of even greater importance in today's changing world. Most of them have persisted in some form or in some areas of practice; some have already re-emerged into prominent positions, modified and adapted to the present-day milieu. The shifting perception and nomenclature of client groups as "consumers," the development of peer-group perceptions of worker and group engagement particularly at the community level, a renewed concern with explicit value orientations of agencies and groups, with growth and health and with citizenship participation in community development efforts, are all indications of the living, growing quality of these ideas.

It is my position that in the brave new world of the future these are the concepts which have the potential for vitalizing social work and for addressing some of the problems ahead of us. Rather than radical and spectacular changes occurring in the provision of social work services sparked by technological changes, I believe the real effect on practice will come from just such changing perceptions of client groups, of the professional worker's position in the helping relationship, of broadening perceptions of needs and professional purposes, and recognition of the human potential for action in behalf of self and others.

Moving forward to a renewed concern with growth and maintenance of health of invidiuals throughout their life cycle and in their interactions with the shifting social milieu, we see a special place for social group work practice. In a world characterized by transience, diversity and novelty, the "normal" process of growth and development becomes highly problematic. Life's developmental crisis periods intensify their demands on the individuals for successful resolution. The rapid-fire presentation of self to new, shifting groups, coping with novel situations, moving in and out of occupational and social relationships make the everyday life of each individual a hazardous journey. The achievement of a stable identity; a consistent set of core values; a sense of self-actualizing direction; and a capacity for intimacy which reaches beneath the superficial level of transient social relationships may require special social services beyond the institutional arrangements of family, church and school. Emmanuel Tropp points out that the concept of "optimum functioning" has not yet taken full hold in any field dealing with man's well-being.[15] Yet in the future world we visualize, ordinary coping will require optimum functioning. There will have to be social provision of experiences over time which help stabilize the personality, giving it depth and meaning; short-term experiences which help with the task of change; and "common goal" endeavors which help individuals together to cope with the forces of change. The personal capacities will have to be enriched and, to quote Tropp, "Group work, is, in effect, the primary social work practice in a position to meet people at the point of average functioning, and the primary one with the structure and method to undertake the task." [16] To this we may add Clara Kaiser's words, "Social group work has its major contribution to make in focusing on building ego strengths of individuals and on the social health of groups." [17]

As social group workers, we will probably have to give renewed attention to the social group experiences of children. Will the child who is constantly stimulated by fast-moving, novel situations, prodded by change-ridden and changing parents, and growing faster in practically every aspect of his development, have the time he needs really to "grow up" in self-knowledge, interpersonal competence and social responsibility? Will there be time and place to achieve for the pleasure rather than the necessity of achievement, to experience friendship in more than transient terms, and to have opportunities for the kinds of peer group activities which contribute to the development of values through experiences which are beyond self-seeking, opportunistic conformities? Given novelty and diversity as features of the new society, we can expect an increasing array of groups and values presented for individual choice; and if together with this, transience in family relations means shorter marriages and changing marital partners, the potential value discontinuities for the growing child can be a threat to development of a stable value core for the personality. The "wholeness" and autonomy of the person who is to survive in a rapidly changing world will need to be compounded not only of skills which permit mastery of this environment but also of a morality which informs and directs the exercise of mastery.

We may need to revitalize the youth-serving agencies whose "character building" function has embodied value premises which, though often laughed at or derided as "middle-class," yet have been concerned with self-actualizing behavior and social responsibility goals. Perhaps these older agencies and new ones to come need to take on a stability-building or "shock-absorbing" function. For example, they could be closely related to schools, be organized to serve the child over several years' span, and might take over some parental functions, possibly offering residential, group living services, somewhat on a camping model, for short or long-term periods but during the school year. Such organizations might differ in their ideologies and/or program emphases, offering choice according to individual tastes within a given geographical community; but intergroup emphasis would be on cooperative rather than competitive activities, or, understanding instead of unwillingness to understand and on equality rather than elitism. They would be communities in which there would be real tasks and decisions to be made with "a deliberate sharing of power and responsibility as the growing competence of the child enables him to use it"; [18] and a value milieu based on reciprocal obligations and respect for others in child-adult as well as peer social interactions and transactions. They might be deliberately organized as heterogeneous communities, providing a real-life experience for their members.

This type of service should be under the direction of social group workers who would bring to it the combination of knowledge about the socialization needs of childhood, especially the role and meaning of the peer group, the humanitarian values of social work, the understanding of group process, the skill in effecting it to create a growth-inducing environment, and creative knowledge about programming to facilitate the acquisition of values and skills through experience. The changing structure of the profession and changing roles and functions of the MSW level worker should mean a renewal of an earlier emphasis on the program design, training, supervisory and administrative skills of the master's degree holder, with the direct service function carried by the BSW, aides, volunteers or others.

For adolescents, the importance of the peer group is well-recognized as a medium through which the young person seeks to gain separation from his parents, development and confirmation of his identity and movement into adult status in the society. Clausen writes, "by adolescence, the nature of the socialization process has markedly changed. The child has become far more active in defining his own goals and in seeking the kind of socialization experience that will help him achieve them. . . . He is likely to be much more *au courant* [than his parents] with changes occurring in social patterns and moral norms. . . . If the child alone is aware of the contradictions in norms that are presented to him in various settings . . . the whole task of resolution and synthesis remains with him to accomplish without assistance. In the last analysis, of course, only he can achieve such resolution, but this is a place where skilled socialization agents can offer guidance and enhance understanding." [19] Any social group worker who has worked with adolescents knows the uses made of the nonparent, mature, understanding, helpfully disposed adult who is available to them. Yet, if the rapidly changing social norms widen the gaps in understanding between generations, then the peer group becomes increasingly important to its members and the exclusion of adults is more likely to occur. With this increased utility of the peer group to its members, and with the smorgasbord of behaviors and norms characteristic of various groups to choose among, along with the importance of peer *relationship* as the objective of affiliation, inevitably many young people get themselves misplaced in a group. They experience enormous conflict in conforming to group norms for the sake of acceptance, and often want and need an understanding adult to relate to for help to find their way through their dilemmas of relationships, personal morality and social development. We have already begun to see the formation of highly attractive groups which offer opportunity for personally destructive and social unproductive behavior. Along with this have come a number of creative programs by youth-serving agencies to provide helpful resources for those youth who wish to use them. These new-type services may be prototypes for program designs for the future, where the services of professional workers, or those under professional guidance, are made available to youth groups and individuals for assistance in finding their ways out of dilemmas. "Pathfinder" services, we might call them.

In discussing adult socialization, Brim points out that "The socialization experienced in childhood is not enough to meet the demands of later years. . . . In these rapidly changing societies (e.g. the United States), . . . the younger adults must find new models, or develop new styles of life without them; meanwhile, the older adults try to adjust to the conflicts created by the rapid rate of ideological and technological change." [20] In the ordinary course of life, the average nondeviant adult must change and must be socialized into new roles; he must meet the demands for change made by others and the demands he makes on himself. He has many self-initiated ideas and role prescriptions for his own personality and behavior change.

Again considering Toffler's projections of transience in jobs, home communities, family relationships and social groups, the problems of changing roles and meeting one's own and other's role expectations can be expected to increase beyond today's experience. Given the tendency toward self-initiated socialization, which Brim speculates "may already be on the increase because of greater affluence of the average adult and the greater leisure for experimenting in new areas of life," [21] perhaps there is another cue here for program design in which groups become key media.

Job orientation and training seminars will undoubtedly continue and multiply and a variety of adult education and retraining courses be available on a self-selection basis through educational institutions. But beyond occupational role adaptations lie a number of other challenges to the adult self: marriage, stages of parenting, retirement, and various citizenship and social group roles and interpersonal relationships. The transience, diversity and novelty of many of these experiences pressure the adult into seeking new ideas for ways of dealing with the demands; but also, as Brim says, "New ideal states for the individual's personality evolve and can be seen just ahead; thus the individual directs himself toward these new ends." [22]

Toffler suggests that a variety of short-term groups will be needed in the new society through which individuals will seek solutions to specific types of problems which face them. Brim and Wheeler support this in their observations on the use of informal, primary group relationships by adults to test out, compare and socialize each other in relation to new interests and roles.[23] The group and its members may actively assist the individual with the change he seeks or may merely provide the conditions within which his own developmental purposes can be pursued. Aside from the growth in entrepreneur or self-organized groups, provision of group services to meet adult socialization or resocialization needs is already a feature of many social agencies. Offerings to their actual or potential clientele ranging across the remedial, supportive, preventive and developmental purposes, from young adults to the aged, in institutions and out, and focused on a host of special problems and concerns. There is no reason to assume that in the future world there will be any lessened need for such services, although the content of the group experience and the target groups may change. In all these groups, however, the supportive interpersonal relationships are the key elements and the direct or consultative services of the social group worker are pertinent.

While the demands of role performance in handling day-to-day tasks are important, a continuing thread of concern is the deepening meaning of one's self in interaction with others, the reaching for intimacy in human relationships, the eliciting of response from others that confirm the reality of the self. In the rock musical *Godspell,* there comes a moment when the clownlike characters who have romped their ways through a fun and games interpretation of the New Testament parables turn to each other and in a tender, caring way wipe the grease-painted clown faces off one another. From this point, real selves revealed, the action takes on seriousness and depth. In a way, the world we do and

shall live in makes it possible to move through life with surface presentations of self, while the need for deeper investment and revelation of
self may be sought through experiences which promise "instant intimacy." The T-groups of the training laboratory movement, originally
organized for role training purposes, have been seized upon, often with
religious zeal, as potentially offering therapeutic group experience for
"normal" individuals. A proliferation of personal growth labs, encounter
groups, marathon groups, "feelies" and their variants have sprung up.
For some individuals, this may be a genuine seeking of release from the
isolation and impersonality of a machine culture; while for others the
appeal may be in the novelty, the manipulative, contrived experience—
consonant with a machine culture—in which one experiences one's self,
or takes apart others and is taken apart by them and hopefully put back
together again in a way which runs better.

There is no doubt that the need for primary group experience in
which one can find and become one's real self will be a continuing one.
It is also probable that the short-term, controlled and manipulated media
for this experience will continue to develop. This is the direction in
which knowledge moves us. For the social group worker, as for other
professional helpers working in treatment settings, the value premises
for the development and skilled use of increasingly precise manipulative
methods for restorative purposes may be clearer than when similar
methods are used outside these settings for purposes of enhancing normal
social functioning. Is a contrived, artificial experience as effective as a
real-life one? If so, under what circumstances and for what purposes
will we choose one or the other? And how can we or should we assure
that "voluntary" participation in such experimental groups is really
voluntary? [24] Perhaps in twenty years, artificiality of environment will
be so much a part of our lives that any professional change agent will
be expected to use these artificial micro-environments and to manipulate
them for controlled outcomes. It seems clear that as we move inexorably
in the direction of having more and more specific manipulative techniques available to us, the values and ethics of the profession must be
strengthened to provide the essential boundaries of practice.

The stream of practice developed around use of groups for treatment
purposes will continue to grow, for the individual casualties of a fast-
paced, changing society are heavy and the group treatment milieu has
great utility. Studies during the 1960's of populations in two large eastern
cities estimated the incidence of persons handicapped by emotional disturbances as from 20 to 25 per cent of the total.[25] Their distress handicaps them in their work, their personal relationships, their family life—
in various ways they are experiencing an inability to cope with life's
problems. Not only will tomorrow's world create new problems of stress,

but new services are already being designed to extend help to greater numbers of those experiencing problems of coping than in the past. The usefulness of the group as a treatment form does not have to be debated here, but various aspects of present-day organization and use of groups may need examination, experimentation, and reconceptualization. Henry Maier, for example, suggests that homogeneity as a basis for group composition (i.e., persons in similar functional dilemmas) may not be as advisable or clinically necessary in the contemporary world as heterogeneity. "A group has to bring together a wide spectrum of age ranges and persons of different segments of life because living with diversity, coping with the predictably unpredictable, and finding a personal integrity amidst many others are the challenges of today." [26]

In sickness and in health, for self-centered needs of individuals and for expression of their social responsibilities, for maintenance of stability and for creative forms of engagement with change, for self and social development, the group has meaning and utility. Historically, the core content of social group work has enabled its practitioners to move with professional ease into activities centered around these various purposes, acquiring the additional appropriate learnings as needed. With the expansion of knowledge, trends to specialization, and new patterns of curriculum organization in schools of social work, perhaps the logical development of education for social group work will be task-oriented training for the volunteer and aide, generic education for the undergraduate and, for the graduate, specialization in individual need-oriented group work or in work with community-focused groups. The major problem with this latter division could be the loss of a core group of professionals concerned with the development of social group work, examining and refining practice and developing and testing concepts which bridge the potential distance between the personal and social purposes.*

Group work's special uniqueness lies in concepts relating to (1) the group as entity, its development both as a tool for assisting individuals with their growth needs and as an instrument for the individual's expression of his social responsibilities; and (2) the use of program content and task as media for engagement, growth and change for the individual as well as the group as a whole. In short, both what the group *is* and what it *does* are of significant utility in helping individuals and their society. Instead of passage from peripheral status to a loss of

---

* Maier gives an example of this connection in his suggestion that social action by means of client activation, group confrontation, and advocacy efforts become legitimate and essential features of a clinical approach. "The focus is upon vitalizing the client's own competence in effectively entering into the change effort of his changing society. . . . The stress is upon the client's competency in effecting change rather than upon societal change *per se*."

identity through integration with stronger, higher-status social work methods, which many present practitioners and educators fear, group work should move into a central position among the modes of social work engagement. It is a method of work which represents a bridging concept between work with individuals and work with communities, with content and values distinctly its own, applicable with different emphases to the various purposes and tasks of social work, and important enough to have its unique context preserved and developed for continued enrichment to professional practice as a whole.

9

Community Organization

ELIZABETH L. PINNER

The world will be different in 1993 and so will community organization. If we practitioners in community organization are to do more than keep up with events, if we are to have some signficant effect on them, we must be willing to move quickly and effectively into new modes of professional activity.

Most of the future is beyond our imagination. However, current trends do indicate some of the dimensions of the problems which will be ours in 1993. There will be more people in the United States in 1993. They will live just outside the urban centers of today. Core cities will continue to lose population and tax support, but gain in demands for service. The expectation of an even better quality of life and environment will be found among an increasing proportion of our people. People will expect to have an impact on their world rather than be content merely to survive in it. They will have more time to devote to this goal since they will spend less of their lives in bare subsistence income-producing activity. Demands for service will change; auspices will change as more people become more informed about social service needs and programs. New criteria of effectiveness will be proposed, tested and used to guide the flow of resources. The information explosion will continue at ever-increasing rates. Advances in computer technology will inundate current systems of fact utlization. Community organization practitioners will have to retool not once, but several times to keep up with and influence these events.

One of the issues community organization workers must face at once is change in the organization of the profession. How can we organize to cope with the jobs we now have and build in the necessary flexibility to change and change again by 1993? Several possible ways are being hotly debated today. Community organization could merge with the other social work practice methods in a generic practice. Community organization can cease to exist in a professional arena in which the workers are not required to have any particular professional identity or credentials. Community organization might merge with the other professions in the general planning field while social casework might become a part of the individual therapies. It is the purpose of this paper to present and evaluate each of these plans in light of two criteria for future practice—flexibility and effectiveness. A combination of these plans will be presented as a possible new direction for the profession of social work and community organization.

Generic Practice

Social work has already experienced fluctuations between emphasis on specialization in a particular method and generic or generalist practice. When the National Association of Social Workers was formed, it incorporated different special practices in casework as well as group work and community organization. In the recent past the three practice methods have continued to develop almost separately. There is now considerable interest in reducing or eliminating specialist methods practice and expecting all social workers to be able to carry out the same tasks to achieve the same goals. Several schools of social work are teaching social work methods as a unity. The generic practitioner is expected to deal with problems on several levels at once. He must be able to diagnose the contribution of individual pathology and see to it that the client gets the help he needs. The worker must also understand the contribution of society and service systems to the problem and be able to undertake the professional actions to modify these. Further, he must decide which of these tasks to undertake in a particular situation. He must have the diagnostic skills and the treatment skills required by both levels of professional activity.

Generic practice provides an opportunity for social workers to be quite flexible in their definition of a problem as well as in their selection of possible actions. A particular worker might help individuals cope with and/or modify their environment. He might help citizen groups improve their ability to effect change in society. Or he might exert the influence of his own expertise in bringing about change. An agency or sponsor of practice could be quite flexible in the assignment of staff to tasks and in the selection of problem areas for attention. New problems could be handled by existing agencies if the agency and its staff were able to carry out genuine generic practice.

A particular advantage of the generic way of organizing practice is that it preserves and emphasizes one of social work's contributions to the helping and planning professions. There are few other disciplines which have included both the skills of helping individuals and the skills of modifying social systems in their professional purview. It has been an uphill struggle to try to understand a practice which involves diagnosing and treating people in interaction with society as well as in modifying that society and its service provisions. Different language, different value priorities and different theoretical assumptions seem to underly helping individuals as opposed to planning services. The struggle is still with us and will probably continue to be in 1993. True generic practice will require that this struggle continue and intensify. The results cannot be other than salutory for generic practice if the combatants can survive. Social work generalists can insist that insights from planning practice be available to helping practice and that knowledge gained in helping individuals be used in planning.

Because of the vast range of possible problems and the extensive specialists, method generalists tend to become problem specialists. This is not because social work practice in the health field is essentially different than in housing, argue the generic practitioners, but that the "facts of the field" are different. As anyone new to the housing field can attest, the federal, state and local regulations affecting a project are astounding in their complexity, confusion and internal contradiction. The skills involved in helping people solve their housing problems may be the same as those involved in health planning but the "facts of the field" are different. With the information explosion this will probably be even more a fact of 1993 than it is today. Thus, it seems most likely that method generalists will become problem specialists.

There are things that all of us in social work might do to mitigate the difficulties in communication among the various workers in the social problems fields. All social workers should make sure that the regulations and research reports in their own field are clear and stated in language that more people can understand. New ways of organizing and codifying information will have to be developed. It is important that we not make service delivery any more complicated in an era when many aspects of living will become almost unbearably complex. If social work is to become a genuine generic practice this must be done, at once, lest we substitute extreme specialization in problem areas for extreme method specialization, and fail to be as flexible as we must be.

One of the requirements of an effective practice is that it make use of new knowledge as it becomes available. Further, practitioners must be able to demand that research efforts be undertaken which will help them solve practice problems. The generic practitioner will have the opportunity to carry out a variety of professional actions which will make it possible for him to be more flexible, but what about his ability to be effective? Adequate measures of effectiveness are yet to be devised for most of community organization. More about the problems of assessment will be considered below. Here the generation and utilization of new knowledge will be discussed as it relates to effective practice.

Generic social work practice is similar to general practice in medicine. The medical general practitioner is backed up by a group of medical specialists. Most new medical knowledge is developed, evaluated and first put into practice by the specialist. The general practitioner has too many bodies of knowledge, too much research and too much literature to peruse to become an expert in any one of them. Even with the organization of the medical specialty, general practice, only limited new knowledge has been developed by general practitioners. The ability to focus on one specialized interest seems to be essential for research programs that yield results. Social work knowledge and theory development occur in the same manner.

If we move to generic practice and abandon the specialized practice methods, we will run the risk of losing an arm of the profession which can update our facts as well as our theories. Such access to new knowledge is essential if we are to continue to improve the effectiveness of our practice. Social work is not like medicine in the degree to which we separate general practice from special practice. For example, specialists in social work do not have more education than the generalists, they have different education. Community organization now uses the findings of research efforts undertaken by those who do not consider themselves as basic scientists for our practice. Translation of research findings into practice skills is carried out in the schools of social work, in agencies, and by individual practitioners. This function of adapting basic research to practice is not as systematized nor as consistent in social work or social work community organization as it is in medicine. Generic social workers will have to be even more aware and astute if they are to keep abreast of new developments without the benefit of the new knowledge developed by social work specialists, and the translations of this knowledge into practice skills.

Generic practice will have a particulary unfortunate effect on the practice skills now called community organization. Community organization theories or "mind holds," according to Chin,[1] are not at the stage at which they can serve a practitioner throughout his career. A doctor can learn about circulatory systems as a way of organizing a body of information and then be able to update his facts as new ones become available. We lack these enduring "mind holds" in community organization. Considerable research, assessment, evaluation and just plain thinking must be done before they evolve. Meanwhile practitioners will have to make do with what was available when they went to school. It is much easier to update existing "mind holds" with new facts than to learn new ones. Those of us who learned the "old math" have experienced the difficulty of learning new theories when our youngsters brought home "new math" homework from school. Their teachers were right, most children would be better off if they did not ask their "old math" trained parents for help with homework. Community organization will require some "new math-like" thinking if we are to be effective with future problems. It will be difficult if not impossible for generic practitioners to keep up to date with these changes if planning and community intervention is only part of their professional responsibility. Because of the lack of theory in community organization, the generic practitioner will find community organization a most difficult method with which to keep current. The natural tendency to do what one knows best how to do and learn more about that which one already knows will result in community organization aspects of the generalists' practice failing to keep up with new knowledge and new theories. The generic worker will inadvertently become a methods specialist in those methods for which he has been able to learn enduring "mind holds." They do not exist in community organization.

Generic practice will require mature workers. They must be able to be sufficiently self-aware to distinguish their own motivations from those of clients, to be able to undertake appropriate action rather than familiar action; they must be able to relate to the inarticulate as well as the articulate, and to the powerless as well as the powerful. This definition of practice makes it almost impossible to develop a hierarchy of problem complexity, or even of task complexity. All of the generic worker's duties require maturity, self-discipline, and knowledge. There is no room for the inexperienced, the immature or the uninformed worker. Many professions including social work are considering career ladders as a way of making it possible for tasks demanding less skill to be performed by the less skillful. As an individual develops more skill, and every effort is made to make it possible for him to do so, he can undertake tasks commensurate with his skill. Career ladders are easier to develop in a stable professional field. It is not by chance that paramedical professions developed before social work paraprofessional opportunities. Career ladders once instituted tend to freeze professional activities. It is more difficult to redefine and reassign tasks once they have become the professional property of some rung on a career ladder. Perhaps flexibility cannot be achieved in professions with extensive career ladder opportunities. Generic social work practice may be an illustration of such a principle. In any event, we in social work will have to take a hard look at career ladder possibilities for social work. If we do not move in this direction, other professions will and they will incorporate tasks and skills we now consider to be our responsibility. Are there sufficient remaining tasks to support a separate generic social work practice or must we find some way to accommodate the principle of efficient use of manpower with the flexibility the future will require? It looks as if we must seek the accommodation of the goals of efficient use of manpower and flexible practice. Flexibility and efficiency are difficult to reconcile.

Generic practice seems to offer the flexibility that will be required by a rapidly changing society. There are some real difficulties which can prevent workers and agencies from maintaining both problem and method generic practice. The realities of the information explosion and new theory development may make it impossible for workers to remain competent in such varied fields. They can become inadvertent specialists. The major advantage of generic practice is its flexibility. Efficient use of manpower may become a goal of greater importance than flexibility. If so, generic practice will cease to be an important way we might organize social work practice.

Anti-Credentialism

The anti-credentialists propose that the organized professions be abolished. Workers will undertake tasks and learn what they need to know to accomplish their objectives. As the worker's skill increases he could undertake more varied and more complex tasks. The worker would decide what he needed to know at any point in time and seek help from a variety of sources. He would not accumulate credits as symbols of new learning, but would demonstrate new competence in his practice. Promotion and larger responsibilities would go to those who had demonstrated competence, not to those who merely accumulated credits. Workers would be free to seek whatever knowledge they needed. They would have access to the special knowledge and skills now thought to be the province of doctors, lawyers, architects, psychologists, city planners, economists and social workers.

This argument makes some sense to us in social work. We have long known that field education increases a student's readiness to learn. Real people with real problems that require real solutions right now, sharply increase a student's eagerness to find out what he must know to be of service. Today's students call such information relevant.

One of the difficulties in preparing students for lifelong practice at the beginning of their careers lies in the inability to learn for the future. Another difficulty lies in the inability of the faculty and accrediting bodies to assess what that future will be. Student objections of irrelevance can arise from their lack of experience or from real awareness that future practice will not require a particular bit of information or skill. Faculty members of schools of social work all over the country are being challenged to decide which of these reasons might underlie charges of irrelevance. Social work educators are further troubled by the need to see clearly into the future of social work and convince students that they need to learn new things to deal with these potential problems. This whole experience is a strong argument for continuing education. Continuing education is the hallmark of the anti-credentialist's program. Along with generic practice, anti-credentialist practice has the potential for needed professional flexibility.

There are major disadvantages to this plan for the organization of professional practice. Anti-credentialism suffers from the same limitations as generic practice. In fact, anti-credentialism is a radical form of generic practice. There are additional matters which make it unlikely that anti-credentialist practice will be possible by 1993. If worker effectiveness is to be the sole criterion for continued practice and promotion, we must be very clear about who determines goals, what the goals are, and how we measure effectiveness.

Goal determination is a complicated problem in community organization. Our clients can be our employers.[2] Welfare rights groups and communities which employ urban renewal consultants can serve as two examples. Our clients can be groups a sponsoring agency wishes to serve. The settlement tradition of service to neighbors is an example. Or we may be employed to serve amorphous population groups. Health planning can be an example of planning for an amorphous population group.

When our employer is our client we have the least difficulty in goal determination. The client determines the goal, modifies it with our assistance, but maintains the final authority. If we find we cannot operate within the limits imposed by the goals, we seek other employment. The question of advocacy does not become crucial; our employer is our client.

Some of us in community organization practice in situations in which our employer is not the client and the issue of who determines goals becomes more complicated. The sponsor may impose wider or narrower limits on the kinds of goals workers may pursue if client groups are interested. The goals may range from the wide-open goal of helping people participate in making the decisions which affect them to the more narrow goal of helping people make wise decisions about how to implement specific programs such as literacy. The fact that sponsoring agencies do impose limits is sometimes forgotten, particularly when the limits are wide rather than narrow. Real difficulties have developed when workers understand their task as that of employee of the client group, when agencies construe the workers' task as implementation of agency goals. Only in the situation in which client groups and sponsoring agencies have very different goals is the issue critical. This seems to be happening more frequently and the trend will continue. However, in the future the client groups will be increasingly able to hire their own workers, lessening emphasis on this dilemma.

When we have amorphous population groups as clients, it is impossible to seek client goal determination. We use the device of client representatives to deal with this problem. We make the interesting assumption that all clients are alike since they have experienced the need for a particular service, i.e. they lack income, they may be potential users of service, they live in a particular neighborhood or they belong to a particular ethnic or racial group. Without having any systematic contact with or accountability to their amorphous constituents, their voices are taken to be those of the people. Elected public officials are at least accountable to a defined electorate and that electorate has some ability to influence the officials' behavior. When we use representatives to speak for amorphous client aggregates the accuracy of their statements about goals can never really be tested and they become the goal-determining body. In this case the needs of the people are what the representatives say they are, unless different representatives are selected.

Workers for whom the sole criteria for continuance and promotion is goal achievement must be able to be very sure that the client group can be defined, and that it has a stable mechanism for policy formulation and goal determination. We have not been so clear in the past and we are only beginning to clarify our thinking at the moment.

Not only must uncredentialed workers seek employment where the authority for goal determination is clear and stable; they must also find clear statements of goals. In community organization, we are just beginning to question what have been our traditional goal statements. Citizen participation can serve as an example. Does citizen participation mean "power to the people"? Does it mean that the expertise of users of service is a unique point of view which should be used in the formulation of better social policy? Or do we use the words to indicate that participation of the citizen compensates for internal feelings of powerlessness and frustration that occur when many people live interdependently in densely populated areas? Do we mean that participation in planning for a service will result in motivation to make use of that service? Unfortunately we sometimes mean citizen participation as a pseudo activity to keep the vocal citizens occupied while the experts implement the solution they believe will be effective for a particular problem. Is citizen participation a value, a right, a strategy, a therapy, or an "opiate of the people"? The words mean these and many other things in the literature of today. Before workers accept assignments to improve citizen participation, both the worker and the sponsor must be very clear about what is meant by the words. They will have to agree about who the citizens are who should participate. Are they representative? If so, whom do they represent? They need to agree about the role and authority of participants and limitations on strategies the sponsor may impose. These are easy questions to ask and almost impossible ones to answer well. Private consulting firms in the community organization field are now being very careful to draw up contracts which are as specific and clear as possible about goals of their service. They have to be. Future contracts will depend upon satisfied customers. The anti-credentialist workers will have the same problem.

Clear goal statements are a necessary condition for evaluation of outcome, but are not the whole story by any means. No matter how well we define goals, social work tasks and social work community organization tasks are complex. Evaluation of complex tasks is equally complex. New and improving ways of measuring effectiveness are on the horizon. Cost benefit analysis makes it possible to weigh the cost of various kinds of programs against each other. Our definition of cost is clearer than our definition of benefit. The application of such analysis makes it impossible for us to substitute actual achievements for proposed achievements when the time comes for evaluation. Quality control devices have long been used in industry and are beginning to be applied to social work activities. At the moment they tend to ensure equal treatment of clients rather than effective differential diagnosis and treatment. Planning, Programming and Budgeting Systems (PPBS) originated by the Defense Department includes continuous feedback or monitoring capabilities. Monitoring is an important feature of any evaluation scheme. The tasks in community organization have not been defined discretely or sequentially, making monitoring of effectiveness difficult, if not impossible, before the completion of a program. The investment of time and resources necessary for most programs make it essential that incompetence be identified and pinpointed long before the end of the project. Program Evaluation and Review Technique (PERT) is one way of monitoring an ongoing project to be sure that difficulties are overcome before they result in the failure of the project to achieve the objective. These are all beginning efforts in community organization and are by no means to be taken as infallible techniques of evaluation. The development of adequate techniques to measure effectiveness is an important goal for community organizers. It is essential if anti-credentialist practice is to remain truly anti-credentialist.

If there are no organized professions of any sort, a new profession will of necessity develop. This profession will be responsible for carrying out the monitoring, discipline-ensuring functions now partially carried by the organized professions. It will eventually perform certifying and credential-conveying functions. This will be true particularly for those practices for which the client is assumed to be unable to evaluate competence or in those fields of practice in which failure would be devastating. Perhaps the universities or professional organizations (ACSW) are not the best organizations in our society to certify for practice, but until effective service is self-evident to every client accrediting bodies will exist. Anti-credentialism means no credentials, not the substitution of one kind for another. It seems important that the organized body of professional social workers take part in the design of measures of effective service rather than abandon this effort to those who know less about practice and who may be less sympathetic to the value base of social work.

Specialist Practice

There are social workers, both in and out of community organization, who think that community organization practice is based on such different theory, uses such different skills, and requires such different ordering of value priorities that it has no place among the helping professions. Community organization has more in common with community development, city planning, economic planning and applied sociology and anthropology than it does with social casework, social group work, psychology, psychiatry and clinical psychology. According to this plan, there would be no social work in 1993, but in its place a complex career group of those interested in community planning and another completely separate career group composed of those in clinical practice. Through each of these groups would run a career ladder that would make it possible for those with less skill and knowledge to practice in the profession, as well as those with more skill and knowledge. An extensive continuing education program would make it possible for each worker to keep up with new knowledge at his current level of practice and to move to more responsibility and remuneration when he was able. The career ladders would be relatively stable and backed up by an organized and inexpensive continuing education program and a program of certification for practice. We could make efficient use of money and manpower. Successful practice at a prerequisite level could be used as an alternative to educational certificates. Anti-credentialists would find this modification of our current credentializing system to their liking, but they would object to the right and the ability of the powerful accrediting body to set up and administer such a program.

The thrust of this bifurcation into specialist professional groups is toward definition of profession by nature of target system and method rather than problem area as proposed by the genericists. As we use these words in the future, it will be wise to note that generic practitioners tend to become problem area specialists, and method and target system specialists tend to become problem generalists.

Organizing all the planners under one professional roof has the advantage of increasing the pressure for more and better research. New knowledge will have to be organized and presented to these practitioners for whom it can be professionally useful. The jargons which now separate us and make cross-discipline communication extremely difficult will have to be modified. The accrediting body will be confronted with the impossible task of assessing practicing competence. They too will demand that new knowledge about measuring effectiveness be a high priority in the research centers. At the moment the new centers of urban studies seem to be moving in the right direction. They may become the research centers for a new professional complex of planners. Their development is still in the future, however, and should not be taken as a sign that the differences among community planners can easily be ironed out.

One of the difficulties among planning professions is that of value priorities. Those in social work community organization who hold that citizen participation is a value requiring no further justification have a difficult time with some city planners who think of citizen participation as a strategy. A strategy which will result in the prompt implementation of the best possible plan devised by experts. These two groups of workers have different value assumptions and different opinions about the role of experts in the planning process. This is no mere error of semantics. The same disagreements exist today within community organization and community development as well. The battle would become even more fierce if community organization were to become a part of a planning profession in which the majority felt that citizen participation is primarily a strategy. It is not enough to smooth over this dispute by asserting that means and ends are inexorably intertwined (strategies and values are the same). Means and ends are distinguished in professional practice.

There is another major difference between community organizers and other planners. One of the skills all social workers are expected to bring to their jobs is self-awareness. This skill makes it possible for the worker to distinguish between what he thinks and what his client thinks. Social work community organizers are expected to be able to separate their own world view from that of others. To be able to identify differences in value assumptions or ideas about how things happen, and to respect such differences, requires that the worker be self-aware. In an era that promises increasing polarization, rhetoric and pluralism, community planners will need to be able to appreciate how those quite different from themselves think and feel. Self-awareness is not among the educational objectives of any of the planning professions except social work community organization. The ability to win the trust of others is a skill requiring self-awareness. Thoughtless manipulation can result if workers are not aware that differences exist. Distrust of all professionals results when this type of manipulation is defended under the guise of professionalism. It is difficult to recognize and certify self-awareness. It is impossible to do if the accrediting bodies do not recognize it as a professional skill along with self-discipline or the ability to communicate. If we are to move in the direction of a career ladder in the community planning and action fields, social work community organizers will have to be both alert and skillful so that self-awareness is included among professional skills required for certification.

The specialist method of organizing practice tends to emphasize the unique characteristics of worker methods and target systems. In fact, they are sometimes presented as if one set of methods or worker actions were applicable to social systems, and a completely different set to individuals. Just as we have not carefully assessed what skills and knowledge are applicable to all target systems in generic practice, we have not assessed what skills and knowledge are unique to the target systems of specialist practice. Our lack of attention to this problem is due partly to our tendency to disguise real differences by global concepts or to create differences by our use of jargons. The matter will require attention if we are to increase effectiveness, no matter what organizing plan we adopt.

Another of social work's contributions to the professions will be lost if the specialist plan is adopted. Social work has focused on the interaction between individuals and small groups and social systems. Continued focus on this difficult problem area is a strength of the generic plan for organizing practice. The specialist plan will increase attention on the problem of interaction between social systems, which we desperately need, but it will be at the expense of the former. Social work must continue to emphasize the relationship between man and his society as the area in which we find our professional tasks.

Specialist practice in some ways has just the opposite advantages and disadvantages as generic practice. Career ladders will be required in specialist practice and as a consequence flexibility will be more difficult to achieve. Such a highly organized profession will be able to command the research resources necessary for new knowledge and better goal statements and criteria of effectiveness. Continuing education can be required by the accreditors so that practitioners can make use of the most recent research findings. However, some of the advantages of flexibility will be lost and some of the unique contributions of social work will almost certainly be lost. The cost will be high.

Another Approach

Specialization versus generalization, university credentials versus practice credentials, flexibility versus stability, all are issues with which any organizational plan must deal. Some of the possibilities for future organization have been discussed above, but there are others as well. However, there is another way to prepare for the future. We might begin to analyze the functions which must be carried out if we are to have an effective, flexible practice. In each of the sections above, certain necessary functions were highlighted as of particular importance if that method of organization were to be pursued. If generic practice is to be effective there must be a more systematic effort to discover new theories and organize existing information. This is particularly true for community organization. Anti-credentialism will require a new system of certifying workers for practice. This will be based on practice performance rather than academic performance. To do this we will need much better methods of evaluation. Specialist practice may result in a loss of the emphasis on practice values and techniques which are vital to our society.

It is possible that the organized profession of social work and specifically community organization might provide for the performance of these functions and let the actual organization of the profession change as times change. One possible method of doing this is to create five national commissions to carry out the functions The five functions are certifying practitioners, evaluating projects and practice, education and continuing education, research and information collection, and finally, trend analysis and goal setting. These functions must be performed if our profession is to continue to meet the challenge of change. There would be a sixth commission to coordinate the work of the other five.

Certification of Practitioners

Organized professions have certifying bodies. In some cases, governmental agencies carry the full responsibility. In others, the organized profession administers the certification program under the assumption that it will be responsible for disciplining members who do not practice in an ethical or effective manner. Professional organizations, including the National Association of Social Workers, have not been as aggressive in identifying and eliminating poor practice as they have been in upgrading the certification requirements for entry into the profession. It is very hard for professional organizations to require increasingly more effective practice of fully certified members. The functions of certification for practice and recertification at set intervals might better be separated from other functions performed by professional associations.

It will be hard for those of us who have devoted much time and effort to the elevation of social work to genuine professional status to devote future effort to the identification of aspects of practice which do not require extensive education. However, hard as it may be, the task must be done and redone if we are to remain as flexible as we need to be.

The new practitioner certifying agency might begin by identifying the existing certifying techniques and criteria. Can these be regularized and simplified? Can we make better use of letters of reference, performance ratings, exam results, and educational credentials in our current certifying practice?

The immediate next step would require some codification of existing tasks social workers or community organization workers carry out. Such a scheme might identify those tasks that require extensive information and the ability to communicate it to a particular group of people. Community workers who help their neighbors find their paths through the maze of social services are performing a job that requires extensive information of a temporary nature. Other tasks require special skill, but less extensive temporary information. A worker who is helping a citizens' group learn how to organize will have to be particularly skilled in guiding group process but may not have to be so knowledgeable about particular services. Other tasks may require great skill, maturity and knowledge. A community planner who is attempting to involve citizens in a planning process may have to possess a great deal of technical information about social welfare planning as well as be skilled in guiding group process and decision-making. The certifying procedure and criteria could be very different for each of these kinds of practice.

Another task for the certifying agency is to undertake ongoing study of improved methods of identifying skill when the candidate has it and of noting its lack when the candidate does not have it. These new methods could then become a part of the ongoing certification program. The Academy of Certified Social Workers entrance exam is a start in this direction. Could we now put our attention to the creation of continuance exams?

The practitioner certification agency could be financed partly out of fees charged to applicants, partly from dues paid by members of the profession, and partly by agencies who request professional status information on a particular individual. The over-all policy decision might be made by a board composed of members, representatives of employing agencies and experts in the field of practitioner credentialing. This group would require a paid staff of great skill and integrity, beyond influence of those who seek credentials. It would be accountable to the coordinating committee for its actions and responsive to its demand that there be a continued review of criteria and methods of accrediting in keeping with the changing demands the profession will have to face.

Evaluation of Programs

The second function, that of evaluation of programs, should be financed differently and should be separately accountable from the certification of individual competence. These are related processes but different in crucial ways. The role of an individual professional, however well he fulfills it, may not have significant impact on total outcome. Professional actions, well performed, within the requirements of the program, may not be effective because the program itself may be poorly designed, an inappropriate solution to the problem at hand. The questions for the evaluation agency to examine are: What professional actions are effective to achieve what goals under what circumstances? It is not concerned with how well any individual performs in professional practice.

Funding for the evaluation agency could come from a number of sources. The federal government requires evaluation of many of its grant programs as part of the grant itself. It would be relatively easy to set up a social work or community organization program evaluation agency empowered and equipped to carry out these evaluative functions. Local agencies could contract with this agency to fulfill this grant requirement. Other funding agencies also seek independent evaluation of programs they fund and they are willing to finance such program evaluation by agencies known to be impartial and competent. Many private corporations are offering to conduct program evaluation services today, particularly in community planning. The organized profession might be able to tap this source of funds as well as to provide a valuable service. However, the public nature of this agency's operation as a function of social work will not bring it into competition with the private firms when the private firms will be able to offer confidentiality of findings. All findings of the program evaluation agency in social work must be public information. Published reports might be sold for a small charge to help defray the cost of printing, but nothing should be so expensive as to prohibit wide distribution.

Many people will be interested in findings. Those responsible for social work education will need constantly to keep current on new information about effective strategies. Funding organizations, including the government, might be increasingly guided by evaluative findings as well as political realities in decisions to fund or not to fund services. One of the charges to this agency is that it make concerted efforts to inform decision makers about the results of evaluative studies it has undertaken.

The program evaluation agency would be further charged with the responsibility of updating our current evaluative techniques and of developing new ones as new tasks are defined. Its board of elected professionals would have to make sure that in addition to carrying out evaluative studies for other organizations, it also evaluated the programs given high priority by the profession. Had we such an agency when we first began to offer programs for the drug dependent, we might have a much better idea of program effectiveness and limitations than we now have. Effectiveness is a difficult matter to conceptualize, let alone measure. However, if we do not tackle this problem now, we will be not further along in 1993, and may as a consequence no longer have a profession.

Education

Education and continuing education must also be carried on well if we are to have a flexible, effective professional practice in 1993. Included would be the institutional accrediting function now carried out by the Council on Social Work Education, although this would be but a small part of the educational agency's responsibility.

It would have to anticipate what educational experiences would best prepare practitioners for new kinds of practice. Not only will workers want to improve their skill and income, they will have to continually learn in order to keep up and they may have to learn entirely new tasks as the need for former skills attenuates.

Educators have the task of translating new knowledge into practice skills and finding the best method for teaching. Some educators feel that unless a teacher carries out research and publishes it, he is not making maximum use of his opportunities to enrich his teaching. In this program, teaching and research would be carried out in different places by different people. The assumption is that teaching and research are becoming sufficiently technical that specialization is both necessary and desirable. Teachers would have the opportunity to participate in research efforts, if they were sufficiently competent in research, and would be required to keep up with the findings of the research agency of social work along with the reports of the practitioner accreditation agency and the practice evaluation reports.

Various funding sources would be required. Universities could continue to offer the bulk of pre-entry education. This education is general in nature and provides the necessary basic understandings upon which the worker builds as he continues in a particular practice. Since our profession requires a minimum of special facilities with the exception of libraries and perhaps computers, we ought to be able to make decentralized educational opportunities widely available. We can offer courses in evening schools, in agencies, in church basements, anywhere. The courses could be required for recertification for practitioners and provide opportunities for advancement, new information, new research findings, or new practice techniques. Teaching techniques must be constantly revised and improved. The teachers cannot be less up-to-date than the students. The cost of these programs can be borne by the agencies requesting it, the students themselves, educational endowment funds, and scholarships.

The idea that one prepares for a profession during some period in an educational institution and forever after is considered competent to practice that profession will be the most difficult impediment to the efforts of the educational agency. The realities of a recertification program may be the spur we need to make social workers understand that we mean it when we say that social work education will be a lifelong responsibility.

Research

This function includes theory building as well as testing new methods of data collection and coding. Its efforts should be cumulative and of special importance to social work. The focus will not be to add new knowledge, but to add new knowledge as requested by the other functions and the organized profession. It might be possible to use existing research centers in various parts of the country on a contract basis. A central research facility could carry out the projects which cannot be subcontracted to other institutions. Contracts could be assigned to practice settings as well as to university-based research facilities. Agencies now unable to afford research programs would have an additional resource for money and expertise.

The following strictures would apply to all the projects financed by the research agency. All results must be made public. The agency would include funds for the publication of all findings in every grant. All data would become part of the permanent library of data available for authorized research purposes. Even if a project defaulted and was not completed, all data and materials would become a part of the permanent library.

All research must fit in the scheme of the policy thrust of the organized profession. It must build on what has already been done. It may become apparent to the trend analyzers that there is an increasing gap between the expectation people have about their ability to influence their society and their actual ability. One programmatic research thrust might be on the relationship between aspirations and behavior, aspirations and socialization, aspirations and effectiveness in social change.

Funding for such an agency might come from private grants, government research grants, universities, members' fees and from small amounts charged for published reports. The agency would have to be aggressive in seeking grants that it could fulfill within the goals of the profession. It would have to exercise great restraint in not accepting those which would lead its efforts away from a general programmatic plan or into areas not of primary importance to the profession. Its primary goal is to build better theory which is needed by social workers or, if not done for the whole profession, by community organizers.

Trend Analysis

The final function which must be performed if we are to have a viable profession is that of trend analysis. A sort of Distant Early Warning system which might alert us to changes in professional duties far enough in advance so we might have a chance to conduct research, propose professional actions, teach people what they need to know to perform these tasks and evaluate effectiveness. Had we had such warning about the increasing use of drugs, and had we heeded it, we might be much further along in our practice in the drug field. What new trends are appearing now for which we can prepare? What is the role of a community organizer in the ecology movement? Should there be one? What would he need to know to do the job?

Legislative trends as well as newly passed legislation could be summarized and examined for implications for practice. If the OEO Poverty Program job descriptions for community workers had been used for a guide, a helpful continuing education program might have been mounted before the workers experienced the frustrations they did. The Comprehensive Mental Health Act mandated that certain types of health services be provided in new ways. We did not move fast enough to set up the educational experiences which could have been most helpful to the professional staffs of these agencies. Urban renewal experts found themselves unable to carry out reasonable "element seven" (citizen participation) programs when their experience had been in business administration or the building trades. Continuing education seminars might have been designed to meet this need.

The trend analyzers can also alert the research agency of the need for new emphasis as new problems become important. Could we have anticipated the War on Poverty? We might have been prepared with adequate summaries of the facts as well as studies of causes and evaluations of existing programs. Social workers have been concerned with poverty for a long time. We should have been able to provide better answers with more credibility than we did. Perhaps a professional DEW line agency will help us to move more quickly in the future.

The primary funding for this agency should be members' dues. Its function is to inform and alert members and the other agencies. Members should be prepared to pay for this direct service. The agency might be located in a research center as it will need access to computers, but its funding and function should be independent of the research center. All its reports should be public. It should have considerable responsibility for informing legislators, members of the profession, and other staff of supporting agencies of the implications their analyses have for practice, legislation, research and professional goals.

Summary

All five of these functions, research, education, certification, evaluation, and trend analysis, are now performed in some manner by all professions. They are essential if a profession is to remain viable. Each of the ways of organizing practice mentioned in the first section of this paper emphasized the need to improve in one or more of them. If these functions could be well organized and operated reasonably well, social workers could organize themselves in any number of ways. Some might be generic workers, others in specialized fields. Some might specialize in a particular method while others specialized in problem areas. Community organizers might practice in the planning field with city planners, economic planners, policy planners and systems analysts without losing the important contributions of social work.

By 1993 our profession may have changed so much that we would not recognize what is done then as community organization or social work. The goals for 1993 are not that we be recognizable but that we be effective and flexible. If these functions are performed well, we might achieve these goals.

10

Social Work Administration

HARLEIGH B. TRECKER

Administrators of the nation's social welfare enterprise have been under mounting attack in recent years. They have been caught in the bind of activist groups demanding more services and conservative groups demanding cutbacks in service and financial retrenchment. Some administrators have decided that the struggle is not satisfying for them and they have stepped aside. Overworked, underpaid, and often misunderstood, they have felt that perhaps others might do a better job than they have been able to do. Their replacements have usually found that after the "honeymoon period" they too are caught up in never-ending conflict situations which soon exhaust their energies and stifle their creativity. Thus it cannot be said that social welfare administration is an endeavor of much appeal during these troubled 70's.

Any assessment of social welfare administration as it is practiced today raises more questions than it answers. For example, if we ask, Are today's social welfare services well administered? we would have to answer yes and no. Yes from the standpoint that a remarkable array of services is available with only limited financial resources, no from the standpoint of the inadequate financing itself which seems to be evidence that such services are not as yet universally accepted and valued. Yes from the standpoint of many needs being met at least partially, no from the standpoint of poor coordination of services, unmet needs and waiting lists, and the persistent maldistribution of services. Yes from the standpoint of honest, dedicated, hard-working administrators, no from the standpoint of inadequate educational programs to prepare the next generation of administrators. Yes from the standpoint of the continuity of services, no from the standpoint of very limited research and evaluation of how much good continuing programs do. Yes from the standpoint of more and better professional staff workers, no from the standpoint of personnel utilization especially insofar as nonprofessionals are concerned. So it is really hard to say how effective administration has been or is, but it is clear that the administrators of the future have their work cut out for them. Many of the men and women who administer the nation's social welfare enterprise will not be so doing in 1993. Some will have died, others retired, those still serving will be in the latter stages of their careers. What they do now in the 70's and 80's will sharply influence the 90's.

The Climate of Administration

It is important to try to understand the atmosphere or climate within which administrators will work during the next twenty years. Most of the points that follow are but continuations of existing situations and trends. It seems clear that rapid technological change will continue but that social changes in the human services field will at times lag considerably behind technological developments. While we read much about the swift rate of change, the opposite seems true in our field because change is so slow and crablike in coming. Certainly the rate of change is quite uneven and is markedly slower in the human realm than in the technical realm. Hence, it would seem sensible to observe that it is unlikely that there will be a "giant leap forward" in the human services field and that slow progress will have to suffice.[1]

There is much uncertainty about population changes in the upcoming decades. It seems clear that population growth will continue but at a much slower rate than had previously been forecast. In any event, there will be more people to serve and it is unlikely that population zero will arrive immediately in spite of the declining birth rate. More and more people will live in the cities and in metropolitan areas. The flight to the suburbs has not been arrested and in many of the larger cities the central area is gripped by decay, declining tax revenue, and a residual population with extraordinary needs. The urban crisis will not abate and there seems to be little inclination to rebuild our cities even if sufficient money ware appropriated to do so.

Tax reform so badly needed on all levels of government will be widely discussed and it is possible that some piecemeal action will be taken. Yet there is no assurance that massive reforms will be enacted during the immediate period ahead because of the deeply entrenched special interest groups that are sheltered by the existing tax systems. In spite of the declared need for much more tax revenue to support public purpose programs at this moment there seems little inclination on the part of the lawmakers to face up to the reality of starving social programs. Without doubt the financing of social welfare programs and services will be parsimonius until the tax structure is rebulit and until more revenue is forthcoming.

The struggle for equal opportunity so much a part of the 60's and early 70's will continue during the next two decades and possibly beyond. Racism in all of its ugly aspects will have to be eradicated if much is to be accomplished in solving the problems of poverty, unemployment, underemployment, poor housing, inadequate education, slum housing, and limited health care. While progress has been made the rate has been discouragingly slow and much remains to be done. It is hard to see how any social welfare enterprise can reach maximum effectiveness in its service offerings unless at the same time it is fighting to eliminate racism.

Challenges to the "system" or to the "establishment," so pronounced in recent years, will continue and will be stepped up.[2] Every administrator can expect this to happen and some will welcome such challenges because through them the system may become more responsible. Every one of society's institutions will continue to be challenged. Business, industry, government, unions, churches, colleges and universities, and social welfare agencies are all undergoing the vigorous scrutiny they have so often said they invited. While the consumer may not yet be king he is no longer the serf of the past.

There is a growing concern with the matter of national, state and local priorities particularly in the light of limited financial resources.[3] One can expect that there will be continuing conflict between foreign and domestic needs, between expenditures for defense and war and expenditures for peacetime social improvements. Already there is a struggle going on between the environmentalists who are rightly concerned with the problems of pollution and the humanists who see large areas of unmet human needs. It is increasingly clear that incremental objectives will have to be established over a period of time because there is no way of meeting all of the national needs at once.

The growth of government responsibility in the human services has been pronounced over the past several decades. There is reason to believe that this growth will have to continue because the large problems of health, welfare, and housing, and education cannot possibly be handled on the local level or by the private sector of the economy. It is unlikely that there will be great expansion of the private agencies and it is evident that more and more they are seeing their roles as advocates of planned social change.

The issue of agency control is a major one. Persons are asking penetrating questions as to who really own, runs, and decides matters in our human service enterprise. Already there is more involvement of people in the decision-making processes of the agency and it is not likely that this trend will be reversed. In fact, it is a healthy recognition of the need that agencies have to create a much broader base of support, understanding and responsibility spread. While many institutions continue to be in the control of the elite, these institutions are under question and challenge and there is bound to be an "opening up" of the hitherto closed corporations of the past.

The issue of service organization, delivery and accessibility is a prominent one which will continue to receive much consideration. One can expect the growth of multiservice agencies employing multidisciplinary methods. There will be consolidations and mergers of smaller agencies and there will be new clusters of agencies with outreach programs geared into new systems of mass transportation to facilitate accessibility.

There is much discussion of the centralization-decentralization issue with little clarity as to what direction the organization of human services will take. On the one hand there is increasing recognition of the need for strong central planning, resource allocation and control, while on the other hand there is a strong movement for building up local responsibility for the day-to-day operation of services. Quite likely the centralization-decentralization conflict will be with us for a long time with the need for both forms of organization continuing to be manifest.

The new "populism" of the early 70's is mentioned with mounting frequency but no one is quite certain exactly what is meant by it. Nor can it be certain that it represents a real trend and shift in the thinking of people. Perhaps it is primarily an election-year catch slogan which will fade rapidly after the election is over. In any event, there is seemingly much disenchantment with the operation of government and the apparent lack of responsiveness on the part of government. Numerous groups are advocating working within the system to change it and these groups of consumers, youth, women, minorities, the aged, blue-collar workers, and so on represent potential new coalitions. Whether or not this comes to pass is as yet unclear. Nevertheless, there are many changes under way in the power structure and mechanisms of this country and it is to be expected that far-reaching shifts will occur in the next two decades.

Therefore, administrators will have to continue to relate their agencies and programs to over-all metropolitan operations and state and regional planning requirements. From the mid-1960's on, federal aid programs mandated by Congress were increasingly inclined to require local projects to be seen in the broader terms of the metropolitan or regional geographic area. For example, the Housing and Urban Development Act of 1966 called for increased attention to regional planning. Title II, Section 204 of the Act reads: "All applications made after June 30, 1967 for federal loans or grants to assist in carrying out open space land projects, or for planning or construction of hospitals, airports, libraries, water supply distribution facilities, and water development and land conservation projects within a metropolitan area *shall be submitted for review to any area-wide agency which is designed to perform metropolitan or regional planning for the area within which the assistance is to be used."* While this is seen as only a review procedure it has been evident that such reviews have tended to make localities develop their programs with the wider area in mind.

In 1968 the Congress passed the Omnibus Crime Control and Safe Street Act making federal monies available to units of local government but *only through a state planning agency.* The new agency, the Law Enforcement Assistance Administration in the Department of Justice, was designed to bring about a better coordinated and intensified program of law enforcement on the local level.

The securing, allocating, and accounting for financial resources will continue to be a major issue to be faced by administrators. The ravages of an inflationary wartime economy have already been felt and serious financial problems face every agency in both the public and private sectors. It is not known at this point how much time key administrators devote to "getting the money" with which to operate but it must be considerable. It is not going to be any easier to obtain resources in the period ahead; in fact, it will probably become more difficult. There is no long-range planning going on at present on any level of government, so it is impossible to see just what will be needed and where the money will come from. Incomplete and fragmentary policies of public subsidy for private institutions result in highly uneven treatment of various fields of service. The responsibility of the individual to pay for services when he is able is under extensive review in the private sector. Never has there been more concern and less light as to how to proceed financially in the human service field. Administrators can expect to lose more sleep over this in the period that lies ahead.

Metropolitanism, regionalism, and the like have become issues only in the recent past. Yet, more and more attention is being given to the development of services for the populations of more than a single locality. This is a vital issue to be faced because inevitably intergovernmental bodies have to be created and responsibilities allocated to them. The same holds for consortia of private agencies who wish to expand their boundaries.

In some of the large city and state public welfare departments there is a trend toward replacing social-work-trained administrators with persons from the field of business or from schools of business administration. Porter [4] reports on New York City in this connection. It is too early to know if this trend will continue but it is important and no doubt reflects a kind of national "get tough" with welfare recipients approach. In a way the advocates of the business approach seem to be saying that the social work administrator is "too soft" and "too easy" on the public assistance client and the business administrator will be tougher. Advocates of the business management approach contend that public welfare agencies are too large, too costly, and that welfare is a business. Hence, the business approach should be used. This generally means that the objective is marked reduction in welfare costs. Advocates further claim that there is a vast body of management and systems technology which has grown up in recent years and that this new knowledge should be put to work in the welfare field. They further claim that the management-trained person can be more "objective" because he has no real interest in the welfare client. The clincher to the management argument is that social-work-trained administrators have not reduced the welfare load so they should be replaced. It remains to be seen, but it is to be doubted that the management-trained administrators will be able to make much of a dent in the increasing welfare population. Advocates of the social-work-trained administrator feel that public welfare services are not a business but rather human assistance programs which must keep the needs of people central. They agree that management technology has a place in welfare administration from a procedural standpoint but it is a technical rather than a professional contribution. Those who believe that social work services should be administered by social workers point out that to administer any human enterprise one must have had experience with it and must operate in terms of explicit human values. They feel that schools of social work should provide more professional education for social work administrators and should not turn the welfare system over to the business group by default.

Some schools of social work have developed specialized programs in social work administration at the master's degree level. For a discussion of the field practice component in one such program see Neugeboren's useful report.[5]

The issue of the "right to services" is more and more brought before the courts. This is true in a wide range of fields including public welfare, mental retardation, health care, and the like.[6] With a strong trend toward equality of opportunity and availability of services for all it can be expected that former strict limitations often imposed by law or custom will tend to vanish or, at least, recede. The legal assistance programs born during the 1960's under the auspices of the Economic Opportunity

Act have challenged many prevailing patterns of service and funding and have frequently overturned existing structures. One can expect that administration will have to be closely related to the law and intimately informed as to the legal basis which underlies much of the human services field.

Of striking significance in recent years has been the role of administration around issues of conflict resolution. There is scarcely an agency that has not been embroiled in conflict whether with constituents, staff, the community, or some group. This has called for keen administrative skill in problem analysis and definition and in providing channels for the processes of accommodation and conflict resolution to take place. It is likely that one of the central skills of the administrator of tomorrow will fall in this area of conflict resolution. This skill will have to be founded on deeply felt values as to the rights of human beings to participate in the affairs which affect them.

The issue of accountability has emerged as one of the salient features of the human services in the 1970's. After the vast expansion of the 1960's there came the retrenchment of the early 1970's. This has forced administration to pay more attention to the establishment of better means of quality control, accountability, and determining the cost effectiveness of programs and services. More and more social programs are being challenged and questioned by persons who claim that these programs do not accomplish what they are supposed to in spite of their increased growth and funding over the years. It is entirely possible that some programs have had unrealistic objectives or have tried to accomplish impossible goals. It is also possible that various constituencies have had conflicting expectations as to the purposes of these programs. In any event, one can expect the questioning to continue and possibly become sharper and more penetrating. This would seem to specify the need for far more evaluative research on the part of agencies and for administration properly armed with reliable data to justify the efforts of their institutions. While it will never be easy to "cost-account" the human services, much more can be done and must be done. The social audit and the human audit are just as important as the financial audit and much creative work must be done along these lines. Even this will tax the administrator who must keep the work going under the pressure of dwindling resources.

There is some evidence to support the notion that the era of the large "superagency" has already dawned. Agencies that embrace a wide range of programs and services have come into being and some of the more specialized smaller agencies have been merged or absorbed. Those who advocate the large superagency stress that it is more efficient, eliminates duplication of services, provides for better coordination, makes possible better equality of services and greater accessibility, and brings into focus multidisciplinary techniques. They have some impressive arguments on their side. Opponents of the large agency see it as unwieldy, excessively bureaucratic, and dangerous from the standpoint of so much centralization of power. They regret the loss of specialized expertise which seems to diminish when brought into huge conglomerates. They worry about the vulnerability of the single large agency and see greater security when agencies are separate. They argue that the superagency tends to reduce the level of services for large populations and that instead of having many high-quality smaller agencies the community becomes acceptive of a mediocre mass approach to its needs and problems. So far there has been little experience with the conglomerate social agency and it is difficult to forecast how effective those now in existence will be. It is true, however, that they represent a challenge to existing forms of agency organization and if they continue to develop will require a much different kind of administrative leadership.

In some of the larger agencies there is a trend toward separating long-range planning from day-to-day administration by setting up departments of planning. This approach, long used in industry, is claimed to have many advantages for the social welfare field. Advocates say that the information input is so great in this computer age that only through a separate department can it be processed and fed into the program development process. They argue forcefully that the day-to-day tasks of most administrators are so demanding that they have little time for long-range planning even if they had the inclination to work this way. They feel that a separate planning arm can be more objective because it is *not* involved in the sticky decisions of ongoing operations. They suggest that different skills are needed for planning and stress the need for current social science background. Opponents of separate planning departments feel that it is both unwise and impossible to separate the planning process from the administrative process and that divorced planning bodies become too theoretical, unrealistic, and nonrelevant. They also argue that when planning is removed from administration there is a serious loss of ready information input. It is evident that there is much discussion under way and that major decisions affecting the next several decades will be made. In substance it seems clear that more planning is much needed and the issue is how planning services should be organized and integrated into the over-all administrative structure.

One of the most vigorous debates now under way is that between those who believe in a highly centralized administrative organization and those who feel that the decentralized system is better. The advocates of centralization claim that it is more efficient and more economical. They add that it makes for a uniformity of standards and quality of services.

They point out that centralized authority is more defined and thus more accountable. They claim that decision-making is more rapid and that decisions are more uniform in their impact. They claim that when authority is centralized it is possible to bring about an earlier mobilization of forces and to bring them to bear on problems with greater weight. The advocates of decentralization of services, programs, and authority feel that their way is more efficient because people in the neighborhood who understand the problems faced know much more than do people who are a great distance away and as a result better programs will be offered. They see greater flexibility and variety in programs which are tailored to the conditions of the particular locale served. They also feel that decentralized authority makes for greater individualization of programs in relation to the special needs of community people. They suggest that the decentralized program administrator can be held accountable for his area of service more easily and more completely than the remote central office. They see quicker decisions made more realistically because people on the scene are involved. They argue that many decentralized agencies will actually have a greater impact on funding bodies because of the many more people involved who can be organized to exert influence.

It is evident that it will be an interesting time for administrators, even an exciting time in spite of strains and ever-present pressures. There will be a real need for highly qualified and able persons to man the administrative posts now open and to open up in the period ahead.

Goals for Administration

As social work administrators work together during the next two decades it is to be hoped that they will achieve a number of goals at least in part. Although this list is far from complete it may be the beginning of thought in the goal realm which can be refined and expanded as time unfolds.

1. The Goal of Clear Definition of Administration

It is of great importance that efforts be made to define administration of the human services in terms of its unique characteristics. It is not satisfactory to think of administration only as an area of knowledge. It must be seen as a method of social work practice.

Sarri had put forth a concise definition of administration with these words: "Administration is defined as a *method of practice* rather than an area of knowledge or research. It is a method which is concerned with the following activities: 1. Translation of societal mandates into operational policies and goals to guide organizational behavior. 2. Design of organizational structures and processes through which the goals can be achieved. 3. Securing the resources in the form of materials, staff, clients, and societal legitimation necessary for goal attainment and organizational survival. 4. Selection and engineering of the necessary technologies. 5. Optimizing organization behavior directed toward increased effectiveness and efficiency. 6. Evaluation of organization performance to facilitate systematic and continuous problem-solving." [7] This clear declaration that administration is a method of practice concerned with specific activities is an important contribution to the growing trend that schools of social work include administration sequences in their programs.

2. *The Goal of Competency and Skill Qualifications in Relation to Defined Administrative Responsibilities*

Much more work needs to be done in the way of defining more clearly the expectations attached to the administrative job and the kinds of competencies and skills needed by persons who aspire to administrative positions. Unfortunately little has been done in a definitive sense in social welfare administration and no one really knows much about what is involved in modern administrative leadership in the welfare field.

It is interesting to note that in a recent informal study of educational administration six competencies were mentioned as essential for the administrators of the nation's schools. They included: "(1) human relations skills; (2) knowledge of educational hardware, especially computers; (3) ability to assess scholarship; (4) understanding of finance; (5) ability to persuade verbally; (6) capacity for decision making, and (7) a grasp of the legal aspects of institutional administration." [8] It would seem that these competencies would apply with equal weight to the entire realm of human services.

Bennis declares that a key task of the administrator is "building a climate in which collaboration rather than conflict will flourish. An effective collaborative climate . . . should include the following ingredients: flexible and adaptive structure, utilization of individual talents; clear and agreed upon goals, standards of openness, trust, and cooperation, interdependence, high intrinsic rewards, and transactional controls— which means a lot of individual autonomy, and a lot of participating in making key decisions." [9]

No matter what philosophy of administration one holds it would be enormously worthwhile if there could be a comprehensive nationwide study of administrative jobs as they are now defined and a companion look at the administrators in terms of their qualifications, skills, competencies, areas of adequacy and inadequacy, and their needs for further training. It is to be hoped that this goal may be accepted as one worthy of much consideration.

3. *The Goal of More and Better Professional Preparation*

During the next two decades it is likely that there will be an expansion in the opportunities for students to secure professional education for social welfare administration. It is to be hoped that most of the schools of social work will provide a concentration or specialization in administration on the master's level. In addition, it would be worthwhile if eight or ten regional centers for doctoral work in administration could be established. This might call for the pooling of resources and the exchange of faculty and specialized staff. At issue, of course, is the extent to which the substantive content of social welfare is seen as an essential element in the program of professional preparation. Even though this writer holds that it is indispensable there are others who think differently. In any event, this matter must be clarified.

Another goal is the establishment of a National Center of Training in Social Welfare Administration attached to a university and set up to provide research, publications, and advanced study on a short-term but continuing basis. While this would be initially costly to fund it would help to produce the kind of leaders so very much needed.

In talking about leadership in the future Bennis says, "This new concept of leadership embraces four important sets of competencies: (1) knowledge of large complex human systems; (2) practical theories of intervening and guiding these systems, themes that encompass methods for seeding, nurturing, and integrating individuals and groups; (3) interpersonal competence, particularly the sensitivity to understand the effects of one's own behavior on others and how one's own personality shapes his particular leadership style and value system; and (4) a set of values and competencies which enables one to know when to confront and attack, if necessary, and when to support and provide the psychological safety so necessary for growth." [10]

4. *The Goal of Dynamic Organization and Structure*

There is increasing agreement that administrative structure and organization must meet certain basic criteria. Some of these criteria are: The roles and responsibilities of all units within the agency (board, staff, executive office, etc.) must be clearly stated and understood. The overall policy and operating decision centers must be clearly identified. There must be well-established channels of communication, horizontal and lateral, formal and informal. There must be the means and mechanisms of coordination clearly placed in the executive office. There must be ways of getting input from the service population and the community relative to the needs to be met and the effectiveness of the programs. The responsibility of the chief administrator and assistant administrators must be known and accepted by all. Systems of delegation must be worked out so that the work load is properly distributed. Appropriate media of interpretation are in use so that there is a growing understanding of the work of the agency and an increasing willingness to support it. There are carefully prepared ways of program evaluation. There is a built-in system for periodic review of the agency structure.

As Bennis points out, "Organizations of the future . . . will have some unique characteristics. They will be adaptive, rapidly changing *temporary systems,* organized around problems-to-be-solved by groups of relative strangers with diverse professional skills. The groups will be arranged on organic rather than mechanical models; they will evolve in response to problems rather than to programmed expectations. People will be evaluated, not in a rigid vertical hierarchy according to rank and status, but flexibly according to competence. Organizational charts will consist of project groups rather than stratified functional groups as is now the case. Adaptive, problem-solving, temporary systems of diverse specialists linked together by coordinating executives in an organic flux— this is the organizational form that will gradually replace bureaucracy." [11]

5. *The Goal of a Meaningful Information System*

One of the goals for all administrators is the establishment and operation of an *information system* [12] which will produce rapidly and completely the data needed to make wise decisions. Many administrators feel buried by material which they can neither read nor digest. The flood of reports originating within the agency and coming from the outside swamp even the best intentions to "keep up." Fortunately, the computer is now beginning to play an important role in helping to make available, and if need be to retrieve, information so vital to the day-to-day work of the agency and for its long-range planning. In developing an information system the administrator must identify the sources from which needed material is coming, select the essential data and rank it in terms of priority, arrange for transmission and distribution, and of course arrange it for purposes of instant retrieval. Important historical data regarding past performance must be tied in with present service statistics and future service projections. It is likely that each agency will set up an Information Department, appropriately staffed, and tied in with the office of central administration. While the start-up cost might be substantial, especially in large agencies, the payoff would be great in terms of better planning.

6. *The Goal of Wider Participation in Decision-Making*

The power centers in many social welfare enterprises are confined to small self-perpetuating groups of people who tend to exercise tight control over agency purposes, resource allocation, and service designs. While this situation is changing it is still a worthwhile goal for many institutions to seek wider participation in the decision-making processes both long-range and short-range. Every agency should make a careful study of the extent to which various groups and individuals have a real voice in the affairs of importance to them. A review of vital decisions over the past decade might reveal that only a very few have been involved and should this be the case fundamental change is needed. Balanced decision-making which rests on proportional representation of all agency interests, community, clientele, staff, board and administration will inevitably result in a far more viable and realistic program. Furthermore, it can result in much broader support and in the discovery of new resources of both money and talent. The goal of wider participation in decision-making cannot be ignored and must be achieved.

7. *The Goal of Better Long-Range Planning*

In any list of goals for the future it is important to include long-range planning. Social welfare services have tended to evolve from crisis to crisis and often in an overlapping piecemeal fashion. While much data of a social need indicator type is available it does not get used because too few administrators concern themselves with the hard work of long-range planning in relation to fundamental purposes.

It is urged that every agency have a long-range planning mechanism of some kind firmly placed within the office of administration. The chief administrator must give over-all direction and supervision to such a mechanism even though he may delegate actual technical operations to assistants. Most likely the Long-Range Planning Committee will become a regular and permanent part of agency structures during the period ahead and this is all to the good.

8. *The Goal of Evaluative Research*

Closely tied in to the long-range planning goal is the need for evaluative research of agency operations including administration. Few agencies today have a continuous research effort or input rendering data on the degree of success of program services or administration. Small agencies may not be able to afford such research services but they can form consortia and pool staff and resources to this end. Few practitioners can be expected to be researchers in a scientific sense, hence there will be a need for administration to secure qualified research staff and support them with sufficient funds. Research advisory committees with interdisciplinary social science representation will be essential. It is to be hoped that by 1993 every agency will have far better notions than they have today about the real value and effectiveness of their services in relation to their avowed purposes.

No one can tell what it will be like twenty years from now but it is to be hoped that social welfare administrators and those who seek to educate them will diligently formulate the goals they wish to pursue and earnestly strive to attain them in the period that lies ahead.

11

Social Welfare Planning: An Essay

JACK STUMPF and **BEN P. GRANGER**

I. Introduction and Definition

The purpose and scope of this essay is to raise some questions and to make some suggestions on how to guide social welfare planning between 1973 and 1993, so that some of our most serious social problems will be reduced significantly and some of our most important social goals will be realized during that time. A further aim of this essay is to stimulate the evaluation of social welfare planning itself by identifying some of its major conceptual guides, so that during this twenty-year period there may be a careful examining of the utility of the concepts. If in that time we could learn which social science concepts and which professional principles can result in effective planned social change, and which do cannot, the prospect of reducing the social problems and realizing the social goals of the next century will be much more encouraging than it now can be. This essay is not intended to be predictive although it will discuss selectively some alternative choices and some probabilities of goal setting and goal achievement as perceived by the writers. There is no safe way to foresee the future, although there are ways to explore the future and thereby identify possible trends and options. On occasion we will try to extract from present concepts, as tested by accumulated experience, some lessons of what not to do, what have been blind or circuitous paths which have not led to social welfare goal realization, and what paths seem to have potential for goal realization. Our capability of doing this is limited by the research on social welfare planning and by our own experience, biases, and preferred conceptual guides. Because of the recency and scope of Dr. Robert Morris' chapter on "Social Welfare Planning" in *Five Fields of Social Work Research,*[1] and the recency and scope of the books developed by Dr. Arnold Gurin and Associates in the Community Organization Curriculum Study [2] this essay will not attempt to summarize their findings although their influence will be evident in some ways. This essay purposely avoids some of the main concepts and issues which social welfare planning shares with community organization practice in social work; another chapter of this volume deals with them.

The remainder of the first section will provide a suggested definition of social welfare planning. Section II will consider some of the fundamental assumptions and concepts about social reality, social change and social welfare planning. These assumptions and concepts may shape the structures, processes and professional practice of social welfare planning and thus, its capability of realizing selected social goals. Section III will identify some of the issues which transcend any social progress and institutional development, issues out of which come major social welfare goals as well as the major resources and restraints for realizing them during the next twenty years or more. Section IV will raise some questions and discuss some possibilities on social welfare goal selection and realization. Section V will suggest some conclusions.

Definition

Social welfare planning is the intentional guiding, generating, and influencing of those social processes and programs which reduce the damage to human populations, increase the opportunities for the social development of human populations, and restructure their organizations and institutions so that the forces which concretely support social justice for the one and the many prevail over the counterforces in society. The guiding, generating, and influencing are usually directed toward change and sometimes toward continuity.

The first task of social welfare planning is to *define and redefine* social justice with general and specific populations. This definition is usually made by the identification of specific social goals. The second task of social welfare planning is to *design and redesign* social policies, programs, organizations, and institutions with characteristics and qualities intended to reduce social problems and to realize social goals. The third task of social welfare planning is to *align and realign* the required social power, and with it the reallocation of required resources, for the redirection of social processes to change concretely these programs, organizations and institutions. The realization of sufficient power is, in large

measure, the development of a set of effective strategies aimed at influencing the present sources of power to support selected social goals,
or the redistribution of powers in ways favorable to these goals, or the
converting of micro-powers into macro-power for use in the specific
situation where social justice is at risk. In social welfare planning the
possibility of sufficient social power is enhanced if the private interests
can be ethically linked with the version of the public interest implicit
in the specific goals. The fourth task of social welfare planning is to
evaluate and re-evaluate periodically, if not continuously, the impact of
the planned changes and the unplanned effects upon the intended and
other populations. With such appraisal made on the basis of research
and authentic responses of the populations whose human conditions and
destinies may be affected by the planned change, the fifth task of social
planning is to *initiate* responsibly the tasks of redefining social justice,
reassigning social programs, organizations, institutions, and realigning
power so that resources may be reallocated and social processes may be
redirected toward the revised social goal.

Social welfare planning is thus a circular and spiraling process, rather
than linear. Its movements in a given society, community, or organization are not, however, necessarily or even preferably gradual in timing,
regularity of stages, or neatly connecting of one sector with another.
The social changes resulting from social welfare planning may be, and
too often are, small or incremental; or they may be major changes in
quantity within the present continuity of program; or they may be, and
hopefully more often will be, major changes of quality or what is referred
to as major discontinuities due to social invention.

Social welfare planning is conceived as being responsibly enacted
within a continuum of social research, planning, and action or implementation. Social welfare planning cannot viably function without the
guidance from research or without the serious intent to implement the
plans. Social responsibility calls for the delegation of authorities, or
awareness of self-initiated authorities, among a set of organizations and
actors which makes the continuum of research, planning, and action a
reality. Sometimes, in a given situation in which a certain social goal
is sought, one organization may maintain the continuum, although one
alone often requires the support of others to succeed. Without regard to
organizational structures, the triadic processes of social research, social
welfare planning and social action are often referred to elliptically as
social welfare planning, sometimes as social welfare planning and action,
and sometimes within certain contexts as social planning and action.
Lack of clarity and presence of stigma have made difficult a commonly
acceptable labeling of terms in both the professional literature and public communications.

Social welfare planning includes but is larger in scope than health and welfare services planning, or human services planning. It is also larger in scope than most of the current conceptions of human resources development planning. The concept of social welfare planning discussed here is larger than these not out of any desire to build empires or be idealistic, but rather out of the requirement of conceptual integrity and ethical responsibility. The first dimension of social welfare planning is the design and development of social welfare services or programs of human service. Health and rehabilitation services, public assistance, individual and family services, group services, correctional services, recreation services, housing services, educational services, reduction of racism services and the many other kinds of social services under public, voluntary or mixed auspices clearly require planning.

The populations who are damaged, or lesser developed than is their capability and right to be, usually require some social services which are planned to be available and effective in reducing the damage, recapacitating, reimpowering, developing and redeveloping them in such ways as to better manage current and future problem situations. The planning and conducting of such social services is clearly the social responsibility of the community, local or cosmopolitan, and clearly inclusive in any concept of social welfare planning. The present definition of social welfare planning preferred here has as a second dimension the prevention of damage to people. The reduction of social processes which create negative human conditions, and their redevelopment to enhance positive human conditions are also clearly inclusive within any concept of social welfare planning that purports to be socially responsible. Therefore, the scope of social welfare planning includes the shaping and reshaping of social welfare policies pertaining to generic and specific social problems and social programs. To effect either or both, social welfare planning has a third dimension, the processes of developing, changing and sometimes conserving organizations, institutions and social systems of various kinds and sizes. This breadth, to repeat, emerges out of conceptual integrity and ethical responsibility. The gestalt of social welfare planning includes the situational analysis which, in turn, includes the analysis of the human condition and the power arrangements which permit or encourage the particular condition. The situation analysis gives some guidance to the formulation of new policies, the design of the service and the restructuring of the service-providing organization and system. Furthermore, none of these changes are possible unless approved, or at least not disapproved, by the present powers. Any policy affecting the broad population or intending to change radically the structure, processes or rules of influential organizations and institutions clearly requires considerable planned changes in the power arrangements or in what the existing powers are willing to support. To conceive of social welfare planning as health and welfare services planning without the complementary planning to gain the required power so that social action or implementation occurs is sterility. Social justice is not possible on a planned basis unless social welfare planning and action are connected with social power. Social welfare planning is more concerned with the change or continuity of valued organizations and institutions than in changing individuals. It is the institutional arrangements and provisions which enhance or do not enhance the human condition. When social planning is focused upon changing individuals, it is focused on those actors in major roles who, with others, make decisions in organizations and institutions. In social welfare planning the changing of individuals through rational argument, political influence, or replacement is a means, not an end.

This conception of social welfare planning and the present emerging conceptions of social administration are quite similar, and are moving toward each other in theory and practice. The writers believe that this trend will continue, and that the theoretical basis for each within the organizational, community, decisional, and community-decision-organization concept will result, before 1993, in the articulation of social welfare planning and administration as being one process and one professional practice. Some graduate and advanced educational programs already treat the two similarly or as one concentration for study, practice and research.

II. Some Fundamental Assumptions and Concepts About Social Reality, Social Change, and Social Welfare Planning

This section will discuss the importance of basic assumptions held about the world because they give latitude and limitation, resource and restraint, possibility or impossibility to any kind of planning, including social welfare planning. This section will also suggest some of the possible choices of concepts about complex social reality, social change and social welfare planning. The raising to a conscious level of assumptions and concepts of the social welfare planners is imperative if planning is to be socially responsible and effective. Assumptions geniunely held and concepts actually utilized determine the scope and direction of planning. Intelligent choice of concepts can only be made after a full exploration of the implications of the possible guiding concepts. Since assumptions and concepts guide planning behavior, their choice makes a critical difference. In a changing world especially, assumptions and concepts are more important in guiding planned change than are facts. Amid social change, concepts provide framework, give relevance or not, last longer and span wider social entities than facts. It is the search for ideas, not facts, that will likely determine if the social goals between now and 1993, and in the period after 1993, will be realized. Cox has observed: "In general, we don't have enough data about society to know what, in detail, is happening to us, much less what will happen to us, especially as a function of technological change." [3] And T. H. Huxley warned: "Those who refuse to go beyond facts rarely get as far as facts." [4] Facts obviously have great importance in specific situations after the guiding concepts are chosen and the relevant questions are posed concerning how to convert the present situation into the desired changed reality within a given time span. However, time and timing are crucial, for elapsed time tends to corrode the validity and reliability of social facts.

The critical exploration in planning is for the *implications* of the aspirations and problem perspectives of the populations and institutions to be affected by the plan and *the search for a concept that provides coherence and allows for flexibility* in the plan. The initial study is of the aspirations, problem perspectives, current priority problems, preferred forms of organization of the particular populations, and the study of the manifest and latent goals, resources and restraints, and potential power of the institutions and organizations which will be most affected by the eventual plan. The implications of these findings derived with imagination and courage give latitude to the search for the guiding concept. The guiding concept, it is to be remembered, is more than an instrument of the planning phase. It is also the vehicle for the plan to lead real people and organizations toward a new synthesis. As we shall discuss later, the most difficult problem of social planning is how to achieve synthesis, or perhaps better stated, how to plan to enhance the occurring of synthesis within the particular system and among the other systems affected by the plan. The choosing of the guiding concept is a critical act either toward or against that combination of coherence and flexibility which leads to a new social synthesis.

To clarify our assumptions and guiding concepts is an act of simple responsibility that we now believe is imperative where shared understanding, decisions, and actions are required. It is a responsibility that is often breached in planning, as in other aspects of community life. Because any kind of planning aims to modify the present reality into some different reality, the view of the reality that is held by those persons guiding the planning is of fundamental importance. The assumptions one holds, expressed or not—and often they are unexpressed and taken for granted—tend to shape one's aspirations, problem perspectives, goals, plans and optional prospectives of realizing plans. The central assumptions held by a population, and the decision makers and planners within a community, are of even more importance in determining the destiny of that community. Because of this it may be worthwhile to explore one of the most basic assumptions of all which probably all persons have: *a dominant view of reality.* The authors are aware of no better formulation of dominant views of reality held by Western peoples than the following by J. Samuel Bois,[5] who first labels the epoch in which the view emerged and then provides the essence of the view:

The Age of Primitive Realism (to 650 B.C.)	The world is what I feel it to be.
The Age of Reason (650 B.C.–350 B.C.)	The world is what I say it is.
The Age of Science (1500–1900)	The world is an immense machine, and I can discover how it works.
The Age of Relativism (1900–1966)	The world consists of the probabilities that I create by my way of looking at them.
The Age of Unity (1966–)	My world has a structure that no formulation can encompass; I conceive of the world as my own total experience within it, and I play with my own symbolic constructs in a spirit of easy detachment. (Anthony Athos suggests the substitute "uneasy attachment.")

While to some extent each of these perspectives may be held concurrently by a given individual, probably most thoughtful individuals prefer one over the others. Certainly persons responsible for initiating and maintaining planning processes ought to know their preferred assumption or view of reality and its implication for planning. While this essay is not intended to examine thoroughly the planning implications of each of these dominant views of reality, it will suggest some implications and urge that the reader pursue this exploration further.

The view that "the world is what I feel it to be" seems to have these implications, among others, for planning: I do not influence the world; I feel that it influences me. Therefore, I do not feel I want to try to change it or plan it; rather, I plan to adapt to it, especially I feel I want to please the mysterious forces, as I fear them most. If any planning is to be done it must be done by the priest-king, with the assistance of the sorcerer, for central planning of this realm is among their most important duties. Anyway, the feelings I have about the world which concern me most are anxieties about the present. The past is gone, and I do not feel much for the future. The view that "the world is what I say it is" seems to have these implications for planning: "What counts most is the description, the label, the diagnosis and the prognosis I devise and state. The world makes some sense: at least as far as I have reasoned it out. If I can explain it clearly as it is now, perhaps I can figure ways to change it. Therefore, planning may be possible and desirable, especially if others agree with my reasoned view of the world.

The view that "the world is an immense machine, and I can discover how it works" seems to have these implications for planning: Planning is possible if, as in physical science, we take the time to discover what the parts of the machine are, how they are structured, how they function, how they fit together and work together, and how they test out when using standardized measurements of quantity and quality. One problem is that the scientific examination of the immense machine called "world" has been done, in the main, by those interested in only the physical parts. There is question whether the seamlessness of the social aspect of the world makes it as readily subject to classification, the testing of its parts, and simply testing without being unnecessarily disruptive or actually changing that part of the social reality being tested. Another risk is that planning based upon physical science notions tends to put heavy reliance upon facts. In the social system—which many simplistically interpret as anything that is not part of the physical world—facts often change even before the plans based upon them may be implemented. In general, predicting future social facts has not been accurate, not only because the indicators and instruments used are faulty, but also because human conditions and social conditions are more shaped by the overarching issues of the times and the social system as a whole than anything seemingly implicit in the conditions or problems. However, looking at the world as an immense machine has produced many ideas which led to planned and accidental technological advances. Just probably, looking at the world as a complex social system could produce ideas for planning great social advances.

The view that "the world consists of the probabilities that I create by my way of looking at them" seems to have these implications for planning, among others: The probabilities in the form of concepts, imaginative goals and strategies, imaginative options and statistical or qualitative estimates of chances of realization are the creation of humans. They are not imbedded in the immense machine called "world" and awaiting discovery. The world "out there" is really what I and we say it is, and it hangs together or not by the concepts we choose to use. Whatever meaning the various multiple realities have depend upon the theoretical, philosophical, professional and personal intellectual lens we use. Planning, therefore, is not only possible, but desirable and necessary. The relatedness and relativity of things may be there, but we can perceive ways of improving the relationships and qualities of life by selecting one conceptual scheme rather than another. Our concepts and probabilities give us present perspective, future prospectus and a proposed process for converting the real present facts into the desired future. Questions abide but most facts are too transitory and causality in social affairs too uncertain for planning. What is most practical in planning is a guiding concept. What is most important if we really want a task accomplished is a clear and urgently wanted goal coupled with the belief that it is probable. The probabilities we create by our intellectual vision are culture bound and time bound, therefore effective planning tends to be more for the present and immediate future, rather than long-range. Anyway, may not social progress be retarded if one generation tries to impose its probabilities on future generations?

The view that "my world has a structure that no formulation can encompass; I conceive of the world as my own total experience within it, and I play with my own symbolic constructs in a spirit of uneasy detachment" seems to have these implications for planning, among others: My view of the world is exclusively personal, probably impossible to share with others, and inconceivable to adequately describe or understand in commonly shared concepts. Each person finds, and must find, his or her own experience with the chaos of the world. Planning and most other public policies are not likely to be achievable since there is no commonly held or formulated concept, except that of allowing personal views to abide even amid some prevailing insecurities. Whatever unity or order or plan exists, is in my synthesis, and the other person's; it is neither in what is "out there" in the chaotic world or what is achievable by the deliberations, planning behaviors of collective populations, or other communal playing with symbol constructs. Only a generic public policy is required to guarantee everyone complete choice of meanings and options to plan and do his individual thing so long as it does not diminish or damage another person or delimit his doing his thing.

The reader may quarrel with some of the suggested planning implications of the five important views of the world, or believe that the writers went beyond what is implicit—and they may have. The expressions were intended to emphasize and illustrate the importance of explicating the assumptions of the planners and decision makers in society, because *it is their assumptions, behind theories,* that guide behaviors, rather than what is reported to be the intentions and explanations for actions. In addition, these paragraphs hopefully reflect the possibility and importance of using imaginatively concepts to guide planning behaviors.

Assumptions About Change

There are other fundamental assumptions about social change which, in the writers' views, make a vast difference in whether social welfare planning can be effective and how it can be guided between now and 1993, and how social welfare goals for 1993 and beyond may be formulated. These assumptions come from a blending of many sources of study, of professional experience in social welfare planning, and of observations so that they seem robust enough to ask others to consider. These assumptions are briefly presented.

Social change is possible. Persons who live with the assumption that change is not possible tend to accept their life and their lot as fate, and do not attempt to initiate change, engage in planning earnestly and hopefully, are not discouraged with failure and may learn from their past judgments and actions.

Social change is widespread, and pervasive, but occurring and possible in some aspects, with less resistance and more quickly than in others at a given time. Intentional change depends considerably upon whether the problem is currently perceived as important and urgent by a large public or by powerful groups.

Social change is apparently accelerating, but more in technical ways of doing tasks and in interrole relations than in institutional forms and functions. Planning is increasingly concerned with, not only what to change, but what to continue.

Intended social change of a given condition may be more dependent upon the concurrent issues of the period, the competition for attention and resources with them, and the trade-offs among issues in the body politic or the specific organizational settings, than dependent upon the qualities implicit in the given condition itself. Inherent rationality for the internal system is one test of value; another is political acceptability in the external system.

Intended social change almost always has unintended effects, some of which may be positive and some negative. Side effects, or unintended consequences, are difficult to monitor and more difficult to foresee even when one wants to assess them.

The monitoring and assessing of unintended consequences is a part of social responsibility. The negative side effects are to be minimized and controlled, and the positive side effects are to be maximized and enhanced. Sometimes a great social benefit can be realized through careful enhancement of a positve consequence that was originally unintended. Sometimes the social cost of a side effect cancels out the benefit of the intended change.

The estimate of volume and impact of unintended change may be greater than it actually is because of not knowing the source of the change and the intention behind it. Ignorance of source of intent is no reason to judge a change as happenstance, incoherent, or unintended. Whether the world or a community is being shaped and reshaped principally by unintended changes or by a concatenation of unknown intended changes, although either may produce chaotic situations, is probably not ascertainable. There is ready agreement that the impact of intended changes toward social development appears all too little. Either the technological advances have outstripped the capacity of most social institutions to function to enhance social justice or we have not learned to harness technological progress to produce social progress in many situations.

Intended and unintended social change are critically important. Some observers emphasize the superior influence of unintended change, noting the incoherence of so much in the world or in any given community. Other observers emphasize the superior influence of intended change, noting the relationship of so much. The problem of taking sides on this is that no one has a wide enough or penetrating enough view to know what is intended or not, by whom, and whether the unintended effects outweigh or not either positively or negatively the intended goals. There is a question, under any circumstance, whether at the present time coherence of social change is more related to intentional change and incoherence is more related to unintentional change. Neither the logic nor the reality is that neat. In our view, there is such a volume of uncoordinated and incoherent intentional change that, despite the rational intentions of planners in a given situation, there is in fact substantial chaos. The social system is so complex it is only possible to map and trace some aspects and even fewer sources of initiation of cause. The sorting and weighing of multiple causes is frought with uncertainties and ambiguities which are too complicated for most persons to manage and furthermore consume a great portion of the time and energy available for problem reduction. On the other hand, the attempts to reduce complexity to single causes (such as economic interest) give little guidance to social planning.

Amid the chaotic conditions of society and the complex situations of communities, social development and justice may be sought without ascertaining the causes of social problems. The use of research and planning in that effort may be more effective in seeking intended change than the search for causes. The notion of cause as used in the physical health field may be a misleading notion when used to determine how certain social conditions became the way they are. It is significant to note, however, that some fields of physical science are now dropping the search for cause and instituting the search for purpose of matter and phenomena. In our view of social history and social planning history, in particular, most of the significant social changes which have occurred by intent were those initiated by individuals and organizations which were absolutely clear on their purpose and goals, able to organize others to support them and capable of convincing those who allocate resources that realigning these goals was in their combined public and private interest. The social conditions we have may be analyzed by some persons on the basis of causality, but most people support proposed change or resist it on the basis of its purpose. The formal or informal analysis of costs and benefits almost always seems to include the personal and the public, the weighing of goals and means as they affect the various roles of self and others significant to the self in the various systems.

We assume and emphasize the importance of social research for purpose and goals. The study of human aspirations and concerns, the analysis of various problem perspectives, the delineation of preferred organizational and life-styles of different populations, the measuring of social resources and effectiveness of organization, is, we believe, a far more fruitful path to social progress than the search for causes to problems. The rapidity of change may well render findings on causes irrelevant on the basis of outdated facts, already changed conditions, and already changed actors. What "caused" poverty and crime in the 1960's may not "cause" it in the 1970's. The systems and the people change. And we have long observed that similar situations seldom produce similar behavior responses. More importantly, we have long observed that the society or community cannot and will not plan to modify itself to prevent all the different conditions in which people and populations find themselves and to which they attribute their problems. What a society and community is prepared to do is to select from a range of goals some which are more important than others, and reallocate from time to time power and resources to try to achieve the selected goals.

III. Transcending Issues

There are at least six issues which transcend all social advance and institutional development in the United States, and possibly other societies as well. We see these permeating and pivotal issues as being generic social welfare issues, the conflict source from which social goals are formulated and selected. In addition, these issues and their resolution will condition the resources and restraints for the reduction of all social welfare problems and the realization of any specific social welfare goal. In that sense these issues may be perceived as either overarching or undergirding the entire society and not just the social welfare system. These transcending issues are:
—war or peace as the pivotal foreign policy;
—racism or positive transracial action as the pivotal people policy;
—elitist rule or citizen governance of the major institutions and organizations as a pivotal institutional policy;

—institutional and bureaucratic obsolescence or bureaucratic change or replacement as a pivotal institutional policy;

—conflict or collaboration among the adherents to the three fundamental approaches to systems changes—evolution, revolution and evaluation—as the pivotal social change policy in given problem systems; and

—poverty amid plenty or no poverty as the pivotal social welfare policy.

The writers thought for some years that another overarching issue was whether the United States would develop essentially as a capitalistic system or a socialistic system. Although the topic is often discussed as an issue, the issue now seems to be resolved at the federal-national level with the marked blending of the two philosophies and practices in domestic and foreign programs. We see this trend as pervasive and gradually influencing state and local, public and voluntary decisions in almost all systems.

The connections of these issues with social development are generally apparent but may need some clarification. In the first place, issues of war and peace, racism, systems change, are themselves social planning issues of the greatest magnitude requiring the attention of the highest political leaders. They are also social planning issues of the most basic kind which affect the daily lives of all persons, groups and organizational decisions. It is probably at the organizational and community range of social planning that conscious social intentions are most specifically identified and choices of strategies are shaped by these overarching issues. Local planning has a tendency to be chiefly, but not always consciously, a reflection of national aspirations and priorities of the current federal administration. Organizational and institutional changes are especially subject to the review, criticism, and control of the political system; in part through charter, tax exemption and other legal means and in part through direct or indirect controls of potential fiscal resources, both means constituting superordinate legitimation or not of institutional patterns of the society.

War or Peace

The relationship of war or peace to human welfare and social planning prospects is, perhaps, most clear as it pertains to injuries, deaths, fears and dislocations of both combatant and noncombatant populations. What may not be so readily perviewed is that a very small war is expensive and may be used as the reason to reallocate very large portions of the gross national product of a people and to postpone indefinitely very large social and cultural goals of a people. One of the positive proposals of the student-organized moratorium of the war in Vietnam was that the United

States has the capacity and therefore must continue to increase domestic programs at the same time as waging war. Again, we must try to develop, as some groups attempted fifty years ago, a "moral equivalent" to war. President Kennedy's Peace Corps was a small beginning in that direction, but it got diluted by the larger anti-youth movement in retaliation for youth's anti-war movement.* The search for a "moral equivalent" to war could be one approach to social goal setting during the next twenty years. If successful, it could make a most significant difference in how the American and other societies use their power and resources from 1993 onwards. The subject of social goals pertaining to the issue of war or peace is one which the National Conference on Social Welfare and the National Association of Social Work have dealt with seriously but not persistently. Each edition of NASW Goals of Public Social Policy has included goals pertaining to peace as a professional social work goal but only after debate at Delegate Assemblies on whether peace was or was not a social work goal. The majority has always, to our recollection, agreed that it is, but a sizable minority has always disagreed, apparently not perceiving the impact of this issue upon specific social advance.

Racism

The issue of racism or positive transracial actions has been long, but not universally, acknowledged within social welfare and social work as a major issue affecting human development and social services. In general, however, it has been dealt with as a specialized field or problem, rather than as a transcending issue as proposed here. By racism is meant the assumption for arbitrary reasons by one population grouping that another population grouping is inferior, with consequential treatment of the latter grouping by the former with prejudicial attitudes, discriminatory actions and inequitable distributions of opportunities and power intended to enact a real superior-inferior status and stature.

Racism is here perceived as a generic process that includes negative population relationships along "lines" of race, ethnicity, national origin, regional identity ("the Appalachian," "rural folk," etc.) as well as along lines of age (youth, aged), sex (male chauvinism), and social class (white collar—blue collar, professional—working, etc.).

Racism is expressed by individuals and institutions. Institutional racism is the more serious, we think, and the appropriate focus of social policy and planning. The substantial progress seemingly made by many individuals to reduce their individual racist behavior is threatened unless there is great progress in reducing institutional racism. It is not just that

---

* There have been other programs introduced as moral equivalents to war. The Marshall Plan was certainly a moral equivalent to the conqueror's right to the spoils of war, and was a reverse twist that also expiated some American guilt for "overwinning" with atomic bombs.

the two forms of racism reinforce each other. Institutional racism is prevailing social policy which locks the society into practices which are essentially *anti* human development and *contra* social justice, both immediately for the oppressed population and in the long run for the oppressor population as well. Institutional racism structures inequity, binds the oppressed groups into situations of diminished opportunities, and double-binds them by disallowing any additional power to change the situations. It is, therefore, the oppressor populations which must change their policies if the structures, binds and double-binds are to be changed. The major question is how power will be used or redistributed to make the policy changes possible. Obviously the initiatives for changing power can come from either or both oppressor and victim populations, and the strategies can involve either collaboration or conflict. The most important initiative is that of setting as a social goal the substantial reduction of institutional racism in absolute terms. We think that there are ways of perceiving institutional racism in absolute conditions; therefore, there are ways of measuring its reduction absolutely in given situations.

The setting of a social goal to reduce institutional racism substantially and measurably, say on the order of 25 per cent every four years, can be done. It could best be done by collaborative planning among the leaders of the respective populations, including those political leaders who are in administrative roles affecting all peoples and the organizational leaders of the major racial-ethnic populations. Obviously, there are already laws and regulations regarding racism, although they tend to be expressed as "to eliminate racism" or "there shall be no discrimination on the basis of race, color, national origin (etc.)." Likewise, obviously, the various racial-ethnic organizations which assume responsibilities in the black, Chicano, Puerto Rican, native American, and other oppressed populations, have goals to reduce institutional racism. These are often expressed with insufficient specificity to permit measurement. What is especially needed now is the statement of measurable goals to reduce racism in certain nationwide institutions or systems in specified ways. As practical illustrations we suggest the following:

a. to structure the governing bodies of each institution and organization in such a way that there is authentic, not symbolic or token, representation of the different racial-ethnic populations affected by the decisions of that institution or organization, setting as a minimum goal (not quota) the proportion of the total nonwhite and non-Anglo populations existing in the general populations of the defined community;

b. to require those institutions and organizations affecting the development and quality of life of nonwhite and non-Anglo populations to employ in administrative and program positions professionally qualified nonwhite and non-Anglo staff during the next five to ten years until the ethnic proportions of such staff about equals the proportion of the ethnic populations groups served by the organization. (The initiation of a positive employment program to enact long-standing nondiscrimination policies in hiring is a responsible step that social welfare organizations by now will have taken.)

c. To require all institutions and organizations purporting to provide services to nonwhite and non-Anglo populations to evaluate critically their programs biannually, and to adapt their programs to fit the aspirations, problem perspectives and organizational styles of these populations. (The notion that one human service can be designed and administered for all populations and evaluated by one set of criteria which are expressive only of the majority population's will is itself institutional racism.) A pluralistic society could, and we think should, require each organization to have pluralistic adaptations of programs. The alternatives to this are a much wider latitude for individualization of service, which administratively has not been feasible, or the establishment of parallel organizations for every program for each racial-ethnic population, which does not meet other social requirements for positive transracial action of a pluralistic society. The proposed evaluation and adaptation of programs and administrative machinery require the appropriate participation by the receivers as well as the providers of service. Each population grouping could be given special attention in, say, a two-year period out of every six years, so that not all programs were being evaluated or redesigned at the same time and so that administrative stability may be maintained.

The setting of some such specific goals (as illustrated above) could be done at federal, state, and local levels and in the public and voluntary sectors with viable participation by white, black, Chicano, Puerto Rican, native American and other populations. But if this is not possible due to the prevalence of white racism generally, then, at the minmum, the socal welfare system and the social work profession could set these goals for their own.

If this is done the functions of social welfare and the tasks of social work become more clear and crucial, possibly along two main thrusts:

a. The first thrust is to develop the capacities, to harness the motivations, and to increase the power of the nonwhite and non-Anglo populations, individually and collectively, so that they can themselves increasingly influence the society or community to reduce institutional racism wherever it exists, to adapt all programs for racial requirements, and to increase positive transracial actions. (In effect, as we see it, this is what social work espouses as its normative task for all people; to enhance the fullest possible social development and realization of social well-being goals through individual and institutional changes, and especially to compensate for long deprivations and damages to given populations. This is the social welfare planning thrust related to the task responsibility to provide relevant high-quality services.)

b. The second thrust is to motivate and organize the leadership of the white majority population and those institutions which are essentially operated on the basis of the aspirations and criteria of the white experience to redistribute power, reallocate resources, and redesign programs to satisfy the new definitions of social justice implicit in the goal of substantially reducing institutional racism. (In effect, as we see it, this is what social work espouses as its institutional task in a critical period: to advocate with and on behalf of the damaged or less powerful populations to the end that the social policies of the society and communities are changed fundamentally, in this instance, so that in the long run, the nonwhite and non-Anglo populations have their full and equitable share of power, resources, and opportunities. This is the social welfare planning thrust related to the generic process responsibility to develop better institutions and organizations committed to social justice.)

While social work has an immediate responsibility for the management of social welfare institutions and providing services to damaged populations, it also has a persisting responsibility for the public criticism of, and proposing correction for, those policies and practices of any institution or organization which damage or restrict the development of people. The services providing institutions in which social work practice is located are more readily accessible, and some persons may wish to limit professional responsibility for such changes to these institutions. The other institutions with which social work practice is inevitably connected, yet not located in, such as the family and profit business-industry, are not actually so accessible to the professional social worker even though their patterns of behavior may drastically damage or restrict the development of individual people or ethnic population groups. These institutions will require time, energy, and strategies hardly foreseen today by the professional or volunteer workers in social welfare.

Elitist Rule

The issue of elitist rule or citizen governance of the major institutions and organizations as a pivotal policy is a generic one of which the resolution will either undergird or undercut the American version of democratic processes and republican forms. For purposes of clarity and brevity, we delineate this issue as whether or not the citizens and persons affected by the decisions of the institution or organization may really and directly engage, not symbolically, in the setting of the social goals and the making of the major decisions of resource allocation by the given institution or organization. The question is not a choice among three types of democracy: participatory democracy, or elected representative democracy, or symbolic democracy in which elites tend to self-perpetuate their group through control of appointive and elective processes. The question appears to be how to increase the first type, participatory, and to decrease the third type, symbolic or elitist, while improving the quality of the second, representative.

The social welfare planner, indeed any planner interested in social justice, can really perceive this issue as a question of means, rather than ends, and we propose citizen governance as one of the major *process goals* for the next twenty years. It is one possible way of correcting many of the specific social injustices, maldistributions of opportunities and resources, and continued misuses of power as viewed from the social welfare prospective. This increase in real citizen participation, to repeat, must be accompanied by the improvement of the system of representation of populations and interests in the governance of public and voluntary organizations. The practical limit of citizen governance depends chiefly, we think, upon the social awareness level of citizens, the availability of time and financial resources to get themselves prepared and present at the right places to express themselves effectively, and their capability or willingness to organize so they convert their diffused micro-powers into focused macro-power in given situations. There is no question, in our judgment, that most ordinary citizens can competently express social goals, including specific objectives of institutional change. That is one of the major learnings of the 1964–1970 federal anti-poverty program at the community level. The questions are whether most citizens care enough to determine, or assist in determining, social *goals,* and whether ordinary citizens know enough to assist in determining *means* to these ends. The experience of many programs, including the anti-poverty program, suggests a negative answer to both questions. The response of most eligible Americans to opportunities to participate in governance, including crucial elections and referenda that are well publicized and readily accessible, and to attend and express themselves at organizational meetings, is certainly not encouraging when the real is compared to the possible. Does this mean that most Americans do not care sufficiently to participate?

That aspect of the issue of elitism or citizen governance pertaining to determination of means and participation in the administration of programs requires further comment. Some observers believe that most citizens simply lack the knowledge, experience, and perhaps judgment to assist in determining means, whether they be administrative mechanisms or regulations, strategies in attempting to influence other centers of power, or programs of human service. The most common position of administrators and professional persons is that only those with capacity to think in policy terms, competence to manage, and ability to make professional judgments should determine means and methods to achieve social goals. This, we emphasize, does not exclude volunteer workers and leaders. The differentiation is that volunteer workers, while either ordinary or extraordinary citizens, have a known and demonstrated commitment to a particular social goal, a sustained affiliation with a particular organization or institution, and intensive and recurring education and training to guide their actions and judgments in specific administrative or program roles within the organiaztion, and regular opportunities for participating in the assessment of the organization's and program's effectiveness, including their own effectiveness. The qualified volunteer and the professional person tend to share responsibility for determining *means* and *methods* for achieving social goals in this society. Whether the ordinary citizen should engage increasingly in that aspect of governance is an issue that the nation will be facing more and more as citizens and population groups become more and more dissatisfied with specific organizational functioning and specific programs effectiveness. The rise in recipient and consumer organizations in many fields will tend to expand citizen governance, we believe, from only determining social goals to also influencing the choice of means and methods. Citizen governance will be pressed further with continued charges by racial and ethnic groups, and by youth and the aged and women, that the American system has too much hypocrisy so long as these large populations have so little influence in *how* their destiny is determined.

One further comment on this issue of elitism or citizen governance: The role of administrators and professional persons exists with either choice, but what makes a significant difference is the identification of the administrator-professional with either the elitist group or the citizen population. The administrator and professional roles are always somewhat in between, and some define the chief executive role as among the elite and the lower personnel classifications of professionals as among the citizenry. What seems to count increasingly in determining identification is the sustained commitment to the social task or goals of an organization and the capacity to demonstrate purposeful effort toward that interpretation of the goal as expressed by either the elites or the citizens. There is evidence to suggest that most professionals of any field identify themselves, and are most identified by others, as a part of the elite. On the other hand, the journals of various professions seem to reflect a growing proportion of each profession wanting to identify, and be identified, with the citizens and consumers. One of the trends which may influence this is the growing number of nonwhites and non-Anglos entering the various professions, and their identification with the aspirations and problem perspectives of their respective racial ethnic population.

Bureaucratic Obsolescence

The transcending issue of institutional and bureaucratic obsolescence or bureaucratic change or replacement is another fundamental issue of which the resolution will shape one way or another the capacity of the society and the community to realize its social welfare goals. Actually, this issue gives us some important social goals, such as: institutions work as their manifest goals intend them to work; certain organizations change in specified ways; certain organizations need to be replaced (having out-lived their usefullness, or failing to respond effectively to human aspira-tions and social justice); and new institutions capable of performing certain sets of social tasks need to be designed, launched and legitimated. There is increasing recognition that for an institution or organization not to change is to obsolesce; to remain the same in goals, rules and pro-grams is to fall behind and fail. At the same time, there appears to be relatively little support, especially from centers of power, for institutions and organizations to change. There is especially little organized power and resource to design, launch and legitimate new institutions, and thus universalize their access. To illustrate, we note that certain well-tested, broadly required and socially just programs such as Head Start, Aged Protective Services, Legal Defender for the Poor, Consumer Protection Services, Crisis Centers and Ombudsman are not yet stably institution-alized in most states and communities. Are institutional and organiza-tional change and replacement to be little expected because institutions and organizations are chiefly where power is located, because bureau-cracies allocate and manage most of society's resources and do not like either to change or to face competition from other old or new bureau-cracies?

If it is accurate to say that all bureaucracies have two basic goals, to accomplish the task for which they were established, and to maintain and expand themselves and thereby enhance their own power and prestige, then the best future course of change may be to hasten the demise of the ineffective ones, rather than to try to change them, and to establish com-peting alternative ones. The emergence of even small alternative organi-zations during the past few years may have done more to influence resource reallocation, to initiate improvement in old large organizations, and to enhance the quality of human services than any other approach. The fear lingers, however, that these new alternative organizations may also quickly become obsolescent. Can the bureaucratic system become essentially *ad hoc?*

Conflict–Collaboration

The issues of conflict or collaboration between or among the adherents to the three general approaches to social change—evolution, revolution and evaluation—is one that is often not perceived as a serious issue, al-though we believe that it is one. The adherents of each approach not only tend to assume their position to be superior; they frequently assume that no other approach counts for much and is likely to be used. The issue merits much more attention than it is given by the major actors in decision organizations, including those doing social welfare planning, and by professional persons concerned with social development and justice.

Social change tends to be perceived in three approaches or processes: evolution, revolution and evaluation. Characteristically, the public usually refers to approaches to change as being either evolutionary, that is, a series of quantitative increments and qualitative gradual change; or revolutionary, that is, large-scale and relatively quick qualitative change in which there is a discontinuity between some present pattern and initiation of a new pattern. In some contradistinction to this, most professional persons tend to prefer evaluative approaches which may then lead to either evolutionary or revolutionary changes. Evaluation presupposes consciousness of purpose and a freedom to identify the options and to select a preferred one. The adherents to each approach tend to assume that their way brings certain progress. Evolution has not always resulted in either guranteed or universal progress, and has sometimes been retrogressive or damaging. Revolution has not always resulted in progress, and has sometimes brought social damage. And rationality or evalutation is certainly not inherently self-implementing.

Revolutionary social change does not require violence, but it does require social conflict or a competitive force-counterforce (resistance) between the seekers of change and the defenders of the established status. Social conflict has many positive uses, and those engaged earnestly in social welfare planning soon learn that the positive use of conflict is essential. Social change as it pertains to the well-being of people and the effectiveness of social welfare institutions is not traceable along an ever-improving evolutionary line. Social development at this time is not expected to be wholly evolutionary, even when based upon evaluation. We are inclined to be guided in our assumptions on this by one of the most distinguished historians, Karl de Schweinitz, who noted the tendency for a cycle of flowering and withering of social welfare conditions and programs, with reflowering of some at a somewhat improved level or quality. The improving is not generally to be accounted as evolution in the sense of some pervasive bettering influence but rather by intentional efforts and often little-known complex influences. A point which seems to require emphasis is that probably most adherents to one or another of the general approaches—evolution, revolution, evaluation—are interested in a wide array of common social goals, such as the reduction of poverty. Yet they are just as likely to be in conflict over the means by which to approach the problem as they are to be in conflict with the anti-goal forces. It is as though the process or means is more important than the goal or ends. They are convinced that the other approaches will worsen the social situation. Whatever the thinking or attitudes, this situation tends to confront the society and each community with a major block and further resistance to change, even change of those seriously damaging social conditions which most people, powerless and powerful, declare that they want changed. The issue of conflict or collaboration among the adherents to major approaches to social change thus becomes a major resistant force to planned change. It can be and is used that way by some powers who do not want specific changes. This is an issue that bears much attention by those interested in social welfare planning and can become the grist for selecting strategies. We add that the issue at the present time presupposes the use of some conflict strategies and some collaborative strategies if any major social goal is to be achieved.

Poverty

The issue of poverty amid plenty or no poverty is an overarching issue in this society that tests whether the American concept of social justice means social justice for all people or for some people. The issue also tests whether the economic system can be trusted to produce and be the chief means for achieving major social goals. The issue further tests whether the individual shall continue to be held accountable for his situation while the evidence mounts in all aspects of social life that the complex inter-systems control the major access to resources and opportunities. When economically successful persons are praised for beating the system, while economically unsuccessful persons are blamed for being beaten by the system, the issue of poverty or no poverty amid plenty of this nation is important to its ethics or morality and not only its condition of human well-being. But we prefer to keep the issue fundamentally on the fulcrum of social justice, on the question of whether economic progress can be relied upon to produce social progress, and on the weighing of individual and institutional or systems influences in a complex modern society. Briefly, we believe poverty is unjust and unnecessary, that accumulative history demonstrates that generalized economic progress cannot be relied upon to produce all of the important social goals, and that institutions will take their toll on some individuals in the growing system of individual-institutional interdependence unless the system is corrected. The correction in the case of poverty, or rather no poverty, will be major changes, not just adjustments. Furthermore, the gravity of the problem, its scope and seriousness to millions of families suggest compelling and swift changes in various systems to reduce poverty.

The issue is already joined as there are many persons and many systems which do not agree with that assessment or conclusion. Many statements are made in support of reducing poverty, but what counts is those actions not taken, or weakly taken, which prolong poverty. The social welfare goal of reducing poverty has been discussed far more thoroughly in many recent writings, so here we wish to emphasize only several of the essentials. First, that poverty be perceived as one of the transcending issues of America. Its resolution will have ramifying effects throughout the society. Second, that the goal be phrased to reduce poverty by a given amount or percent each biennium and to be totally reduced by 1993, the point being that the quantification of the goal will make it considerably more politically feasible than simply proposing eliminating poverty. Third, that the social welfare system and the planning subsystem within it provide aggressive leadership in conceptualizing both absolute and relative measures for assessing the reduction of poverty while pressing for steady and substantial reductions periodically. Fourth, that much public attention be called by social workers to the increasing alienation of the poor, the likelihood of their increasing powerlessnesss as their number gets smaller (as the goal is gradually realized), and the need for social workers and others increasingly to be advocates for the poor in all systems. Fifth, that the present system of public welfare, which combines many values and many faults, not be readily sacrificed until there are, in fact, better alternatives which do actually reduce poverty and increase social justice for the poor. Within the whole effort to set social goals for the 1973–1993 period, it is essential to plan to account for the inter-relationship of certain problems, such as poverty and racism and illness, and to maximize interdependent approaches. Furthermore, it is highly essential to any planning effort to perceive that those social conditions which are most difficult to change—like poverty, racism, mental illness, delinquency and crime, poor housing—are those in which human beings are not only damaged or less developed, but also have much less power, individually and as a population.

There are, no doubt, other transcending issues which permeate the entire American social system (and probably beyond) and thus consti-tute the main issues of the social welfare system as well as the main influence upon the reduction of social welfare problems and realization of social welfare goals. In essence, as we perceive social welfare amid complex society, all other social welfare goals and questions will be chiefly dependent upon the resources and restraints generated by the abrasive working out of the transcending issues. The reader is encour-aged to identify other permeating issues and to weigh their impacts upon social welfare planning and goals.

IV. Some Questions and Possibilities on Goal Selection and Realization

There are many important questions for the social welfare system to examine pertaining to the selection and realization of social goals for the near and more distant future. Only a few of these questions will be discussed in this essay, and the brevity of attention here does not do justice to their persistence or importance.

Before identifying the questions, we believe it is useful to emphasize one concept to which all the questions are related: *social welfare as a subsystem of the general social system.* A social system is a set of interdependent social entities. One may perceive in the general social system the existence of various major subsystems which have major social functions or tasks, but which receive resources and restraints from the environment of the general social system. These subsystems include social welfare, health, education, housing, business and industry, to name a few—although their conceptual scope and label are variously expressed. The notion we wish to emphasize here is that as a subsystem social welfare (as any subsystem, although more than some) is shaped more by the external system or over-all society than by its own internal decisions. In the long run, the resources and restraints of the general social system include general goals and policies, inputs and limitations, evaluation and validation. On the other hand, the social welfare subsystem manages its resources, converts them into outputs of various kinds and qualities, and has the opportunity to influence or try to influence the general social system with its own initiatives, proposals, and products. Once this concept of the interdependent nature of systems and subsystems is understood, social welfare planning is done more carefully and somewhat differently than it is when the social welfare system is perceived to be quite independent, with the general social system not really caring about the direction, scope and quality of social welfare. With this conception of social welfare as a subsystem, both goals and means are selected with consideration of the external and internal systems and the potentials inherent in their interdependent relationship.[6]

We now identify some of the questions pertaining to goal selection and realization.

Social Problem: Collectivity and Process

How to "get hold" of a social welfare problem seems to become more difficult as we gain more knowledge. Now that is not a regrettable thing to say, we think, because it is precisely the function of professions and professionals to be aware of the maximum complexity of a problem. If we gain in awareness of the complexity of social problems perhaps we will sometime have a real chance of substantially reducing them and managing them.

How to "get hold" of a social problem can be facilitated by changing the dominant concept of what a social problem is. At the present time, and characteristically throughout the past seventy-five years of organized social welfare and social work, a social problem has usually been defined as the collectivity of damaged or lesser developed people. We have tended to say that the population at risk and socially damaged or disabled, with its various demographic characteristics, constitutes the social problem. Most attention in the form of research and services has been focused on that population, since it has been believed that such people could not only be assisted, their condition ameliorated or corrected, but that the problem would also be reduced, even solved. What this conception does is make the damaged population, and often victims, the problem, and fails to account seriously for those processes doing the damaging or not doing the developing. Sometimes the precise institutional process which is supposed to do the helping does the hurting, and yet is entirely ignored in the problem definition.

The concept of a social problem as the social process which blocks the realization of a social value and results, therefore, in a population of damaged or lesser developed persons is a more viable and useful one for social welfare planning. With it there can be attention to correcting or reducing the social process which produces the human damage, as well as the damage itself. The concept also leads social welfare planners to attempt to identify and counter those forces and powers in the society which support the social processes which do the damaging.

Multiple Aspects

Another aspect of "getting hold" of a social problem requires increased thinking in multiples and interphenomena. In brief, what much research and disciplined speculation, from that of Community Research Associates to the multivariate analysis of Hadden and Borgatta, seem to add up to is the authentic complexity of social welfare problems. One way to perceive that complexity of processes, structures, goals, actors, and conditions is to recognize that social welfare problems tend to have these dimensions:

> interpersonal
> interrole
> intergroup
> interorganizational
> intercommunity
> multiprogram
> multiprofession
> and
> multiproblem

Man or Manpower

In complementarity to the purposes of reducing social problems and influencing institutions to enact social justice, what is the essential purpose of planning social welfare services? Is it to develop man or manpower, woman or womanpower, children or future citizens? Or is it all of these? Some systems and professions other than social work have made much further political advance by putting the emphasis on developing manpower and womanpower, that is, productive workers in the economic system and taxpayers, and major contributors to the economy and society. The stating and the meaning of goals pertaining to "man or manpower" is critical.

The Labeling of Human Difference

What is the way to express the human differences which social welfare and social work are concerned with so that there is a maximum of acceptance and support and a minimum of rejection and alienation? There is no question that most volunteer workers and professionals seem to have about the same biases and fears toward human difference as most other citizens. It is a notable failure of volunteer training and professional education in all professions. What is possible is some serious rethinking of the matter of difference, which is interpreted as negative, deficient, or dangerous to others. The social welfare system and the social work professions mostly continue to use the term "deviance" when the concept of *human variance* might be much better. Somehow "deviation" has taken on mostly negative connotations and attitudes. The *normalcy* of variation or variance is not stressed professionally or publicly. The value, the positive benefit, of variance is not emphasized, even though we have historically expressed the desirability of difference. Perhaps what was meant was some difference, enough to differentiate individuality but not enough to require special attention or assistance.

Acceleration of Decisions

Another practice problem which plagues all planning, social welfare planning included, is how to accelerate the making of effective decisions that lead to realization of the goal. The acceleration of decision-making is an even more serious practice problem now than it was in earlier decades. With social changes occurring with such rapidity, social welfare planning is pressed to make much faster decisions and follow them up with faster implementation if the negative conditions are to be counteracted. One alternative is, of course, to predict what the conditions will be and shape the plan to predictions. We can predict single variables sometimes, but the experience so far with social indicators for complex multiple variables is not encouraging.

Widest Range of Options

Just as it is incumbent upon social planning personnel to describe and assist others to describe a social problem in its complexity, so it is a professional responsibility to try to identify the widest range of imaginable options. This problem of every participant in social welfare planning is not alone due to the obviously limited experience or knowledge of any one person. It is intensified by the relatively small literature which has correlated the range of optional approaches to problem reduction, including program purportedly related to each social welfare problem, and the assessments of those options utilized in various situations and measured or "weighed" with some commonly stated criteria. The starting of such a project could give a useful assist to social welfare planning, even though it may also reveal the discouraging effects of many options already tried. However, negative knowledge is important, too, in the quest for social well-being, and many more null hypotheses may have to be tested before positive knowledge can be expanded.

Demonstration of Service

Are social development and social services to be demonstrated by the public or voluntary sector? Regardless of philosophical positions historically held, this question is resolved in practice by both sectors demonstrating just about anything, with each learning from the other and both conducting most of the range of different programs. The major differences in operations are the finding and management of the mass financial assistance and gigantic health research and career development proposals by the public sector, and the tendency to locate politically risky, consumer-sponsored youth development, citizen leadership development, and religious sponsored programs in the voluntary sector. However, to repeat, most of the range of social welfare services may be demonstrated and operated within either sector. Perhaps the main reason for referring at all to this question again is to note the increasing use of the quasi-public organizations to demonstrate and lanuch new services. The quasi-public organization is typically a publicly chartered voluntary association, certified as nonprofit and tax exempt, with a board of directors that combines some prescribed elected or appointed public officials, some officers or representatives of other organizations and other citizens at large, with the organization funded by a combination of public (tax) and voluntarily contributed monies. Often the public officials are in the numerical minority on the board while the public funds are preponderant. The quasi-public agency is sometimes also a consortium of public and voluntary organizations set up for the purpose of social welfare research and planning, demonstrating or conducting social welfare programs. The quasi-public body, whether an association or consortium, has obvious advantages in demonstrating politically risky and unpopular social programs.

Voluntary Funds

Are voluntary or contributed funds for social welfare growing and likely to increase? This question is frequently raised in view of the obvious increase in public funds, and the often-expressed doubts by the less experienced in funding matters. So far as the various official reports show (up to 1971) the amount of voluntarily contributed funds for all social welfare purposes has increased almost steadily for the last five decades. This includes monies raised through united funds and religious federations, and contributions directly to organizations from corporations, individuals, trusts, and foundations, and other sources. Although the experience of any given city may not reflect it, the aggregate total of the united fund goals of all communities in the United States has usually been reached during the past few years, with each year exceeding the former year's amount raised. Also, although the experiences of any one organization may not reflect it, the aggregate total of all foundation contributions to social welfare has tended to increase each year. In summary, the availability of voluntary or contributed funds for social welfare planning itself has increased in absolute figures, and is likely to continue. However, in realtive terms, the situation is not so encouraging for social welfare. The proportion of public and voluntary fund expeditures to the gross national product is gradually declining. The data and the implications of volume and proportional trends are beyond the scope of this essay, except to suggest that funding patterns merit attention generally and require specific study in relation to selecting a social welfare goal. Purchase of service and other contractual agreements between governmental and the voluntary organizations, as well as profit-proprietary firms in social welfare, are expected to increase and may further blur any philosophical distinctions among the sectors. That source of funding of social welfare services which social welfare planning has almost always overestimated, and which trends are a continuing enigma, is the payments by consumers, whether fees for services, fees for membership, or prepayment plans such as in health maintenance. Of these, the approach that appears to be most favorably accepted is the prepayment for health and hospital care and certain social services. These plans are increasing particularly where there is some contribution by the employer and the balance is paid through payroll deduction. One question is whether this kind of financing by the consumer can be applied with consumer acceptance to any kind of human service.

Scaling Goals

How are interrelated and interdependent yet different kinds and sizes of goals to be managed in social welfare planning? Social welfare goals are not all of the same dimension and scale. In general, at least three types of goals can be identified—ultimate, policy, and proximate or specific. Ultimate goals are usually expressed in general, long-range, and sometimes idealistic terms, such as "to eliminate juvenile delinquency" although our preference is to say "to reduce delinquency (say) by 50 per cent in the next decade." Policy goals are those goals for the instituting of new or changed community or organizational policies which together are required to realize an ultimate goal. Illustrations in relation to reducing delinquency are such goals as: to reduce recidivism through rehabilitation of first offenders by such a percent during a given period; to reduce the number of first offenders by preventive means by such a percent during a given period; and to reduce or change the laws and law enforcement or court procedures in appropriate ways calculated to reduce delinquency. The third type of social welfare goals, the proximate or specific ones, are the array of concrete and achievable program or procedural, rule, personnel, facility or resource changes which will make real the implementation of the policy goal. For the most part the proximate or specific goals are the statements of concrete changes intended in administration and program services, and especially the planning and launching of new or revised social welfare services.

Effective planning requires the conceiving of the several dimensions and scale of goals in some interdependent way. One such perception is this:

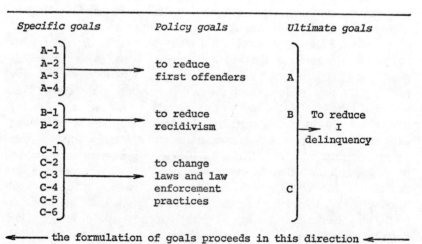

Specific goals	Policy goals	Ultimate goals
A-1 A-2 A-3 A-4	to reduce first offenders	A
B-1 B-2	to reduce recidivism	B To reduce I delinquency
C-1 C-2 C-3 C-4 C-5 C-6	to change laws and law enforcement practices	C

◄——— the formulation of goals proceeds in this direction ◄———

———► the implementation of goals proceeds in this direction——►

One perspective given by this kind of framework for social goal selection is the awareness that the realization of an ultimate goal may require not one but several important simultaneous policy goals, and that each policy goal may require not one but a set of specific program or administrative change goals. That perspective, however, in the illustration given, presumes that we do not in fact know the relative importance of the various policy and specific goals. As research on social welfare problems proceeds, and as evaluation of social welfare planning increases, we can, hopefully, expect to determine what are the most crucial specific goals or variables in the realization of ultimate goals. Obviously, those with the greatest benefit and least cost ought to be selected for earliest and most concentrated attention in planning. A community plan for the reduction of a major social problem could use some such framework for the scaling of its goals, and for assigning various organizations certain shared and individual responsibilities for implementation of the plan. Although we will not deal with it here, a parallel framework of influence of power and resistance needs to be formulated so that the influence requirements are understood in relation to the specific and policy goals. Typically that is where power and resistance are acted out, not around the ultimate goal, at least not openly.

The Relation of Social and Economic Planning

Why is the social progress both slow and small in contrast to the economic capacity of the nation? Whether it results from our ignorance or our unwillingness to reduce other problems is often debated. We believe that there is more a lack of a sense of urgency than a lack of cogency or currency. There is still much we do not know, but the lack of willingness to change institutional behaviors and to change resource allocation patterns seem to be two main impediments to social progress.

The belief that social progress is largely a result or by-product of economic progress bears re-examining in view of the obviously small "trickle-down" social effects to the common citizen in comparison to the social gains made by the economic elites. The notion that social progress automatically proceeds with economic progress, one of the more fundamental assumptions promoted by many economic leaders of the last century, may be not only fallacious but dangerous as well. It can lull us into accepting situations where material gains are socially damaging. The belief that social progress largely emerges from economic progress produces apathy which discourages us from consciously setting social goals and policies of human and social development which merit higher priority than some material, physical environment, technological and economic goals upon which we have focused during the past thirty years.

There is much social planning can learn from economic, physical and technological planning. Perhaps one of the most important learnings is how to quantify goals. Quantification of goals is always more feasible than setting quality goals. They define something less than the universe, something of an imaginable yet controllable size. If the quantification of a goal is valid and legitimate in the first place, then it is possible to establish a scale of possible measurement toward the goal, and perhaps some relative, but not necessarily absolute, measure of testing effectiveness of whatever social program is adopted. The absence of quantifiable goals is almost certainly a main obstacle to the political feasibility of much, if not most social planning, if for no other reason than that political decision makers tend to insist on measurable accomplishment of a program if there are to be continued appropriations for it.

Comprehensive and Balanced Planning

There have been many exhortations that planning be "comprehensive" and "balanced" during the past fifty years in the voluntary sector and the past ten years in the public sector. These terms have been often used without being defined, usually in relation to one another, and almost always implying that they are ideal conditions characteristic of a democracy. The most general meanings of the terms have included the following: that the *whole* community with its various systems (economic development, physical development and land use, social development, etc.) and its various sections (central city, various residential areas, etc.) be considered in planning, with relative equity, each to share in resources without unfair expense to the others, where possible "planning to benefit the greatest number with the greatest good over the longest period of time." There have been more specific meanings of comprehensive and balanced planning. One such meaning is the historic notion of "balancing community needs with community resources" which was expressed frequently as the goal and the process of community organization in social work. Another specific meaning of the terms is the overseeing and control of all planning by one planning body. The public sector has tried to exercise this most recently by the policy of certain federal departments to qualify or approve funding for local planning and program operations only on condition that one local comprehensive planning body review and approve the plans, coordinate them with other plans to which the proposed program should be related, and maintain some casual to close overview for evaluation. The voluntary sector in social welfare has long had various federations or organizations and citizens who have claimed comprehensive and balanced approaches to planning, fund raising, and services delivery as a function to prevent "one-sidedness" or inequitable development of one program over others and to enhance community-wide development over a long period of time. Long-range planning and comprehensive planning have frequently been considered together although they include some mutually exclusive notions. Another specific meaning of comprehensive planning is "planning being done by at least two different disciplines in cooperation for one and the same area, at one and the same time."

There is serious question now, as we consider what is or what has been effective in planned change, as to whether comprehensive goals or balanced planning strategies can be recommended. For the most part, in our view, these concepts have not been workable. There has been no willingness anyplace to allocate sufficient funds or power to one body, public or voluntary, really to test the concepts in application. The concepts lack congruity with political reality. Comprehensive planning bodies are readily feared as being vested with too much control. Those persons with much power see it as risk to their influence; yet they do not want the function overtly themselves as it would openly label them as doing something they may prefer to influence covertly.

The political opposition to comprehensive planning approaches seems to be clearly reflected in the relatively few serious, politically supported and adequately funded efforts reported in the literature. Among those few comprehensive planning efforts which were inclusive of physical, economic and social welfare development were the reclamation plan of the zuiderzee over a 120-year period, the regional development of the Tennessee Valley over the last forty years, and the urban development of New Haven, Connecticut, during the last ten years. Probably the most comprehensively insightful planning programs of the United States federal government were those of the National Resources Planning Board during the 1930's and the early 1940's. The excellence of content of that board's reports, including the analyses, proposed goals and recommendations for implementation, on one hand, and the disparity with what was actually achieved, on the other hand, suggests some of the essential limitations of comprehensiveness in planning.

Five such limitations will be identified. First, the goals or changed conditions sought and the means proposed by those persons directing "comprehensive planning" are typically perceived by other persons and organizations affected by the plans as "control" or attempted control over their destiny. Second, specific aspects of a comprehensive plan are contrary to the special interests of some groups and organizations, and the various anti-forces typically coalesce to change, counter or veto either some parts or all of the comprehensive proposal. Third, the wider and stronger and longer-lasting the comprehensive planning body is the more it is routinely and sometimes ruthlessly subject to the criticism and opposition of other important political interests and other special interest planning groups, and therefore, over time, tends to lose its power first over specific decisions and later, of course, its essential comprehensivity. Fourth, social planning generally and social welfare particularly may be dealt with too much as a by-product of economic, physical and ecological planning within comprehensive planning approaches, often with data that do not distinguish between the crucial and the inconsequential variables (out of ignorance), usually with only casual consideration of the aspirations of the people (although there are some notable exceptions to this), and, tragically, sometimes creating more or worse social problems as a result of giving "higher priority" to some economic or physical plans under the guise of some principle such as "greatest good" or "highest use." The fifth limitation of comprehensive planning is that despite the argument of being able to respond to the most important problems with the most insight and most resources, the comprehensive planning organizations, public and voluntary, tend to define "comprehensive" and "balanced approaches" in such ways as to maintain the status quo of relative conditions and power among the various sectors, organizations, fields of services, sections of communities and social classes. This may result from pressures of the existing powers, rather than the intent of the comprehensive planning personnel. One consequence of this is that comprehensive planning has tended not to allocate sufficient compensatory resources to reduce poverty, racism or other major social problems appreciably in any American city. Comprehensive planning has had a major part in worsening at least one social resource, public parks and playgrounds, about one-quarter of which has been taken in American cities during the 1960's for use in highways, often without compensatory facilities for the population of the area. And what is more widely known, comprehensive planning in conjunction with urban renewal programs has tended to move the poor from old neighborhoods and build better housing there for middle-class and upper-class families, without any appreciable improvement in the housing of low-income families.

In view of the experience so far, social welfare planning has two characteristics which are different from the planning in other aspects of comprehensive planning. Social welfare planning is essentially focused on reducing social problems and producing needed social services, often by designing new programs, delivery systems and institutions. Land use, facilities, physical factors, and economic considerations are, of course, vitally important as means rather than ends. Second, the experience so far indicates that advance in social programs is made mostly by planning spurred by special interest in social problems, by planning demanded by an aroused population due to some crisis, by planning that directly and immediately emerges out of a current crucial condition and opportunity. Even comprehensive and balanced planning within social welfare has not been the effective factor in reaching goals and producing significant changes. In the social sphere at least planning, design, invention, initiation of the new, launching new services and new organizations occur irregularly, with special effort inspired by special interests, usually strongly supported by particular population groups who somehow get sufficient power and support. The public cannot seem to comprehend comprehensive approaches in social welfare or social planning generally.

Community Crisis

A further professional practice question that requires attention if social welfare goals are to be selected well is that of how to identify a community crisis before it is one, how to create a crisis if that is the only way to get imperative attention to a problem, and how to utilize a crisis for ongoing permanent social improvement. The knowledge of community crisis in social welfare in the United States, including those started by nature (flood, earthquake) and by man (fire, explosion, transport accident, disease) is fairly limited; at least so fas as well-accepted implications or learnings are concerned. The knowledge of institutionally created crisis, such as in hunger, poverty, much mental illness, poor education and poor housing, and the breakdown of assistance programs and services, is even less available. It is not only that the dynamics of community crisis are not understood or observed by most, but also it is not clear why one acute problem situation is perceived as crisis while a very similar one is not so perceived. Furthermore, the often-observed phenomenon of the assistance provider in crisis being so criticized and unappreciated is not, we think, sufficiently explained. But what most merits consideration is the use of crisis to stimulate and guide social welfare planning. What is it in the community crisis situation that has significance for social development and social welfare problem reduction? Is there, perhaps, no function or a major function for social welfare planning in social welfare crises? Or is the major question how social welfare planning can generate some crisis on the notion that that is what it takes to get imperative action? Several general observations which have emerged during the past two years may give some clues: first, not until there was clear evidence that the youth of middle-income and upper-income families were using drugs illicitly, and that drug use was not confined to the nonwhite and non-Anglo population, was illicit drug use widely seen as dangerous and considered a crisis in American communities. Second, not until new alternative organizations responded to the critical demand for detoxification and rehabilitative services related to drug use did the long-established organizations acknowledge the crisis and respond. Third, the new alternative organizations were principally initiated by a combination of consumers and volunteering professionals, with the consultation and usually somewhat hidden support of social welfare planning organizations, public and voluntary, not as an agenda item in the usual planning process.

Social Problem Boundary

What is the "best" or most viable functional span or level for social welfare goal selection and realization? The boundary of problems is almost always larger than that of any given community and organization. Federal approaches are not always possible and truly nationwide approaches utilizing a synchronized and coordinated effort among the system of communities and within a community the system of organizations has seldom worked well. Social welfare problems seem to act vertically and horizontally, and readily go across any administrative or abstract boundary established for social planning purposes.

State Planning

The period 1973-1993 will probably be a major testing period for the utility and viability of the states in social welfare planning as in many other functions. The interpositional status of the states between cities with increased powers and a strong federal establishment makes them important in communication and decision-making, but not potent in some fields. The federal government completely dominates some fields for provision of funds, administration, or simple mandating of specific programs. The state governments tend to adopt federally planned programs by accepting federal funds with certain requirements as conditions. The veto power granted governors in some programs (such as anti-poverty) has revived the states' rights issue in social welfare planning and administration.

Most states plan, fund and administer some social welfare programs on their own, but only a few of the larger states have varied programs for the various populations at risk or damaged.

Less than a dozen states have strong state-wide social welfare planning bodies under voluntary auspices. Their emphasis is usually on initiating or influencing state legislation, influencing the administration of state social welfare programs, informing and organizing citizens and leaders from the various communities for common social welfare problems and programs, conducting research and consultation, and either raising voluntary funds or encouraging voluntary giving to support important social welfare programs. Some states have social welfare planning bodies under public auspices, sometimes as an interdepartmental commission and sometimes various citizen commissions for given social problems. Increasingly, the governor's planning office is the state's social welfare planning instrument.

There appear to be several major restrictions of social welfare planning by the state government or state-wide voluntary planning council. The first restriction is that social welfare problems do not fit state boundaries except for arbitrary administrative purposes. What is planned within one state often requires complementary action by adjacent states because of the human interactions across boundaries. The second restriction may be more fundamental; few American citizens have a strong sense of active citizenship toward their state and do not often participate in state-wide problems or programs. The intensity of interest in local community and federal national issues is far greater than in state-wide issues for most citizens most of the time. The third restriction pertains to those states in which the same political party has been in power over a long period of time; social welfare problems in those states are seldom as politically vital issues as they are in states in which there is sometimes a Republican administration and sometimes a Democratic administration.

We are inclined to encourage the expansion and intensification of state and state-wide social welfare planning during the next twenty years. Demonstrations and experimentations of new ways to reduce social welfare problems and to conduct new social programs are required. The states, despite the restrictions mentioned, have a large enough population and financial base to do some such demonstration work. Testing at the state level is often the basis of federal government action. If the state as a participant in social welfare programs is not entirely superseded by the federal government with its regions, and the cities and counties with their increased powers, it may be due in part to the revitalization of the research and planning functions of states, and the capacity for interstate compacts which more nearly cover the territory required for significant social welfare planning.

Profit Corporations

One option which social welfare planning has usually avoided or not chosen is the approach to profit corporations, especially those of business and industry, to assist in reducing social welfare problems, even when there is some reasonable assumption that a particular corporation or set of them is either contributing to that problem or can contribute to its reduction. We have been impressed with how and how well the late Whitney Young used this option, and how the Urban League in many communities has sought and received concrete assistance in reducing certain social problems on which it has focused. An article or two in

every issue during the past three years of the *Harvard Business Review*
has emphasized service to the community as the new goal complementary
to profit. This new espousal needs testing. Social welfare planning has
long involved principal actors in profit corporation roles on important
committees and boards. Now industry and business, like all institutions,
can be asked to change their ways where there is specific knowledge of
those ways damaging human beings or contributing to social problems,
or when an industry is perceived as a specific resource for the reduction
of that problem. If the ecology movement and government can call an
industry to account for air or water pollution, the social welfare system
and government can call an industry to account for damaging people.
What is as important, however, is the perception of profit business as a
possible ally and resource in influencing the social processes which
create damage to people and in making possible better decisions with
more powerful support in social planning.

Strategies

A further question of social welfare planning practice which requires
more attention before major social welfare goals can be confidently expected to be realized is that of how to choose or devise strategies. A
strategy is conceived as "a settled course of action" that is selected because there is belief that the prospects for accomplishing certain goals are
greater than the prospects of other possible courses. We know more
about formulating and selecting social welfare goals than devising and
enacting strategies of change. There has been some tendency to select
strategies one at a time, for application one at a time, rather than in
clusters for simultaneous application. The use of Parson's concept of
"pattern variables," or a set of actions which are interdependent and
applied in a preset configuration, seems to hold promise.

The authors studied two such sets of strategies of community decision-
making, as follows:

a. The object of change: the *individual* or the *institution*.
b. The level and scope of influence used: local *community* or *cosmopolitan*.
c. The sector of influence used: *nonpolitical* or *political*.
d. The mode of influence used: *consensus-seeking* or *conflict-seeking*.
e. The preferred rate of change and thrust: *long-range* preparatory, rehabilitative and preventive service or *immediate* assistance, money now,
and action now. The two pattern variables were constructed, the first options in each strategy comprising one action pattern and the second options
comprising another. In proportions of approximately two to one, a non-
change-oriented group of community decision makers chose the first pat-

tern of strategies and a *change-oriented* group of community decision makers chose the second pattern of strategies.* The essential point intended here is that strategy selection and devising are in great need of improvement within social planning practice, and it can be the object of study itself. The validity or importance of social goals is not enough to get them adopted or enacted. The most crucial of social goals are fundamentally controversial and always have vigorous and powerful opponents. The importance of social goals must be matched by the effectiveness of social action strategies if social welfare advance is to be made.

V. Conclusions

But ours is also a time of new vision and greatness, of opportunity and challenge, to everyone in his daily life, as a person and citizen. It is a time in which everyone is an understudy to the leading role in the drama of human destiny. Everyone must be ready to take over alone and without notice and show himself saint or hero, villain or coward. On this stage the great roles are . . . played out in one's daily life, in one's work, in one's citizenship, on one's compassion or lack of it, in one's courage to stick to an unpopular principle, and in one's refusal to sanction man's inhumanity to man in an age of cruelty and moral numbness.

In a time of change and challenge, new vision and new danger, new frontiers and permanent crisis, suffering and achievement, in time of overlap such as ours, the individual is both all-powerless and all-powerful. He is powerless, however exalted his station, if he believes that he can impose his will, that he can command the tides of history. He is all-powerful, no matter how lowly, if he knows himself to be responsible.[7]

There is convincing evidence that social welfare planners are those who initiate and achieve intended changes in the social welfare system, rather than any given professionally qualified group of actors in roles called Social Welfare Planners. There are some of the latter, too, but most social welfare planners have other job titles, perhaps the most common of which is administrator of some social welfare organization. The planners are not always the chief executive officers, and are frequently in the middle management group. And many of the best proposals for change come from those workers whose chief focus of daily effort is the damaged and lesser-developed populations and who observe firsthand the character and impact of the damaging social processes.

The principal implication of this is that social welfare planning simply must become a larger, more important, higher-quality and required educational experience of all persons entering social welfare professionally.

---

* Jack E. A. Stumpf, "Strategy Selection for Community Decisions," Ph.D. Dissertation (unpublished), Brandeis University, Waltham, Massachusetts, 1971.

The probability that most professional workers will tend to become, in part or in whole, administrators, and the increasingly high proportion of administrative time and effort going into planning makes additional education in social planning concepts, principles, tools and strategies a requirement for professional workers.

All professional workers in social welfare require a working understanding and skill in analyzing social situations and formulating or selecting social welfare goals as part of the development of social policy and their own practice within a program. In addition, many professional workers require an understanding of how to use research findings and identify their implications for goal definition and redefinition, program design and redesign, and the location and realignment of the required powers to effect intended social welfare change. Our concern here is the ordinary practitioners in social welfare who because of numbers and distribution can so vitally and widely effect planned change. We have the distinct impression it is at this level that education generally requires considerable improvement in understanding of and skills in social goal selection and realization. The modification and improvement of advanced education for specialists, consultants, and administrators in social welfare planning has begun in various universities. On the other hand, we must still await the day when the notion of social goal selection is a part of the basic education of all American citizens.

Social welfare planning, to be effective and make a difference in society between now and 1993, will aim at the reduction of specific social problems and specific conceptions of social justice. Its major concern will not be social order although its intention will be to evaluate and redesign situations so that social coherence and flexibility are enhanced. The development of neither individuals nor society is, or for achievement of quality needs to be, orderly, systematic, and controlled. The notion of Alfred North Whitehead that "progress is change amid order and order amid change," a principle which has dominated social welfare planning during the past seventy-five years, requires modification if social welfare planning is to have important impact on the crucial problems of social well-being and social development. Progress can be change or conservation amid order or disorder so long as there is achieved specific advance in social justice and an increasing capacity to reduce social problems.

We believe that social welfare planning can make significant difference by effecting that kind of social progress. Citizens and professionals are required that will be guided by some of the issues, concepts, strategies, imagination, competence and courage suggested in this essay, as modified, of course, by our evaluated cumulative experience.

Our identification with the socially damaged populations and advocacy of the reduction of major social problems which some other systems prefer to ignore or belittle leads often to the social welfare system and especially its professional workers being in unpopular and politically difficult positions. This is re-enforced when we are not as effective in formulating or selecting goals and in realigning the required powers to implement those goals. The position of the social welfare system and its workers, professional and volunteer, earns more positive esteem even while receiving expected specific criticism and enmity, when we act with courage in applying the social responsibility and competence we possess. When we make a social difference by defining problems, generating influence, and attaining specific goals of social justice the task will not be lonely or unsatisfying, but filled with lively people wanting assistance in selecting and attaining other goals toward social justice.

12

Social Work Education 1993

JOHN C. KIDNEIGH

Within a dozen years prior to 1969 each of seventeen schools of social work had celebrated its fiftieth anniversary. The year 1969 marked the fiftieth anniversary of the date when the seventeen schools formed a voluntary association for the purpose of improving education for social work in the United States. By that time the National Conference on Social Welfare (bearing a different name earlier) had been in existence ninety-six years, or forty-six years longer than the association of schools of social work. The lineal descendant of that association of schools is the Council on Social Work Education which came into being in 1952 replacing the previous associations.

The year 1969 also marked the year of intense disturbances in the American society which was expressed by confrontation techniques, violence, and disturbances of social order perpetrated by actionist groups trying to change the status quo—sometimes advocating destruction of existing social institutions and organizations in the naïve belief that change in and of itself would solve problems of discrimination, poverty, status, and power distribution. It was simultaneously a year of great strain in the eighty schools of social work in the U.S.A. Throughout the latter half of the 1960's the schools were under attack by some community groups and by well-organized actionist student groups bent upon wresting from the faculties and the profession the power to make substantive decisions of educational policy. It is probable that the climax of this era of disturbance was reached at the annual meetings of the Council on Social Work Education in January, 1969, and the National Conference on Social Welfare in May, 1969.[1]

No other profession has been more self-critical of its educational preparation or more determined to improve it. The activities and accomplishments of the field in the decade of the 1960's bear tangible testimony to the intensity of effort to improve social work education. It was a decade marked by the production of more studies, more published research on educational matters and more developed curriculum materials than had been produced in the preceding quarter of a century. As a result of this magnificent scholarly production and of the force of the actionists' influence on matters of social policy we could say that the 1970's opened to a markedly changed societal and professional situation. Before we address ourselves to the future let us look at some significant societal facts which serve as context within which social work and social work education must be viewed.

Some of the most fundamental aspects of our society are suggested in population data. In the eight years following World War II (1945–1953) the number of babies born in this country rose by almost 50 per cent. After that the birth rate increased at a much slower rate until 1960 when the total number of births began to drop for a seven-year period. Since 1967 the birth rate remains at that same lower level with few signs of going up. The baby boom of 1945–1953 produced the present-day high supply of young people eighteen to twenty-six years of age. The first part of this wave hit the graduate schools of social work in 1968 or 1969. The tail end of that high wave will pass the schools of social work before 1980. In the decade of the 1980's vigorous recruitment of social work students will begin again as the population supply of young adults shrinks. By the 1990's the trough of the lower birth rate dated from 1967 will be evident in the relatively smaller supply of young people in their twenties.

In 1960 the center of adult population gravity was in the thirty-five to forty age group—substantially older than usual in the history of America. It is probable this phenomenon will appear again by 1990. During the 1960's the center of population gravity shifted all the way down to seventeen—younger than it had been for several decades. Because of the affluence of American families in the 1960's and because of the sheer large size of the youth population, young people were not absorbed into the labor force of the country as had been the case in previous decades. More than half of the young men in the sixteen to seventeen years of age group stayed out of the work force, but remained in school outside adult society and without adult responsibilities. The psychological impact of this situation explains, in part at least, the youth activities which have become known as the youth revolution.

The U.S. Department of Labor predicts that there will be fifteen million workers added to the labor force in the 1970's, bringing the total to 100 million by 1980. Half of this growth will be accounted for by young adults in the twenty-five to thirty-four age bracket. This is a dramatic increase over the last decade which witnessed only 16 per cent increase in that age bracket. On the average one-fourth of the work force will be in this age group and as a group 80 per cent of them will have had at least a high school education and 33 per cent of them will have had some or completed college work. The growth rate of those in their teens and early twenties was a whopping 53 per cent in the 1960's but will decline sharply to a mere 19 per cent in the 1970's. Similarly, it is predicted that the trends in occupational shifts toward white-collar and service occupations will continue with a resulting 50 per cent more in white-collar than in blue-collar occupations by 1980. Social work is one of the occupations toward which this shift is aimed. Furthermore, the trend is also toward greatly increased employment in public agencies (especially at state and local levels) which includes social work positions. There will be fewer workers on farms—the decline to 3 per cent of the work force will be reached by 1980.

It is a well-known fact that seventeen-year-olds are typically rebellious, in search of new identity, addicted to causes and intoxicated with ideas. But young adults from twenty-one to thirty-five tend to be the most conventional groups in our society. It is a time when concern is with immediate and concrete problems—job advancement, career, income, mortgage, furniture, doctor bills and child rearing. It is after age thirty-five that attention beyond the immediate and concrete problems can be undertaken by the majority of adults. This can be called the age when one becomes a liberal. By 1974 those born in 1953 will reach age twenty-one. From 1970 onward the center of gravity of the population will shift upward from seventeen so that by 1975 the dominant age years will be in the twenties. Enrollments in graduate schools of social work of persons twenty-three years of age or older will continue to be high until 1975–76. After that there will be fewer twenty-three-year-olds available. It is perhaps fair to say that student-led disturbances will decline sharply in the 1970's. In the 1980's young people in their twenties will be in relatively short supply and those in their forties will be in relative oversupply.

But the population pressure alone does not account fully for the remarkable change in attitudes about the nature of human nature which took place during the 1960's. It is enlightening to remember that at the opening of this century we lived in the prescientific age of medicine, on the average the educational level of the population was less than eight grades, and many of the service professions (including social work) were as yet unborn. Ideas about man and social welfare were locked into archaic and inadequate concepts which have yielded but slowly to empirically derived, scientifically tested or clinically successful modifications of ideas about the nature of human nature. The poor, the aged, the mentally ill, or the delinquent were mainly classified as hopeless or incurable, and there was no concept of rehabilitation as we have come to view it today. By the 1960's it was beginning to be recognized by the whole population that a poor man was not poor just because he lacked intelligence or morals. The shift of population (in considerable part our nonwhite population) from agrarian to urban life resulting from the industrial expansion of our economy became visible to a considerable proportion of our people. It began to dawn on more than a few that in our haste to expand and mechanize our economy we had inadvertently placed human values in a lower priority. It became evident that man was caught in a vortex of social forces that he could not alone control. The superabundant youth population aged fifteen to twenty-one during the 1960's quite understandably rejected in large part the attitudes of their parents about the meaning of work, about being poor, about the value of established institutions, about the traditional concepts of private enterprise, and about the concepts of individual freedom and responsibility. Simultaneously there seemed to be little recognition of the significant steps taken in previous decades aimed at improving human welfare or reducing human misery. For example, there was little appreciation for the accomplishments represented by child labor laws, workmen's compensation systems, the Social Security Act, to say nothing of the rising standard of living. It was not recognized that the percent of the population defined as poor had declined from about 40 per cent in 1900 to about 7 per cent in 1970. The more than fourteen million constituting the 7 per cent of population were primarily too old (two million) or too young (7.4 million) to be absorbed in the labor market. The idea that the "system" was beyond redemption was sponsored by some, who seemed unaware of these advances, while there was a growing consensus that the "system" must be changed in the direction of enhancing human as something separate from material values. So the 1970's opened with a marked change in attitudes. Social work's long-held values were more generally accepted as valid. At the same time significantly larger numbers of young people sought to enter professional education for social work. Enrollments of graduate-level full-time students in schools of social work in the U.S.A. rose from 3,900 in 1950 to 4,972 in 1960 but took the big leap to nearly 13,000 by the fall term of 1970. According to Reichert's estimate there were 20,000 undergraduates enrolled in social welfare sequences by 1969.[2] By the 1980's these changed attitudes will be considered the property of the aging and the youth born after 1960 will be suggesting a different set, perhaps an improved view of the nature of human nature. If so, enrollments in schools of social work may not decline in proportion to population.

Let us now turn to another set of statements which show similarities and changes in the description of social work education since 1945 as recorded by authoritative authors in certain volumes of the *Social Work Yearbook*—more recently issued as the *Encyclopedia of Social Work*.

In 1945 Miss Gordon Hamilton wrote, "As in all professional education, schools of social work have a twofold purpose, namely advancing professional knowledge, and training in professional skill." [3] She also reported that as of 1944 the essential elements of a professional social work curriculum were to consist of "the basic eight," namely, public welfare, social casework, social group work, community organization, medical information, social research, psychiatric information, and social administration. She said that the general trend in curriculum building at that time seemed to be toward the establishment of broad professional, rather than a narrow technical, base. She also said that "social work can no longer afford to operate within a culture; it has responsibility to contribute to changes in our culture. Students must be exposed to the idea of cultural pluralism; that is, the unity of differences." She contended that education for a profession, from Hippocrates to the present, calls quite as much for growth and change as for knowledge. "Knowledge can be 'crammed'; skill can be quickly acquired; but the growth of a professional self cannot be satisfactorily hastened beyond an undetermined but still real point." A mature attitude toward oneself and others is not easily acquired. Hamilton had summarized a point of view which dominated the thinking of social work educators for more than three decades. The influence of that point of view survives and will probably be one of several that will continue to influence social work education for the next twenty or more years.

In 1949 Sue Spencer said that social work education was in crisis. [4] She attributed the crisis to "a young and rapidly growing profession in which demands of the field far outdistance the resources of the professional schools" and to "basic conflict as to the level of professional education that is both desirable and possible" plus the confusing inadequate organizational problems with which social work education was then struggling. After Spencer had identified those problems, social work educators turned attention to their solution. The 1950's were spent with unimaginable activity aimed at solving the problems of resources for social work education (only partially realized), of mediating the arguments about the levels of educational preparation for the field, and by bringing together all factions of the field in a single national organization concerned with social work education, namely, the Council on Social Work

Education. This latter accomplishment made possible the giant stride forward taken in the 1960's.

Ernest Witte in 1960 pointed to the problems of social work education which then held center stage.[5] He said, "The current period is one portending extensive and fundamental changes in education for social work." He went on to specify the direction of curriculum changes, the manpower problems of the time, the decline in graduate enrollments in the first half of the 1950's followed by a steady increase after that year, the development of accrediting standards with regularized procedures, the growing recognition of the importance of doctoral education and its undeniable association with the development of leadership for the field, and the recognition of America's role in relationship to social work and social work education in other countries and on the international level. In curriculum policy the concept of sequences (public social policy, human behavior, social work practice—including field work—and social research) had replaced the "basic eight." The scholarly task of implementing this new design had begun.

Werner Boehm in 1971 contributed an excellent comprehensive chapter on social work education which every professional and every student should read.[6] He reviews the purposes of social work education (to prepare personnel for performance of social welfare functions), its characteristics and structures (undergraduate and graduate curriculum involving theory and field work generally following a common pattern but showing diversity among the schools), its relationship to the university community (characterized by ties to the community of social services as well as to the university, with a growing impact on other departments in the university), and quality control developments (involving accreditation by the Council on Social Work Education as well as improving quality controls from within on faculty selection, student admission, and curriculum development). He identifies the fact that some schools have begun to move away from emphasis on methods to providing both knowledge and skill in problem assessment and problem solution in conjunction with each other. But he seems to warn that knowledge about social problems without competence in methods of problem solving is insufficient. He points to a central issue of this time—the creation of opportunities for students to acquire either: (a) competence in methods of direct service, or (b) competence in policy analysis and planning (usually community organization sequences, often involving also administration). This development constitutes a break with the past which held that to become an administrator or policy planner a social worker must have practice experience in a direct service method. Questions are being raised about the wisdom of this break with the past. Proponents argue that social work personnel with policy competence will be prepared for jobs that otherwise would go to personnel in other fields from other disciplines. Opponents argue that in the absence of direct knowledge and experience in casework or group work, it is difficult for administrators, planners or policy analysts to know how to identify and develop appropriate policies and conduct programs. They also fear the profession will be split into two groups to the detriment of a unified profession, hence a weakened ability to address problems within the profession and to devise appropriate responses to society's social welfare needs.

We can summarize these four authors, whose statements embrace at least a quarter of a century, by noting that Hamilton in the 1940's emphasized the growth of the professional. Spencer noted the problems of resources and organizational inadequacies at the beginning of the 1950's. Witte in 1960 foresaw the tremendous developments in scholarship and curriculum. Boehm in 1971 identified the shift in curriculum toward problem identification and description, urging the field to develop simultaneously the methodology and skills in problem solving. He also suggested that in a future where more and better social workers will be needed there is a danger of the profession splitting to the detriment of the profession and the clientele to be served.

But there are other dimensions to the unsolved and partially solved problems of social work education. One of these arises from the attempts at curriculum organization which it is believed will produce in the learner an integrated outcome. Not only does this include attempts to show the relevance and usefulness of divergent fields of knowledge (for example, about social policy and programs, about human behavior and the social environment, about cultural differences, etc.) but also it assumes that there exists a set of principles to guide social work practice that would diminish, if not erase, the differences between social casework, social group work and social community organization work (to say nothing of social work administration or social work research) if we could but find them. It is generally accepted that it is more important to "integrate" the curriculum than it is either (a) to bring about a better practice of social work or (b) to get a better student who could undertake the integrative tasks of learning. It is probable that the curriculum organization is the lesser of these three necessary ingredients: curriculum, teaching, and learner.

Certain educated guesses about what will happen in social work education in the next twenty years can be made against the backdrop of what has happened in the last twenty-five years. Let us speculate about the following interdependent factors: (1) the social context and the nature of the concomitant problems; (2) the curricula of schools of social work; (3) the faculties of the future; (4) the students of the future; and (5) the resources for social work education.

Let us turn to a short discussion of the social context and selected concomitant problems.

As we enter the 1970's an economic depression looms as a frightening possibility. The transition from a war economy to a peacetime economy will bring unemployment and strain to a considerable portion of our population heretofore economically self-sufficient. It may take some time to solve that problem especially when one recognizes the relative over-supply of young adults in our population during the 1970's. The inventions introduced into our industrial society have simultaneously reduced the demand for human labor. The effect is to release more people from work for more hours of the workweek, probably resulting in the rich becoming richer while the number of economically deprived increases. This fact makes it clear that a larger share of our national resources, both public and private, will need to be given over to human services. Concurrently, the need for an increase in the number of professional social workers will become evident.

But, assuming that the problems of a postwar adjustment are met, it seems possible that there will be an increase in affluence on the part of all segments of our population. Nevertheless it is also evident that certain segments of the population will be left aside in these developments. It is likely that the aged, the children, and the handicapped will continue to be the vulnerable groups. It is also possible that the minority groups may achieve equality of treatment so that the tensions of intergroup relationships may decline. Although these developments forecast the need for more social workers, another factor may multiply the need. This is the concept that access to social services is an inalienable right everybody should enjoy. As that idea is more widely accepted, social services, and with them resources for social work education, will undergo expansion and change. Social work would then more rapidly add preventive and developmental functions to its already recognized supportive and rehabilitative functions. The resulting effect on social work education would be an expansion of its concern for preparing professionals for roles involving planning in both its epidemiological sense as well as in the sense of structural alterations of social, economic and/or political institutions. It should emphasize the importance of shifting from the philosophical espousal of change as a goal to the development of professional competence for the achievement of human betterment and social change as the goal of social work education. This emphasis is not foreign to many thoughtful leaders in social work education.

The shift in emphasis toward more competence is likely to occur simultaneously with the refinement of the continuing attempts at securing the maximum integrated learning outcome for social work students. As Lowy, Bloksberg and Walberg [7] have pointed out, "Although the literature is replete with references to the desirability of an integrative curriculum, few attempts have been made to distill discrete elements which could be identified conceptually and which would provide an operational point of entry for educators to achieve a more integrative learning environment."

It is small wonder that progress on this task is slow. The wide range of knowledge considered essential to social work education, drawn from diverse disciplines (ranging over the social and biological sciences), expressed in different language from varying conceptual frameworks, has posed a very difficult problem for social work. The task of identifying, selecting, comparing and consolidating into an organized body of knowledge is massive. Furthermore, the rate at which new knowledge is created in those pertinent fields complicates the task. And, more importantly, the forming of an organized body of knowledge from our own sources of knowledge building as well as the incorporation of borrowed knowledge is only a first step. The succeeding or concomitant task of conceptualization so as to produce principles that will guide practice is of highest importance for a professional field.[8]

Another factor to be considered is the relative complexity of duty responsibility to be found within the job functions of social welfare programs.[9] It is now possible to measure the relative complexity of the duty functions of social work at all levels. It seems logical to assume that educational programs leading respectively to A.A., B.A. and M.S.W. degrees would gear curriculum and learning on these levels to duty functions ranging from the less complex to the most complex. It is another of the several goals to be achieved.

However, there is progress being made toward achieving these several important goals. It is likely that considerable achievement will have been realized before the end of this century.

Let us now turn to a few statements about the curricula of schools of social work.

Now that we begin to discern certain effective principles of learning and teaching, it is likely that much that was or is thought to be important will be abandoned because it is not as effective as had been hoped, and certain elements found to be useful will be used, refined and expanded. For example, the use of team teaching—popularly thought to be an effective technique—may disappear, and parallel courses—popularly thought to produce a sense of integrative learning—may be abandoned. Instead the deliberately designed interactions between faculty and student around organized subject matter and a common theoretical framework that uses integrative cross-referencing threads between courses and sequences may be more widely adopted and extended. Furthermore, it will be better recognized that the learning task is the student's task (the teacher is a helper), hence interaction between students as they pursue their educational goals may become more widely used. The linking of common experiences to conceptual theory and principles, although time-consuming and costly, should continue as a central feature of social work education.

Another feature to be mentioned is the relationship between liberal and professional education and its implication for curricula.

For a quarter of a century or more social work education developed with the widely held conviction that a sound liberal education is a necessary prerequisite to professional education. Consequently, professional education was established at the graduate level. But the supply of students completing the graduate program was insufficient to meet the effective demands of the field. Hence, the vigorous efforts to increase recruitment and enrollment combined with the efforts to establish more schools of social work. Simultaneously, the number of young people looking for a career in social work increased. The result of these pressures has brought a decision that instead of a broadly based liberal education there should be an increase of professional education content at the undergraduate level so as to shorten the over-all college and university time span from six down to five years of university- or college-level education. Interestingly, this change has occurred at the time in history when there is an oversupply of B.A.-level graduates and an adequate volume of M.S.W.-level graduates if measured by the effective demand in the marketplace. This reduction of the liberal education base for professional education in social work will probably lead to a profession which will be less well prepared to deal imaginatively with problems of social policy and social welfare practice, although there would remain technical competence to perform job functions in well-defined programs of the social agencies or in quasi-political movements of social action leading to social reform.

An inevitable problem in curricula arises when professional education is inserted into undergraduate liberal education colleges. Normally, professional education is not the primary mission of such colleges, hence professional programs are viewed as foreign agents. In times of financial stress or when impinging policy differences are present, the professional school or program is at a distinct disadvantage in the undergraduate college environment. Consequently, the professional curricula may become warped or the staffing become inadequate. If the development of professional education partly or wholly at undergraduate level continues, the distortion and inevitable lowering of standards could be the outcome.

A few words about the faculties of the future should be said.

Ever since social work education within institutions of higher learning became emancipated from the dominance of traditional academic departments by being recognized as equals within the university, earnest attempts were made to develop content closely related to the practical demands of social work practice. This called for a faculty which, in addition to traditional educational academic qualifications, was clearly qualified by social work practice experience to teach social work practice principles and to oversee the field work component of professional education. Often the available individuals best qualified for this function had not earned the higher degrees based primarily on training in research. The fact that there were few programs leading to the doctorate posed a problem. However, the creativity and activity of faculties in concert with each other under the auspices and leadership of the Council on Social Work Education did produce a sophisticated and balanced curriculum. The deep desire to improve it led to both the development of social work doctoral programs and the recruitment into social work education of a considerable number of social scientists whose experience in social work was limited but whose expertise in research and social science was more sophisticated. Consequently, faculty of a given school might include one or more social scientists (often from sociology, but not infrequently from psychology, political science or economics, etc.) as well as professors of social work practice (casework, group work, community organization), social policy and programs, and human behavior (often including also a full or part-time faculty member from another outside field such as psychiatry). The effect was to create a multidiscipline flavor on the school of social work faculty.

In time, the doctoral programs in social work were expanded in number and in enrollment. These programs vary in focus and content. Some are weighted heavily with social science content but some are devoted to developing graduates who can undertake the important task of developing, organizing and conceptualizing social work knowledge. The doctoral graduate in social work usually becomes a faculty member rather than returning to the field of practice. It is clear that as the supply of these doctoral graduates increases the faculties of schools of social work will have proportionately fewer M.S.W.-level practitioner types and relatively fewer of those whose doctoral degrees are in another field (that is, a social science field, for example). Although many schools which offer the social work doctorate require a block of post M.S.W. practice experience, there are some that do not. To the extent that such doctoral graduates are immediately ushered into faculty positions, the greater is the likelihood that curricula and teaching will become more theoretical and descriptive rather than emphasizing theory and practice problems. Schools which must struggle for a respected place in the university will tend to hire faculty members with the doctoral degree whether or not the candidate has sufficient social work practice experience and competence. This may accentuate the shift of professional education downward. But if scholarship and research is concerned with practice the net effect should be the expansion of social work knowledge.

Perhaps the most important element among all those discussed above is the nature and abilities of the social work student. In the final analysis it is the quality of the student that will inevitably shape social work practice and social work education.

While the field need not be ashamed of the progress and accomplishments achieved so far, the goals of human betterment still lie unfulfilled. In part this may be due to the relatively lower quality of students of yesteryear. During the long developmental years of the field there was a small increment of the total youth population who chose social work as their career. With such a small universe of applicants the schools of social work accepted not only the best and most promising candidates but also many who were marginal in ability and pertient talents. Furthermore, less was known about selecting applicants. Measures calculated to predict success in the field were scarce and the situation remains today in an underdeveloped state.[10] But with a marked change in the volume of young people who seek entry into schools of social work, and the growing sophistication of the selection and admission processes, it is likely that the over-all quality of the student body of any given school of social work will be increasingly higher for at least a decade.[11] This is the most promising aspect of the future. Better students will make better social work faculties which in turn will make for better curricula and better professional education, which in turn will make for better social services.

The resources for social work education have developed in a pattern which involves the cooperation of a number of resources. A major factor is the field work component of social work education which is secured for the school through the cooperation of operating social agencies. Often this contribution is motivated both by a desire to be helpful and a desire to be close to the supply of future staff members so as to reduce problems of recruiting professional staff. But whatever the motivation, the contribution of social agencies by providing placements, supervisory teaching personnel, space, client cases and groups as well as a place where acculturation to the profession proceeds is significant. If the curricula of schools of social work and the kind of student continues to bear a reasonable relation to agency program and needs, one can predict that this major contribution to social work education will continue. If not, then this resource will fade.

Another major resource for social work education is the funds secured under grants from the several granting authorities—mainly public agencies. Obviously, the reason governmental health and welfare agencies provide such financial support is to increase the volume of well-trained manpower needed in the programs of concern to the granting agency. Often these grants are in the form of money for additional faculty as well as funds for student support through stipends and fellowships. As the volume of acceptably trained professionals rises to the level of meeting the manpower needs of the operating agency, the likelihood of continued financial support through these granting mechanisms will decline. At present the outlook for continued funding through training grants is gloomy.

In the final analysis the basic resource for a school of social work must be the university itself. This means that social work education must have sufficient recognition and priority to get an adequate share of the resources of the university. The building (office and classroom space), the library, the salary and expense budget and the like must become an integral part of the university budget if the school is to thrive and survive.

Although man has always sought means to forecast future events in order to prepare himself for oncoming events and problems, he has learned that exact prediction eludes him. It would be foolhardly to state firmly where social work education will be in 1993. But, if we can fully grasp the past trend of events and can assess correctly the present, including all the many factors and variables that influence social work and social work education, we may make guesses about the future which are better than chance guesses. This chapter has touched on only a few of the items that should be considered. It is hoped that what has been included will be helpful to those who set themselves the task of forecasting and planning the future of social work education. There is a complex of factors and resources revealed in the trends in our history that portend a future of greater influence and significance to society than has ever been the case in the past. But there is also the possibility that if the profession does not respond suitably to societal needs, especially to the basic social, psychological and economic needs of individuals and families, then the helping role may be shifted to some other occupational or professional group and social work education will be of lesser influence and significance to society.

13

Social Work Research

ROGER R. MILLER

The recent emergence of a research specialization in social work expresses an old dream. For present at the birth of social work was the vision that scientific inquiry would ultimately provide solutions to social problems.[1] Throughout the formative years of the field, social work research remained an attractive goal; except for the master's thesis project, research was long more a subject for discussion than field of activity. Not until 1949 were social work researchers numerous enough to form a professional organization.[2] Subsequent to that time, social work research has undergone rapid expansion and professionalization. Doctoral programs in social work have recently prepared a noteworthy number of investigators;[3] the dream of a research specialization in social work has recently become a reality.

In considering goals for the future, it is useful to re-examine a dream whose fulfillmment is at hand. For there is reason to believe that the dream still carries some ancient and magical wishes that are at odds with our contemporary reality. And more importantly, there is reason to believe that the dream has led to a social contract which is particularly dysfunctional for the problems we will face in the future.

It is instructive to consider a much earlier version of man's efforts to exploit the power of science for social ends. Through medieval times, the alchemist worked to discover how to transform base metals into gold and to discover a universal cure for disease, the elixir of life. Among the most remarkable features of alchemy is its survival across a span of twelve centuries.[4] The perpetuation of alchemy was made possible by the system of social support it received. So great was the appeal of alchemy's goal, wealth and health, and so limited was knowledge of the study issues involved, as to permit wildly optimistic views about the potentialities of the undertaking. In the social contract between the alchemist and his sponsor each was a victim of a deceit which each helped to create.

The alchemist seems to have derived the lion's share of benefits from this enterprise. By virtue of his command over research technology, the secrecy of which was zealously guarded, the alchemist secured moderately prestigious, nonstrenuous employment. He did preserve and advance some technical knowledge which later made a modest contribution to the cause of science. His patron gained only whatever diversion was offered by an occasional demonstration of experimental work, and whatever satisfaction came from the opportunity to sustain an appealing illusion. The survival of alchemy across the centuries, in spite of its nonproductivity, dramatizes human vulnerability both to the power of a dream and of an expertise that caters to a dream.

It is difficult to escape the impression that there are some uncomfortable parallels between alchemy and social work research. The social work researcher caters to the dream of harnessing the power of scientific inquiry to bring about improved services to people. By virtue of his command over some impressive technology, he secures moderately prestigious, nonstrenuous employment. His sponsor can enjoy the occasional demonstration of his work as well as the opportunity to sustain a belief in the ultimate yield of the undertaking. The social contract which the social work researcher and his sponsor have collaborated in achieving seems distressingly reminiscent of alchemy.

But surely there are some important differences between the social work researcher and the alchemist of old. Alchemy was a private, independent enterprise, whereas social work research is conducted collaboratively by methods open to public review. While the alchemist pursued unachievable goals with futile methods, the social work investigator addresses studiable problems and has available a vast spectrum of research methodology and technology. Because the social work researcher has made useful contributions to the profession, he can scarcely be regarded as the twentieth-century equivalent to the alchemist.

Unfortunately, a critical look at the character of social work research suggests that its differences from alchemy are more apparent than real. For it has been convenient to live with certain illusions about the public nature of contemporary research, about the nature of the relationship between research and social work, about the advantage of methodology and technology, and about the productivity of social work research. A careful look at each of these areas reveals some painful realities that must be addressed if we are to escape the fate of alchemy.

The central thesis of this presentation is that the current contract governing the relationship between social work research and social work rests on some comfortable but costly fictions. If we are to make headway toward the creation of a more effective knowledge-building system for the profession, that contract must be renegotiated.

The Current Contract for Social Work Research

Concurrent with the emergence of the social work research specialist, there evolved a working relationship of the character of social work research. Social work research has come to be defined as the investigative activities of the research specialist. That is, social work research is usually regarded as an elaborate technical activity identifiable by form and auspices rather than by goal or yield.[5]

There are advantages to both the researcher and nonresearcher in this division of professional responsibilities. By locating research with a specialist, the advantages of technical competence can be realized. The investigator clearly benefits from a definition of research that emphasizes the technology under his command. Beyond acknowledging the undoubted utility of research methodology, this view allocates to the investigator a domain over which he can exercise authority, and it provides for his gainful employment. Also, because he can thus dismiss as unfounded the insights or widsom derived by other means, the investigator under this contract escapes any serious competition in the world of ideas and can avoid the struggle required to try to understand quite complex service processes. Under this contract, the nonresearcher is spared the hard work of mastering research technology and the considerable problems that attend a formal commitment to the pursuit of scientific knowledge. Whatever his capacity for scholarship, skilled observation, and creative analysis, the practitioner under this contract can disqualify himself as an investigator and avoid the responsibilities attending such a role.

The working contract which allocates the research function to the specialist contains one important qualifying clause. A partnership between the research specialist and the nonresearcher is widely advocated. Unfortunately, such a partnership has rarely been achieved. In spite of serious efforts to achieve mutually enriching collaborative relationships between the research specialist and his nonresearch colleague, a partnership has seldom been realized.[6]

An early version of the partnership plan expected the practitioner to identify important research issues which the investigator would study.

The investigator's report of the results of his work was then expected to help the practitioner deliver improved services. Unfortunately, the practitioner's curiosity rarely coincided with the interests of investigators and even communication between these colleagues proved unexpectedly difficult. Moreover, the results of investigation seldom proved to be directly applicable to the solution of the problems facing the practitioner. Rather than promoting collaborative efforts, experiences in this model of collaboration seemed to have generated disengagement between the investigator and the practitioner.[7]

Efforts at collaboration via consultation have produced similar problems. The investigator's authority and ability to support whatever model of a scientific method he espouses gave him command over the decisive matter of design. In an encounter between unequally equipped participants to consultation, the practitioner was vulnerable to the technical authority of the investigator,[8] and often found himself conducting someone else's research.

An agency-based research center has been no more successful in creating a partnership between research and the remainder of the field. Often initiated with the hope for mutually enhancing teamwork between practitioner and investigator, members of such "teams" have usually found that the only thing they had in common was the central heating plant and occasionally, when health laws permit, the rest room facilities. While adding a certain luster to the establishment and providing occasional diversion through the demonstration of its work, the agency research center has tended to operate in a world apart from that of the service staff. The encounters between the investigator and practitioner have often been experienced as unwelcomed intrusions into restricted territory.[9]

While the idea of a partnership has retained its appeal, the one matter on which researchers and nonresearchers have best been able to collaborate is in the division of responsibility between these professional partners. In essence, social work research has come to be understood as that investigative activity performed by the research specialist.[10]

Consequences of the Contract

Like the contract for alchemy, the contract for social work research has consequences for the selection of study issues, study methods, and for the meaning assigned to the results of work. For like the alchemist, the social work researcher has preferred certain approaches and is expected to work within certain parameters. As we associate the retort and hermetic seal with alchemy, we associate the table of random numbers and the IBM card with the social work researcher.

The character of social work research shows the influence of research traditions of other disciplines. Evidence of our indebtedness to our mentors is visible in the prominence today in social work research of the survey model and varieties of experimental design.

The activities that have come to characterize social work research articulate quite selectively with the knowledge needs of our field. Some problems can be accommodated easily within the spectrum of usual research methodology, while others cannot. Thus, available models for research can produce accurate and useful descriptions of socially accessible phenomena such as the social characteristics of patient populations. However, our research models have been less coherent with the problems of unraveling the intricacies of service transactions.

Faced with a choice between adapting preferred methodology to a study issue or adapting a study issue to preferred methodology, the investigator is inclined to the latter course. As a consequence, many of the issues that seem most attractive to the nonresearcher are viewed as nonstudyable—that is, incapable of being accommodated within the spectrum of preferred methodology. Some of the issues that are selected because they do fit methodological preferences are viewed by nonresearchers as trivial and uninteresting.

Research as a Source for Knowledge

The achievements of social work research today afford the basis both for some pride and considerable humility. Social work research has been far more successful in identifying problems than in finding solutions to problems. Useful descriptions of who is included within or excluded from our service network, about the characteristics of programs and the services experiences of our clientele have been generated by social work research.[11] Research which has attempted to provide explanations has been a less dependable source of insight. Research has sometimes succeeded in demonstrating the explanatory power of systematic connections among variables in our service activities. Although such research contributes to an explanation for complex events, it is sometimes understood, and sometimes even presented as *the* explanation. Thus, the inverse association between socioeconomic status and the use of service has provided the basis for some extraordinarily simplistic explanations about the nature of complex service activities. The contribution of social work research toward devising and implementing practical solutions to social and professional problems has been minimal.

It is useful to contrast the knowledge yield of formal inquiry with the results of less systematic, informal study. Much of the working knowledge on which social work rests has evolved across time through the interaction of experience and the human mind. Communicated by precept, and in a growing body of professional literature, the knowledge base of social work is continuously tested and elaborated against the experience and judgment of professionals. Like any evolving body of knowledge, it undoubtedly contains errors, as is true also of the results of formal inquiry. The curious feature of our current definition of social work research is its emphasis on the discontinuity between informal and more systematic efforts to advance understanding, and its disqualification of the route to learning that has been reasonably productive for our field. Distrust of experience as a source for learning may reflect our familiarity with the frailties of the human mind as a collector, organizer, and appraiser of data. However, our optimism about the productivity of formal inquiry may reflect too little knowledge about the frailties of research methodology for these same tasks.

Conventional research methodology is designed to guard against error. More specifically, methodology is designed insofar as possible to reduce the kinds of errors that are subject to influence by the procedures employed. Unfortunately, the methodology may operate to reduce certain errors while creating others. Contrary to what we might like to believe, the thoughtful effort to reduce errors may fail and certainty in this enterprise is no more attainable than in any other human undertaking. It is useful to bear in mind that none of the research methodology has any intrinsic value in itself except as it serves to promote accurate understanding of study phenomena. For example, to know that a variable is measured objectively is irrelevant; to know, however, that a variable is measured validly, whether by subjective or objective means, is highly relevant.

The costs that accompany the allocation of research activity to the hands of specialists thus include restrictions on the issues subject to inquiry and the methods by which such inquiries are pursued. These costs are, however, probably less serious than the limitations placed by our present arrangements on the receptivity with which research activity is met. The social contract under which most social work research is conducted virtually assures the ineffectiveness of research as a force for change.

Research as a Force for Change

Implicit in the conception of the research specialist is the expectation that descriptive information and partial explanation produced by research will be a force for corrective action. This expectation, which expresses a touching faith in the decisiveness of logic for directing human affairs, overlooks the influence of the belief systems that enter into research. For contrary to the pretention of scientific purity, social work research is inescapably enmeshed in a cultural context which shapes the choice of study issue, method, and interpretation. The sudden popularity of the subject of race as a focus for inquiry, after years during which the subject was studiously ignored, documents the impact of social forces upon inquiry.[12] But nowhere is the social context for social work research more evident than in the troubled history of evaluative research.

Characteristically, evaluative research is imposed, rather than sought, as a necessary but inconvient condition for securing support for a program in which the planners have invested high hopes. As usually conceived, the mission of evaluative research is to measure the extent to which a program, in its totality, achieves its goals which are characteristically framed in very general terms. An independent and presumably objective outside investigator is then engaged to collect, analyze and interpret data bearing on this politically significant issue. By this point, both the investigator and the program planner have entered the world of make-believe. The sophisticated program planner is well aware that the evaluative result of some investigators will almost always be negative while others can generally find evidence of goal achievement. The program planner is therefore inclined to choose a sample of one investigator on an entirely nonrandom basis.

The investigator, in this circumstance, encounters a number of moral and scientific dilemmas. A program in its totality, with its particular mix of staff, time, locale, and intangibles such as belief or investment in a program, is a nonreplicable phenomenon. Hence, there is little scientific interest in learning about its net effect on a specific and never wholly to be replicated population. But even if it were of scientific moment to abstract a measurement of net effect, the investigator is painfully aware of the impossibility of achieving this goal. By simply selecting different calibration points for measurement or by shifting the focus from immediate and almost inevitable consequences to the remote and unlikely consequences of a program, any program can emerge as either ineffectual or highly successful. The usual compromise found to these dilemmas generates the usual mixture of positive and negative findings about the program.

Whether the outcome of evaluative research is positive or negative, individual convictions then mediate its reception. Negative results when examined by those committed to the program may simply be rejected.[13] Whether discounted on the basis of investigator bias, measurement error, lag in the effects of the program, or due to the impact of other nonprogram influences, research results which depart widely from a developed system of beliefs are negated. Similarly, positive results of program evaluation may be discounted by observers holding different convictions and expectations about the nature of service. Thus, the favorable results frequently cited for behavorial conditioning approaches have excited little interest among practitioners operating within a different theoretical context.

The investigator's efforts to enhance the persuasive power of his work has generally taken the form of expanding and elaborating the inquiry. By making his work methodologically unassailable, it is believed that its persuasive power will be enhanced. The technical purity of the work, however, seems not to be decisive in determining its reception.

The social work researcher, like the alchemist of old, appears to have collaborated in developing a social contract for his work which virtually guarantees his ineffectiveness. By catering to the dream of generating dependable, firm knowledge which will lead to the attainment of our professional goals, by the emphasis on method, and by accepting the role of expert in pursuit of the elixir of professional life, the social work researcher has helped to create a system which adequately serves no one. And our present arrangement for research appears even less capable of accommodating the needs ahead.

Research Needs for the Future

The safest prediction for 1993 is a vastly accelerated pace of change. Social events, many of which are wholly outside the influence of social work, will increasingly impinge on our activities and will require continual adaptation. And along with the increasing tempo of change, the pervasiveness of change influences will impose special new demands on our field. All echelons of our system will be vulnerable to influences arising from outside our field, and from the multiple responsive efforts from within our field as well. Not one of our comfortable familiar practices is likely to escape recurrent challenge.[14]

For negotiating the pressure of rapid change, social work, like all other social institutions, will need to devise ways of preserving useful continuity while achieving useful and creative flexibility.

Research seeks after lawful relationships among variables, and has customarily entertained the goal of establishing once-and-for-all-time the nature of these connections. Progress toward this goal is necessarily slow. And characteristically, research progresses by partializing a complex field of inquiry so as to enhance the study of a selection of the multiple variables at play in it. In the hope of understanding better the influences of certain forces, the investigator usually forgoes the attempt to trace other variables.

For coping with the kaleidoscope of novel circumstances, the kind of knowledge presently generated by research will probably be of limited value. It is quite conceivable that a number of powerful influences on social work will be so transient that traditional research efforts would never capture them. For charting a promising course through the waves of change, ongoing intelligence reports are required. The knowledge needed for social work may constitute a series of approximations based on broad-gauged rapid inquiry rather than more thorough time-consuming study of circumscribed issues.

The generation of timely, relevant approximations will serve the readaptational needs of our field only if we are disposed to use such knowledge. As we know, substantial gaps can exist between the availabilty of knowledge and its application. The usability of knowledge appears to be a function of our location of that knowledge in a general orientation toward error.

Orientation Toward Error

Social work shares with other social institutions a logical positivistic view about the attainability of our social goals. Failures in this context are regarded as the product of human error, either in planning or execution. Error is thus seen as a source for embarrassment rather than a systemic inevitability, and evidence of error is withheld as much as possible from public view in the name of maintaining the image of agency perfection.

It is naïve in the utmost to imagine that an organization can function without error and achieve perfection. Instead, it is realistic to accept the view that the most informed, well-intended choices will miss their mark and will create some problems even as they solve others. The fictional quality of our error-suppressing, perfection-embracing stance is of minor consequence. Of moment is the fact that such a stance deprives us of our most valuable data for readaptation. Vitally needed for our ongoing struggle to achieve the most constructive possible role for social work in the years ahead is an error-embracing stance which enhances receptivity to the clues that can promote refinements and realignments of our work.[15]

Social work researchers experience the same problem with error as is encountered by their professional colleagues. Indeed, the technology of research may be thought of as an elaborate effort to spare the investigator the embarrassment of being found in error. By assigning a numerical value to the probability of his drawing an erroneous inference, and with other appropriate qualifications, the investigator can achieve a state of blamelessness which becomes important only in a context which assigns error to human failure.

There are indications that presently social work is shifting in orientation toward error, in the direction of greater authenticity. As the social work profession has moved from the position of expert entrepreneur to that of collaborator with the community, it has been possible to establish contracts which do not require of social work the pose of omnipotence. Indeed, one of the discoveries of our recently evolving experience with more diverse community groups is the growing intolerance toward perfectionistic pretension. There is some reason to believe that our constituencies will respond favorably to forthright presentations that feature less exclusively our achievements but instead, discuss our readaptational efforts stimulated by our failures. It seems quite possible that in the years ahead, social work may be asked not only "What did you achieve this year?" but "What did you learn this year from your own errors and the errors of others about how not to conduct your enterprise?"

There is no reason to believe that an error-embracing stance can be achieved by allocating to others the task of detecting error. Failures identified by external agents are experienced as an attack. As in the case of evaluative research, critical findings evoke feelings of being misunderstood, unappreciated, and unfairly criticized. The data indicating error are then the stimulus for defensive rather than progressively adaptive responses. Rather than contributing efficiently to adaptive refinements, error data may complicate and impede progress toward professional goals. In contrast, self-detected errors can promote a sense of mastery and achievement. Such error data are plausible, stimulating, and challenge the participant to further adaptive effort. It is this circumstance that most urgently recommends a renegotiation of the contract between social work research and the profession. Instead of remaining an activity of experts, research must become a function intrinsic to a professional role.

Present-day investigators might derive substantial benefit from a redefinition of social work research emphasizing its continuity with less formal knowledge-seeking efforts. In addition to drawing attention to the sociopolitical context in which all knowledge-seeking efforts necessarily occur, such a redefinition of research would provide the investigator with relevant knowledge and experience from practitioners. As the caseworker has learned to relate cautiously to the request "Now tell me what I'm doing wrong," so the researcher might be helped to consider the process through which a collaborative inquiry might best serve constructive ends.

Opportunities Ahead

Advanced in this paper is the proposition that the social work researcher presently caters to an unreal dream about the capacity of an expert methodologist to advance knowledge and promote useful change. Presented as an alternative to the current system is a conception of research as a knowledge-pursuing process, which takes a value-neutral stance toward methodology. In this conception, the relocation of research as a general professional function becomes plausible.

Role for the Research Methodologist

If the research methodologist is relieved of his present burden as investigator for the profession, he would be in a position to make a number of useful contributions in support of a profession-wide research development. In the role of consultant, the methodologist should be able to help his colleagues consider alternatives in the selection of sampling, measurement, and data-processing procedures in the interests of efficiency and productivity. And his technical competence should be particularly useful in devising ways to survive the knowledge explosion which threatens our future. The methodologist should be able to help develop and perfect retrieval systems for identifying and making available the components of our burgeoning literature which are relevant to the scholarly, research, and other professional interests of staff. And in addition, the methodological specialist may make a contribution through his continuing conduct of research in areas that are most suited to his methodological preferences.

Role for the Schools

In the pursuit of academic respectability, the master's program for years featured didactic training in research methodology and a required thesis project. This approach undoubtedly contributed to our present definition of research as methodologically dominated, and promoted the separation between research as an activity and other professional functions. Recent experimentation in which research course work has shifted from a methodological focus to a substantive area seems promising. However, the usual educational objective for the research sequence, to equip the student to become a consumer of research, seems to define the professional as a passive recipient of the research activity of technical experts. And the diminishing emphasis in master's programs on original, studious inquiry seems unlikely to prepare the professional for a career of actively pursuing knowledge.

While few master's students are seriously harmed by course work in research methodology, and there are even some advantages to be gained from familiarity with the technical tools of investigation, the preparation of the learner for a career committed to active, ongoing learning is properly the concern of the total professional curriculum. Students would benefit from models, both in the field and classroom, of professionals whose life and work exemplify this stance toward learning, and would benefit as well from experiences that promote individual initiative in seeking and advancing knowledge. Because of a pressure to equip students with the considerable body of knowledge required for responsible entry into the profession, educators have been drawn toward approaches which are efficient in imparting knowledge and may have given too little thought to the support of the student's own impetus toward active, continuing learning.

Role for the Agencies

Critical to the realization of a viable, adaptable profession is the climate for learning created by the agency. An optimal climate for professional development would feature the expectation of and tolerance for error, along with an expectation for ongoing learning and open communication. Prominent among the advantages of an organizational context for professional functioning is the opportunity we have to learn from each other. Leadership which demonstrates unswervingly an error-embracing, knowledge-seeking stance should help to create a climate in which the benefits of group life can be more fully realized.

Role for the Worker

As a defining aspect of a professional role, every worker should be engaged in the ongoing study of some professional issues. Through following the literature and continuously informing himself of the experience and observations of others relevant to this area, through examination of his own experience, and occasionally through the acquisition of especially created experiences seen as likely to clarify some aspects of the problem, the worker should be struggling with the problem of advancing professionally relevant knowledge. Particular value may attend the examination of failures and limitations in our professional efforts in the hope of clarifying the bases for these failures and exploring alternative courses toward overcoming them. And the worker should accept as a professional obligation the importance of communicating to others the issues he is attempting to understand and the provisional formulations he has developed. In a climate which protects the right to be wrong, the process of evolving improved approximations to the nature of reality could be greatly enhanced.

If this proposal for a new contract between social work research and the profession at large seems demanding and formidable, our history affords some basis for hope that the work can be undertaken. Because of our commitment to another dream, that of a better life for everyone, social work has attempted to address such formidable problems as mental illness, poverty, and the myriad obstacles attending group and community life. If a new contract with social work research will help the profession toward social goals, the challenge it presents will be accepted.

Epilogue: In Summary

In drawing together the ideas presented in this symposium it is impossible to cite or give credit to the specific authors. Most of what is offered here has been said in one way or another by one or several of the writers of the preceding chapters. Yet, it may be helpful to try to organize the material in terms of a summarizing overview.

There seems to be considerable agreement on the problems we face. There is also agreement on the factors that produce these problems. There is somewhat less agreement on our approach to the problems and our role in their solution. This is to be expected.

The Situation Today

It is evident that technological advances, persistent as they have been in our country, do not necessarily contribute to social progress and human well-being. In fact, the opposite may be the case. Consequently, the adapting and humanizing of technology is one of the important goals to keep before us as we move into the latter stages of this century.

As Mesthene put it:

The strains that technology places on our values and beliefs, finally, are reflected in economic, political, and ideological conflict. That is, they raise questions about the proper goals of society and about the proper ways of pursuing those goals. In the end, therefore, the problems that technology poses (and the opportunities it offers) will be resolved (and realized) in the political arena, construing "political" broadly to include economic and ideological considerations as well as questions of more narrowly political organization and tactics. Technological innovation therefore leads ultimately to a need for social and political innovation if its benefits are to be fully realized and its negative effects kept to a minimum.[1]

Mesthene also points out that:

. . . traditional institutions, attitudes, and approaches are by and large incapable of coming to grips with the new problems of our cities. Many of these problems were themselves caused by technological change . . . but existing social mechanisms seem unable to realize the possibilities for resolving them that are also inherent in technology.

Vested economic and political interests serve to obstruct adequate provision of low-cost housing. Community institutions wither for want of interest and participation by residents. City agencies are unable to marshal the skills and take the systematic approach needed to deal with new and intensified problems of education, crime control, and public welfare. Business corporations finally, which are organized around the expectation of private profit, are insufficiently motivated to bring new technology and management know-how to bear on urban projects where the benefits appear to be largely social. Business has yet to estimate the costs of racial discrimination in terms of decreased purchasing power and its consequent depressing effect on the private economy.

All these factors combine to dilute what could otherwise be translated into a genuine public desire to apply our best knowledge, our latest tools, and adequate resources to the resolution of urban tensions and the eradication of poverty in the nation.[2]

Although there will be no turning back from or turning off of technological developments and these developments will continue to create problems, it is to be hoped that their consequences will be better foreseen and dislocations will be lessened.

In the whirlwind that is society today many changes are taking place. There is change in the pace of change itself. It seems to be much faster. Changes in life-styles are clearly evident not only in the case of youth but in the case of other age groups as well. Ideological changes of the past couple of decades are striking. Technological developments have brought about a revolution in the world of work and elimination of work opportunities for many. There is increasing leisure for some and mounting boredom for others. Life's developmental crises have become more serious for many and emotional illness has been on the rise. That there is much anxiety, unhappiness, uncertainty, confusion, alienation, and self-doubt on the part of many people can scarcely be denied.

Although we have built an industrial production system of enormous capacity it pollutes the air and the water and at the same time dehumanizes many of the workers who man it and for many it provides no work at all. We have needless conflict between the indispensable need for common planning and organization and the equally important freedom for the individual to choose a life-style significant for him so long as it does not hurt others. We have distressing discrepancies between huge incomes and wealth for a few and abject poverty for many.

There seems to be some real concern on the part of many people to the effect that both personal and national priorities must be changed. While it is difficult to discern clearly the top priorities and it is only natural that there would be disagreement, it is heartening to note that priority determination is at least being considered and discussed. Perhaps this is due to the relatively recent realization that our resources are not unlimited and choices must be made as to what we will do with them.

We know that significant and possibly enduring development is under way as many people in this country push toward greater autonomy and control over their own destinies and toward much more active participation and leadership in governmental and political processes.

As Reston observes, "a great many people are finally facing the moral dilemmas of power, materialism and war, which were being evaded or ignored just a few short years ago. They are challenging many old assumptions about the rights of governments to make war, and the production of anything regardless of what it does to the human condition, and the relations between men and women, employers and employees, yes, and even the relations between the church and the individual and the highly advertised satisfactions of the secular life." [3]

The peace movement in its various approaches, the continuing civil rights thrust, the student participation developments, the organized efforts of women, consumers, and ecology advocates, as well as welfare clients, are all indicative of a ferment that seems to be more and more deeply rooted in a discontented society. There can be no doubt that the field of social welfare will be greatly influenced by these developments. In fact, social welfare must become a part of the surge for change or it may rapidly decline as a viable force in the struggle for human betterment.

It is clear that unfettered individualism will in no way solve our problems. They are corporate problems and can only be solved by an orderly cooperative approach in which individual and special interest give way to congregate concern for the common good.

We know that individuals and groups in society will become more and more interdependent as people meet their needs only through blending their efforts with the efforts of others. This long-term trend is strikingly evident today and will become more evident tomorrow. While social work will and must continue to focus on the individual, the individual must be seen and understood *in society* in a much more complete way than has been true in the past. The intervening act of helping must focus not only on the individual but on the *interaction* of the individual in his groups and in society. It is known that many of the pressures on the individual are societal in origin and no amount of working *on* or *with* the individual alone can relieve these pressures. Society must be changed.

There is much agreement that the structure and machinery of government at all levels needs considerable overhauling to make government truly responsive to the wishes of the majority of its people. Poll after poll has shown repeatedly that the people are heavily inclined toward a program or position only to find that their so-called elected representatives vote to the contrary.

It is untrue that no one knows anything about the future. We know much about the future. For example, we know that there will be many more aged persons in our society. Will we plan properly for their needs? Will we really work to change the meaning of growing old in America?

We know now that there is a great gap between the promise of our institutions and their performance. But, will we reshape these institutions so that they will deliver up to their potential?

We know that we have an economic system that is responsible for great and sometimes ghastly differences in income distribution and that the discrepancies between the haves and have-nots continue to be serious. Our jerrybuilt income maintenance system must be replaced by a system that is equitable, realistic, and adequate for all.

There is not only wide agreement on the problems, there is growing agreement as to some of the *problem-producing factors* such as unbridled technology, planless urbanization, overpopulation, unresponsive government, and the selfishness of those who control the economic system. These factors are under increasing scrutiny as the nation struggles to find its way.

It is clear that most major social problems are national in scope and know no local boundaries. Hence their solution will require a national attack with government and voluntary initiatives closely coordinated and all available resources harnessed for maximum efficiency. This will require much intergroup communication and a restoration of fundamental trust in our government and in our fellow citizens.

Also, there seems to be agreement that we have not used all of the knowledge we possess and perhaps our failure to come to grips with vast areas of human need is not so much a lack of knowledge as a lack of will to lead and to change.

There may be agreement that there are more than enough agencies, programs, and structures but few are properly coordinated and rarely is there really sufficient funding.

We have tended to identify separate problem areas or zones and then to work on them quite independent of their complex intersystemic relations with other problems. We have repeatedly begun an attack on a problem usually with meager financial support but then we have found the problem we selected was much more difficult than we imagined and would take much more in resolve and resources if it were to be solved. Often we have left the problem discouraged and then we have taken on a new one which may look easier to deal with. Rarely have we really thrown massive resources into the attack on human problems. In the physical realm such as weapons systems, our continuing conquest of space and explorations of the moon we have allocated billions of dollars and have provided handsome corps of research and development personnel. We have not done this in the human problem realm.

Boldness in programmatic conception is essential if we are to solve social problems and it must be accompanied by boldness in funding and personnel allocation. On the latter we have been stubbornly reluctant to commit our huge resources of money and manpower.

There is agreement that what we will be doing in the 1990's depends very much on what we do in the 1970's. Unless our goals or targets are clear to us and unless we are working toward them well in advance we can scarcely hope to achieve the changes that are required.

Goals for Social Welfare

A first step is for the field of social welfare to determine how it views the future of society and what role social welfare will play in shaping its goals. Certainly the future cannot be ignored nor can it be said that the future is entirely unknown. In fact, many things are known or can be ascertained with relative accuracy. There can be no denying that the nation and the field of social welfare are truly in a state of transition. The old and the new are in conflict; that is clear. Many would argue that there must be basic changes made in our way of life or we will continue to decline as a nation of compassion and concern.

How much time does society have to establish new values or to restore credence to older and more tested ones? How much time do we have to create new social institutions or modernize and update old ones? How much time is there to introduce and enforce appropriate controls to prevent the further pollution of water, air, and land? How much time is there to rebudget our dwindling natural resources which when gone can never be replaced? Some would observe that the time is not only limited but all too short. And that there must be more speed in our efforts to foster compelling changes.

In any event, it is clear that changes must be made peacefully and thoughtfully with emphasis on widespread participation on the part of all people and with all people having something to say about the crucial decisions of the decades ahead.

A basic task is to work out some agreement as to how much government control is necessary to save the environment and forward the well-being of the people. There is really no basic conflict between order and freedom provided there is agreement on the fundamental purposes of life.

Another basic task is to discard the theory or philosophy that says the individual is totally responsible for his own fate. This has never been true and it never will be. Hence, change efforts focused only on individual behavior modification without simultaneous system change will fail in the future as they have in the past.

There must be a fundamental shift away from the *separate* problem approach which is no longer satisfactory, if it ever was. Problems must be seen in their *interrelatedness* and totality. More important, *persons* and their needs must once again become the focus of our efforts. Persons with problems are a product of a society that is not functioning properly. Hence, there must be major societal changes.

There must be much more advance thinking and planning before new approaches and programs are adopted. Their objectives must be clearly formulated; their theoretical undergirding must be carefully stated; pilot or test runs must be sought before huge investments are made; strict monitoring and evaluation are essential.

It is very clear that the field of social welfare of the future will be a growing and expanding field of service. Michael sees an "expanding demand for human support services, welfare services not only for the poor but for everyone. . . . The expansion of human support services will engender still greater demands for additional services and for faster development of those already established. As people begin to become more educated, healthier, and more politically aware through exposure to the services now being developed, they will demand still more services pushing their demands with rent strikes, boycotts, protest actions of all sorts, through elections, and, when they deem it necessary, through violence." [4]

We can see a general role for social work in seeking to improve the emotional quality of life for everyone by promoting openness in communication between all people. We can expect social work to do more to help people make effective use of large bureaucratic institutions and we will monitor these institutions to improve their valid need-meeting functions and procedures. Social work services will be practiced in many

diverse settings and will be much more widely available and accessible.
We can expect social work to carry increasing responsibility for advocacy including community organization, legal counseling, and legislative
research, formulation, and promulgation.

What goals do we wish to achieve between now and 1993? There is
no lack of goals for which to strive. At the head of the list is the *creation
of a peaceful world* and the elimination of war as an instrument of national policy. In fact, almost anything we can hope to accomplish in the
social realm depends upon our ability to find alternatives to force as a
means of settling international disagreements. Think what could be done
with the billions upon billions that are now going into armaments. Think
what the millions of people under arms and those who develop arms for
them could do with their talents and intelligence if such were directed
to the solution of serious social problems and the meeting of human
needs. While some might argue that world peace is not a concern of
social welfare, it is clear that without world peace there can be no fundamental reallocation of resources to provide the kind of life people so
desperately wish for and need.

Another goal is that of meaningful *jobs* at adequate wages for all who
are able and wish to work, for without useful work persons are without
essential worth in our society. It is clear that since the economic system
does not provide enough jobs the government must be the employer of
last resort. While some may call this further "welfare statism," few can
deny that it is far better to employ people in productive ways than to
allow their spirits to wither into defeat, anger, and alienation.

It is hoped that in the next twenty years the field of social welfare
can enlarge its role from the remedial and the rehabilitative to the preventive. In fact, the time has come to formulate and launch a vast effort
at the prevention of individual and social breakdown. There is so much
knowledge about the predisposing factors that lead to individual and
societal difficulty that prevention is within our grasp if we would only
move toward it vigorously. Social welfare would thus bring a new sense
of purpose to its work and inspire a new sense of purpose in life.

Ways must be found to bring into society the millions of poor, black
and white, who have been disenfranchised because of racism or discrimination. The Census Bureau reveals that 7.4 million or 32 per cent of the
nation's 23 million blacks lived below the official poverty level of $4,137
in 1971. One and one-half million black families, or about 29 per cent
of all black families, were below the poverty level. The number of whites
living below the poverty level *increased* by 300,000 in 1971 to 17.8 million or 10 per cent of the white population. The number of white families
living below the official poverty line was 3.8 million in 1971 compared
to 3.7 million in 1970. Thus, 8 per cent of all white families are living

below the poverty line.[5] This situation must be changed. By 1993 no American should have to live in poverty.

By 1993 every American should be able to afford and have ready access to adequate health care as needed. Government-sponsored health insurance which covers everyone will be a reality here as it has been for years in many industrial countries.

By 1993 we will have abolished institutions and programs that are not working. For example, prisons as we know them today will no longer exist. Crime and delinquency will finally be recognized as deviant behavior spawned by the interaction of the individual with a society in conflict. There will be at long last the realization that deviant behavior can best be modified in the community-based agency rather than in the isolated and obsolete dungeon.

The operating arm of the social service system must be located in the local community even though funds may come from outside sources, such as the state or federal government. Everything can be done better on the local level where needs can be more clearly seen and services more specifically focused on these needs.

The helping processes of social welfare will continue to strive for a vital balance between genuinely humane goals and rigorous scientific method. Science must be infused with a sense of human values and the attainment of human goals must be sought with the assistance of scientific knowledge.

It seems solidly evident that a great deal of social work will be carried on by means of an interdisciplinary team of specialists in the various helping arts. This is true today in many settings and it is certain that the team approach will grow in usefulness. Given this reality it is reasonable to project far more emphasis on teamwork in the educational preparation of social workers and possibly a merging of schools allied with the several helping professions. While the theoretical foundations of the team approach are still sketchy and incomplete in their formulation at this time, one can expect much work in theory development along these lines.

In addition, a goal for social welfare must be to determine what role it wishes to play in helping bring about planned change. If we really believe in the human potential for intelligent action in behalf of community change, it would seem natural for us to seek to enhance that potential and focus its energy on democratically determined goals. There can be no doubt that new power coalitions are in the process of formation and that long struggles lie ahead as the base for decision-making becomes broader because of the increased involvement of people. It would seem to be a worthy goal for social welfare to accept that it can be only minimally effective by itself and can achieve much more in the way of social change if it joins forces with others of like determination.

Social welfare must restate in specific and explicit terms the values in which it believes and at the same time we must seek to deepen our understanding of the values which guide others who differ from us. They too have reasons for the ways they think, act, and feel. If we ever hope to change them or enlist their support we must have much more understanding of them and must develop new strategies for reaching them.

We will support all efforts for the simplification of service delivery designed to reduce bureaucratic blocks which so often delay or deny services so badly needed by many people.

In a message to Congress on January 24, 1972, President Richard M. Nixon spoke sharply about the absence of coordination of service programs:

> Today it often seems that our service programs are unresponsive to the recipient's needs and wasteful of the taxpayers' money. A major reason is their extreme fragmentation. Rather than pulling many services together, our present system separates them into narrow and rigid categories. The father of a family is helped by one program, his daughter by another, and his elderly parents by a third. An individual goes to one place for nutritional help, to another for health services, and to still another for educational counseling. A community finds that it cannot transfer federal funds from one program area to another area in which needs are more pressing. Meanwhile, officials at all levels of government find themselves wasting enormous amounts of time, energy, and the taxpayers' money untangling federal red tape—time and energy and dollars which could better be spent in meeting people's needs. We need a new approach to the delivery of social services—one which is built around people and not programs. We need an approach which treats a person as a whole and which treats the family as a unit. We need to break through rigid categorical walls, to open up narrow bureaucratic compartments, to consolidate and coordinate related programs in a comprehensive approach to related problems.

Certainly this is a vital goal for the present and an indispensable one for the future.

We will devote our energy to those programs which reduce social conditions that damage people and at the same time we will support all programs that enhance those conditions that seem to offer hope for individual development.

We will consider the desirability of merging social welfare administration and community organization because they seem to have so much in common and can contribute so much to goal implementation.

We will develop more accurate ways to measure the effectiveness of our programs and methods and we will abandon approaches proven to be ineffective.

The field of social welfare can and must take leadership in designing and developing a program for a better future for all people. True, social welfare cannot do this alone and it must work in concert with other groups who share like values and aspirations. We cannot rely on chance or benign neglect to bring about needed changes. Ours must be a leadership of conscience and concern.

It is true that much of what we have proposed in this book will be regarded by some as idealistic. Maybe so. But the goals of establishing a peaceful world, the ending of racism, the establishment of an open society with ever-widening citizen participation, work for bureaucratic change and institutional replacement, the elimination of poverty, and the creation of an evolving social policy are worthy goals. It should also be pointed out that every social advance over the years was regarded by some as being either too idealistic or even impossible when it was put forth. Impossible dreams can come true. We have an unparalleled potential for human betterment. We dare not forfeit the future by default. As Kostelanetz put it, "The crucial question confronting us now is not whether we can change the world but what kind of a world we want, as well as how to turn our choices into realities; for nearly everything even slightly credible is becoming possible, in both men and society, once we decide what and why it should be." [6]

Notes

PROLOGUE

1. Harleigh B. Trecker, "The National Conference—Perspective and Promise," *The Conference Bulletin,* Winter, 1965 (National Conference on Social Welfare), p. 1.
2. James Reston, "Peace in the Heart," *New York Times,* December 26, 1971, p. E9. Copyright © 1971 by the New York Times Company. Reprinted by permission.
3. *National Priorities—Military, Economic, and Social* (Washington, D.C.: Public Affairs Press, 1969). Introduction by M. B. Schnapper, editor, Public Affairs Press.
4. See Selected Readings.
5. Maurice H. Stans, "We Must Handle Future Shock," *Signature,* November, 1971.
6. "Analysts Claim Life to Improve by 80's," *Hartford Courant,* November 19, 1971, p. 31.
7. See Donna E. Shala, *Neighborhood Governance—Issues and Proposals,* National Project on Ethnic America. A Depolarization Program of the American Jewish Committee, New York, N.Y., 1971.
8. *Proceedings of the Federal Management Improvement Conference,* September 21 and 22, 1970 (Washington, D.C.: Executive Office of the President. Office of Managements and Budget). Forum 1: "The Management Demands of Tomorrow—A Frame of Reference," p. 7.
9. President Richard M. Nixon, Message to Congress on Population, July 18, 1969.
10. *Population and the American Future—The Report of the Commission on Population Growth and the American Future* (Washington, D.C., 1972). Chapter 3, "Population Distribution," p. 25.
11. *Ibid.,* Chapter 1, "Population Growth."
12. *Population and the American Future—A Summary of the Final Report and*

Recommendations in Population—The U.S. Problem—the World Crisis, The New York Times, April 30, 1972, Section 12, p. 6. A Special Population Supplement prepared and sponsored by The Population Crisis Committee, Washington, D.C. 20006. Used by permission.

13. "The Harsh Arithmetic of Old Age in America," *Saturday Review,* April 8, 1972.

14. *Population and the American Future, op. cit.* Chapter 4, "The Economy," p. 39.

15. "The President and the Children," *New York Times,* January 31, 1972, p. 41. Copyright © 1972 by the New York Times Company. Reprinted by permission.

16. Gerald Grant, "Higher Education Bill—Universal B.A.?" *The New Republic,* June 24, 1972, p. 13. Reprinted by permission of *The New Republic,* © 1972, Harrison-Blaine of New Jersey, Inc.

17. Daniel Bell, *Toward the Year 2000—Work in Progress* (Boston: Houghton Mifflin Company, 1968), p. 1. Reprinted by permission of *Daedalus,* Journal of the American Academy of Arts and Sciences, Boston, Mass.

18. Excerpted from *The Unprepared Society: Planning for a Precarious Future,* by Donald N. Michael (Basic Books, Inc., Publishers, New York, 1968), p. 5.

19. *Social Speculations—Visions for Our Time,* Edited and with an Introduction by Richard Kostelanetz (New York: William Morrow and Company), p. 20.

20. Alfred J. Kahn, *Theory and Practice of Social Planning* (New York: Russell Sage Foundation, 1969), pp. 15–16.

21. Daniel Bell, "The Year 2000: A Trajectory of An Idea," *Daedalus,* Summer, 1967. Reprinted by permission of *Daedalus,* Journal of the American Academy of Arts and Sciences, Boston, Mass.

22. Edward C. Banfield, *The Unheavenly City—The Nature and Future of Our Urban Crisis* (Boston: Little, Brown and Company, 1970), p. 11.

CHAPTER 1

1. Herman Kahn and Anthony J. Weiner, "The Next Thirty-Three Years: A Framework for Speculation," *Daedalus,* Summer, 1967, p. 705.

2. Gunnar Myrdal, quoted in "Tick, Tick, Tick," by T.R.B. from May 29, 1971 issue of *The New Republic.* Reprinted by permission of The New Republic, © 1971, Harrison-Blaine of New Jersey, Inc.

3. William K. Tabb, *The Political Economy of the Black Ghetto* (New York: Norton, 1970), p. 98.

4. Harvey Wheeler, "In Rise of the Elders," *Saturday Review,* December 5, 1970, p. 14.

5. Bayard Rustin, "Minority Groups: Development of the Individual," in William R. Ewald, editor, *Environment and Policy: The Next Fifty Years* (Bloomington, Indiana: Indiana University Press, 1968), p. 11.

6. Daniel R. Fusfeld, *Fascist Democracy in the Unitde States,* Ann Arbor, Michigan, Conference Papers of the Union for Radical Political Economics, December, 1968, p. 5.

7. *Ibid.,* p. 6.

8. See Ralph Pumphrey, "Past Campaigns in the War on Poverty," *The Social Welfare Forum,* Proceedings of the National Conference on Social Welfare (New York: Columbia University Press, 1964), pp. 158–172.

9. Elizabeth Wickenden, "Sharing Prosperity: Income Policy Options in an Affluent Society," in *Toward Freedom from Want,* Industrial Relations Research Association, 1968. Reprint distributed by the National Assembly for Social Policy and Development, New York, N.Y.

10. James L. Sundquist, *Politics and Policy, The Eisenhower, Johnson and Kennedy Years* (Washington, D.C.: The Brookings Institution, 1968), p. 3.

11. *Economic Opportunity Act of 1964*. Report of the Committee on Education and Labor, 88th Congress, 2nd Session, Report No. 1458, House of Representatives, June 3, 1964.

12. Sundquist, *op. cit.*, p. 6.

13. For accounts of the experience of the Economic Opportunity Act, see Sar Levitan, *The Great Society's Poor Law* (Baltimore, Maryland: The Johns Hopkins Press, 1969); Kenneth G. Clark and Jeanette Hopkins, *A Relevant War Against Poverty* (New York: Harper and Row, 1969); and Peter Marris and Martin Rein, *Dilemmas of Social Reform—Poverty and Community Action in the United States* (London: Routledge and Kegan Paul Ltd., 1967).

14. This material and the quotations are from *Civil Rights: Progress Report 1970, Congressional Quarterly,* 1735 K Street, N.W., Washington, D.C., 1971.

15. Mr. Gardner left his post as Secretary of Health, Education, and Welfare to head the Urban Coalition, and enter a national citizen action group called Common Cause.

16. *Current Population Reports: Consumer Income,* Series Report P-60, No. 77, May 7, 1971, U.S. Department of Commerce, Bureau of the Census.

17. These figures are based on a poverty threshold for a nonfarm family of four of $2,973 in 1959, and $3,968 in 1970.

18. Frances Fox Piven and Richard M. Cloward, *Regulating the Poor* (New York: Pantheon, 1971), pp. 183–198.

19. *Ibid.,* p. 183.

20. *Ibid.,* p. 187.

21. *Ibid.,* p. 198.

22. Alvin L. Schorr, "Income Maintenance and Social Security Ideology," *The Social Welfare Forum,* Proceedings of the National Conference on Social Welfare (New York: Columbia University Press, 1970), p. 34.

23. Gilbert Y. Steiner, *The State of Welfare* (Washington, D.C.: The Brookings Institution, 1971), p. 1.

24. Edward C. Banfield, *The Unheavenly City* (Boston: Little, Brown and Co., 1970), pp. 247–258.

25. Theodore J. Lowi, *The End of Liberalism* (New York: Norton, 1969), pp. 68–69.

26. *Counterbudget: Blueprint for Changing National Priorities, 1971–76,* Robert S. Benson and Harold Wolman, editors (The National Urban Coalition, Washington, D.C., 1971), p. xiii.

27. Herbert J. Gans, "The American Malaise," *The New York Times Magazine,* February 6, 1972, p. 12. © 1972 by the New York Times Company. Reprinted by permission.

28. Steiner, *op. cit.,* p. 153.

29. Roland L. Warren, "The Model Cities Program: An Assessment," *The Social Welfare Forum,* Proceedings of the National Conference on Social Welfare (New York: Columbia University Press, 1971), p. 140.

30. William K. Tabb, *The Political Economy of the Black Ghetto* (New York: Norton, 1970), p. 97.

31. *Ibid.,* pp. 98–100.

32. Lee Rainwater, *"The American Underclass: Looking Back and Looking Up,"* *Trans-Action,* February 1969, p. 19.

33. John M. Romanyshyn, *Social Welfare: Charity to Justice* (New York: Random House in conjunction with the Council on Social Work Education, 1971), p. 407.

34. Harry Ashmore, "Of Charity and Forbearance," Ann Arbor (Michigan) *News,* January 24, 1971.

35. See Wilbur J. Cohen, "A Program to Abolish Poverty," *Congressional Record,* 91st Congress, December 5, 1969, Vol. 115, No. 201.

36. *Consumer Income,* Current Population Reports, U.S. Department of Commerce, Bureau of the Census, Series P-60, No. 77, May 7, 1971.

37. Marris and Rein, *Dilemmas of Social Reform—Poverty and Community Action in the United States* (London: Routledge and Kegan Paul Ltd., 1967), p. 7.

CHAPTER 2

1. The author served as the sixth Chief of the Children's Bureau and was asked to resign to permit the Administration to carry out the changes it desired.

CHAPTER 3

1. Actually the British had pioneered in the development of "home helps," the bringing of services into the home for those unable to manage for themselves and yet not handicapped enough to be institutionalized. Visiting homemakers and "Meals on Wheels" are examples of this kind of service. The U.S., over the years, had tended to emulate the British in the social welfare field.

2. Alfred J. Kahn, *Theory and Practice of Social Planning and Studies in Social Policy and Planning* (New York: Russell Sage Foundation, 1969).

3. Edward O'Donnell and Marilyn Sullivan, "Service Delivery and Social Action Through the Neighborhood Service Center: A Review of Research," *Welfare in Review*, Vol. 7, No. 6, 1969.

4. For an evaluation of these programs, see Peter Marris and Martin Rein, *Dilemmas of Social Reform—Poverty and Community Action in the United States* (London: Routledge and Kegan Paul Ltd., 1967).

5. Catherine Papell, "Youth Service Agencies," *Encyclopedia of Social Work* (New York: NASW, 1971), Vol. II.

6. Here again one might note that the British Citizens Advice Bureaus served as a model. Seel Alfred J. Kahn, *et al.*, *Neighborhood Information Centers, A Study and Some Proposals* (Columbia University School of Social Work, 1966).

CHAPTER 4

1. The history of the entire family social work movement can be reviewed in detail in Margaret E. Rich's "A Belief in People," published by Family Service Association of America, New York, 1956. Or, for a capsulized version, see the article on "Family Social Work" in the *Encyclopedia of Social Work* (National Association of Social Workers, New York, 1965), Vol. 15, pp. 309–319.

2. Churches and other private philanthropic groups have been involved in providing for the poor since earliest colonial days. Their assistance was extremely limited, however. Food and clothing would be provided to the destitute in an emergency, for example, but help to those who were, for psychological, physical or other reasons, always poor usually took the form of the Christmas or Thanksgiving basket.

3. Local government units have traditionally borne the major responsibility for financial assistance to the poor; also medical care and institutionalization of the indigent. It is important to note that neither public nor private organizations have ever provided more than was necessary to prevent starvation and nakedness.

4. This theme runs throughout the social welfare history of this country.

5. Who formed the London Society for Organizing Charitable Relief and Suppressing Mendicancy in 1869, and who, like their American admirers, were worried that England's poor were being rewarded and encouraged to idleness by financial relief.

6. Forerunner of the present-day Family Service Association of America, which was founded in 1911.

7. They later raised funds to be used for this purpose, however.

8. This was not necessarily the result of a wave of humanitarianism. More realistically, the public sector realized it had a great stake in eliminating poverty—

a nation of poor people is death to an economy based on consumer ability to spend for produced goods and services.

9. Although the Social Security Act was amended several times no significant change occurred until 1956 when the purpose of public assistance was altered and officially became directed toward improving the social functioning of the individual. However, even this change did not make available either financial or counseling assistance in the scope needed to combat poverty. As in the past, changes in the law were more directed at protecting the payer against cheating on the part of the payee; subliminally, if not overtly, motives were more focused on elimination of "welfare chiseling" than the eradication of poverty. This self-defeating syndrome still pervades the Social Security system.

10. Significantly, this represents a recognition on the part of the voluntary field that the public sector has failed in its effort to eliminate poverty and it heralds the return of the private agency to this critical area of need.

11. For how this is being practiced today, see Patrick V. Riley, "Family Advocacy: Case to Cause and Back to Case," in *Child Welfare,* Vol. L, No. 7, July, 1971.

12. See Otto Pollock, "The Outlook for the American Family," in the *Journal of Marriage and the Family,* February, 1967.

13. Interestingly, modern families are today increasingly demanding a stronger voice in helping determine the nature of the socialization process. An illustration of this is the present-day confrontations in the school system between parents and educators over the purposes and practices of education.

14. The Family Service Association of America is compiling a bibliography on experimental families. Some sources worth studying are: Margaret Mead, "Marriage in Two Steps," in *Redbook,* Vol. 127, No. 3 (July 1966), pp. 48, 49, 84, 86; "Special Report: The Future of Woman and Marriage," in *The Futurist,* Vol. IV, No. 2 (April, 1970), pp. 41–58, includes the following articles: Jessie Bernard, "Women, Marriage and the Future"; William T. Gay, "The Prophet of Group Marriage"; Theodora Wells with Lee S. Christie, "Living Together: An Alternative to Marriage"; Sylvia Clavan, "Women's Liberation and the Family," in *The Family Coordinator,* Journal of Education, Counseling and Services, Vol. 19, No. 4 (October, 1970), pp. 317–323.

Also see in Herbert A. Otto, editor, "The Family in Search of a Future"; Virginia Satir, "Progressive Monogamy: An Alternate Pattern?"; Albert Ellis, "Group Marriage: A Possible Alternative?"; Gerhard Neubeck, "Polyandry and Polygymy: Viable Today?"

15. Studies of the problems of experimental family forms have been conducted by numerous noted researchers. See: Margaret Mead, "A Continuing Dialogue on Marriage: Why Just Living Together Won't Work," in *Redbook,* Vol. 130, No. 6 (April, 1968), pp. 44, 46, 48, 40, 41, 52, 119; Gilbert O. Bartell, *Group Sex: A Scientist's Eyewitness Report on the American Way of Swinging* (New York, Peter H. Wyden, 1971); Robert Houriet, "Getting Back Together" (Coward, McCann and Geoghegan, Inc., New York, 1970); David E. Smith and James Sternfield, "The Hippie Communal Movement: Effects on Child Birth and Development," in *American Journal of Orthopsychiatry,* Vol. 40, No. 3 (April, 1970), pp. 527–530.

16. In almost every decade since 1900, the proportion of single individuals has declined. For men: 1900, 32.3; 1910, 31.9; 1920, 31.3; 1930, 30.5; 1940, 30.7; 1950, 26.2; 1960, 25.3; 1969, 23.7. For women: 1900, 24.4; 1910, 24.1; 1920, 23.9; 1930, 23.5; 1940, 24.2; 1950, 20.0; 1960, 19.0; 1969, 19.2. These statistics apply to people over eighteen and are adjusted for age and were drawn from the *1970 Statistical Abstract of the United States,* U.S. Department of Commerce, Bureau of the Census.

17. For more discussion see Richard E. Farson's chapter entitled "Behavioral Science Predicts and Projects" in *The Future of the Family* published by the Family Service Association of America, New York, 1969. Also see: Virginia Satir,

"Marriage as a Human-Actualizing Contract," Herbert A. Otto, "The New Marriage: Marriage as a Framework for Developing Personal Potential," in Herbert A. Otto, editor, *The Family in Search of a Future.*

18. Technology's potentials have been studied by many noted authorities. One of the most dramatic portrayals is, possibly, Alvin Toffler's, *Future Schock* (Random House, 1970).

19. Notably China which culturally survived a period of significant technological development as early as the fifth century B.C. China has actually experienced and weathered most Western social transitions including feudalism, nationalism, breakdown of aristocracies and rise of bourgeoisie and various socialist experiments—all centuries before Europe and America.

20. Human beings have withstood any number of social upheavals. To limit ourselves strictly to the United States, consider how people survived the great social crisis created by the Revolution, the Civil War, the great depression, to name only a few. All of these challenged not only the emotional and psychological strengths of the population, but were times of great hunger, suffering and misery, disease and death as well.

21. For a discussion of the human problems related to overchoice, see Toffler, *Future Shock,* Chapter 16.

22. It should be noted that this portrait of the future does not explore the role of family social work should the United States undergo a truly traumatic upheaval such as that caused by a major international war, massive depression, civil war or other catastrophe. The picture drawn herein assumes no major social or environmental disaster, but continued social and economic advancement.

23. The increasing scope and variety of service programs in family service agencies has been accomplished by a shift in their practices regarding employment of direct service staff who do not have a master's degree in social work. On January 1, 1971, 70 per cent of the Member Agencies of Family Service Association of America employed one or more such workers. Five years ago only 28 per cent of the Member Agencies employed in direct service positions persons who qualified as "case aides" or assistants to caseworkers. People in these positions then constituted less than 5 per cent of the total number of employees in all Member Agencies—whereas by 1969 they constituted 13 per cent of the total.

Social work assistants are not being used in areas that require the knowledge, skill and experience of a professional worker such as the skilled counseling service that constitutes an essential part of every Member Agency's program. New ways of utilizing paraprofessionals are being identified and relate primarily to new or broadened agency programs.

In the assignments now being carried out by social work assistants, family service agencies are currently using two general types of personnel. The first type has been employed by a number of agencies for some years and is usually engaged in the traditional family service program. This is the "case aide" and is generally selected from the group of young college graduates. The second type, more recent, is engaged in the newer types of family service programs such as neighborhood-centered services, work with poverty groups, and other programs dealing with social problems beyond the agency's usual counseling function. Workers of this second type tend to be drawn from indigenous neighborhood groups.

24. Today a phenomenon in the field, but not yet common practice. This point of view has been formally accepted by the Family Service Association of America in its 1972 statement of "Proposed Goals" for the family service movement, an official policy document.

25. For an in-depth discussion of family-centered counseling and how it can be used to bring about system change see Elsbeth Herzstein Couch, *Joint and Family Interviews in the Treatment of Marital Problems* (Family Service Association of America, New York, 1970), pp. 279–297.

26. See *The Personal Service Society* edited by Paul Halmos (Schocken Books, New York, 1970).

27. A national family policy has been formulated by FSAA and has, since 1960, been proposed and publicly advocated numerous times.

CHAPTER 7

1. Clarence Day, *This Simian World* (New York: Alfred A. Knopf, 1920).

2. Mary Richmond, *Social Diagnosis* (New York: The Russell Sage Foundation, 1922).

3. Carel B. Germain, "Casework and Science: A Historical Encounter," in Robert W. Roberts and Robert H. Nee, editors, *Theories of Social Casework* (Chicago: University of Chicago Press, 1970), pp. 5–32.

4. Even as early as the 1880's, leaders in the Conference of Charities referred to themselves and others as social physicians engaged in *social therapeutics* for the diagnosis and cure of *social diseases* such as pauperism, trampery, alcoholism, and crime. See, for example, Conference of Charities *Proceedings,* 1881: 124–131, 163–167; 1883: 11–18, 314–356; 1885: 316; 1886: 186–195; 185–188; 1888: 120–130; 1889: 24–35.

5. Talcott Parsons and Renee Fox, "Illness, Therapy, and the Modern American Family," *Journal of Social Issues,* Vol. 8 (1952), pp. 31–44.

6. For detailed discussion of the uses of metaphor, see Collin Murray Turbayne, *The Myth of Metaphor* (New Haven: Yale University Press, 1962).

7. Gordon Hamilton, *Theory and Practice of Social Case Work* (New York: Columbia University Press, 1940; 2d edition, revised, 1951).

8. There have been notable efforts in recent years to overcome this obfuscation by such approaches as family treatment, group modalities, experiments with types of milieu therapy, etc.

9. The most characteristic response of social casework to emergent needs in the past has often seemed to be to offer quantitatively more counseling and therapeutic functions, combined with a search for greater knowledge and skill to perfect them, rather than to develop qualitatively different modalities and service systems. See Philip Klein, *From Philanthropy to Social Welfare* (San Francisco: Jossey-Bass, Inc., 1968).

10. It may be partly a result of this antithesis that the 60's and 70's have seen a revival of anti-intellectualism and a revulsion against the life of reason in favor of the Romanticist emphasis on the immediacy of feeling, impulse, and experiential action.

11. Heinz Hartmann, *The Ego and the Problem of Adaptation* (New York: International Universities Press, Inc., 1958).

12. See *Daedalus,* Winter, 1965, "Science and Culture."

13. Germain, *op. cit.,* p. 17.

14. Gordon A. Hearn, *Theory Building in Social Work* (Toronto: University of Toronto Press, 1958).

15. William Gordon, "Toward a Social Work Frame of Reference," *Journal of Education for Social Work,* Vol. I, No. 2 (Fall, 1965), pp. 19–26; William Gordon, "Basic Constructs for an Integrative and Generative Conception of Social Work," in Gordon A. Hearn, editor, *The General Systems Approach: Contributions Toward an Holistic Conception of Social Work* (New York: Council on Social Work Education, 1969), pp. 5–11.

16. Lucille N. Austin, "Trends in Differential Treatment in Social Casework," *Journal of Social Casework,* June, 1948. Printed also in the *Proceedings of the National Conference of Social Work 1948* (New York: Columbia University Press, 1948) and in Cora Kasius, editor, *Principles and Techniques in Social Casework* (New York: Family Service Association of America, 1950), pp. 324–338.

17. Mrs. Austin quoted from Franz Alexander and Robert French, *Psychoanalytic Therapy* (New York: Ronald Press, 1946), p. 102, as follows: "No insight, no emotional discharge, no recollections can be as reassuring as accomplishment in the actual life situation in which the individual failed . . . fostering

favorable experiences in the actual life situation at the right moment in the treatment tends to make for economical psychotherapy, bringing it to an earlier conclusion than otherwise."

18. Grete Bibring, M.D., "Psychiatric Principles of Casework," *Journal of Social Casework,* June, 1949.

19. Fritz Redl and David Wineman, *The Aggressive Child* (Glencoe: The Free Press, 1957). See also Joel Vernick, The Use of the Life Space Interview on a Medical Ward," in *Social Casework,* Vol. XLIV, No. 8 (1963).

20. Kurt Lewin, *Field Theory in Social Science* (New York: Harper Torch-books, 1964).

21. See, for example, Bruno Bettelheim and Emma Sylvester, "A Therapeutic Milieu," *American Journal of Orthopsychiatry,* 18:91 (1948); Alfred Stanton and Morris Schwartz, *The Mental Hospital* (New York: Basic Books, 1954); Max-well Jones, *The Therapeutic Community* (New York: Basic Books, 1953).

22. John Cumming and Elaine Cumming, *Ego and Milieu* (New York: Ather-ton Press, 1966). Milieu concepts, while not termed as such, have long been a part of casework in areas of placement activities, consultation and provision of resources. Milieu instruments are described by the Cummings as: (1) someone who acts as the therapist's agent in the milieu; (2) someone who is added to the milieu or removed from it thus changing the nature of the relationship within it; and (3) resources and facilities added to the milieu (p. 248). Probably casework has not yet begun to make sophisticated and imaginative use of these three instru-ments but continues to rely on largely traditional forms.

23. Erik Erikson, "Identity and the Life Cycle," *Psychological Issues,* Vol. I, Monograph 1 (New York: International Universities Press, Inc., 1959).

24. Thomas Gladwin, "Social Competence and Clinical Practice," *Psychiatry,* 20:30–43 (1967).

25. Brett A. Seabury, "Arrangement of Physical Space in Social Work Settings," *Social Work,* Vol. 16, No. 4 (October, 1971), pp. 43–49.

26. Bernard Bandler, "The Concept of Ego-Supportive Psychotherapy," in Howard J. Parad and Roger R. Miller, editors, *Ego Oriented Casework* (New York: Family Service Association of America, 1963), pp. 27–44.

27. Louise Bandler, "Some Casework Aspects of Ego-Growth through Sub-limation," in *ibid.*

28. Eunice F. Allan, "The Superego in Ego-Supportive Casework Treatment," *Smith College Studies in Social Work,* Vol. 33, No. 3 (June, 1963).

29. For the application of principles of socialization to social casework, see Elizabeth McBroom, "Socialization and Social Casework," in Roberts and Nee, *op. cit.,* pp. 315–351. For a particularly imaginative approach by an individual caseworker see Evelyn A. Lance, "Intensive Work with a Deprived Family," *Social Casework,* Vol. 50, No. 8 (October, 1969), pp. 454–460.

30. Eleanor Pavenstedt, M.D., *The Drifters* (Boston: Little, Brown and Co., 1967).

31. Robert White, "Motivation Reconsidered: The Concept of Competence," *Psychological Review,* Vol. 66 (September, 1959), pp. 297–333.

32. Lydia Rapoport, "Crisis Intervention as a Mode of Brief Treatment," in Roberts and Nee, *op. cit.,* pp. 267–311.

33. Howard J. Parad, editor, *Crisis Intervention: Selected Readings* (New York: Family Service Association of America, 1965).

34. See Bruno Bettleheim, *The Informed Heart* (New York: The Free Press, 1960), Chapter 3, "The Consciousness of Freedom," pp. 65–105.

35. David Rapaport, "The Autonomy of the Ego," *Menninger Clinic Bulletin* 15 (1951); "The Theory of Ego Autonomy," Menninger Clinic Bulletin, 22 (1958).

36. Robert K. Merton, "Continuities in the Theory of Social Structures and Anomie," in Robert K. Merton, *Social Theory and Social Structure* (New York: The Free Press, rev. enl. edition, 1957), pp. 161–194.

37. Eliot Studt, "Social Work Theory and Implications for the Practice of Methods," *Social Work Education Reporter,* Vol. XVI, No. 2 (June, 1968), p. 22.

38. Carol H. Meyer, *Social Work Practice: A Response to the Urban Crisis* (New York: The Free Press, 1970).

CHAPTER 8

1. Alan Toffler, *Future Shock* (New York: Random House, 1970).

2. *Ibid.,* p. 44.

3. *Ibid.,* p. 107.

4. *Ibid.,* p. 264.

5. *Ibid.,* p. 166.

6. Alfred J. Kahn, "The Function of Social Work in the Modern World," in A.J. Kahn, editor, *Issues in American Social Work* (New York: Columbia University Press, 1959), pp. 3–38.

7. Henry David, "Education for the Professions: Common Issues, Problems and Prospects," *Journal of Education for Social Work,* Vol. 3, No. 1 (Spring, 1967), pp. 5–12.

8. Clara Kaiser, "The Social Group Work Method in Social Work Education" (New York: Council on Social Work Education, 1959), pp. 115–128.

9. Margaret Hartford, "Social Group Work 1930 to 1960: The Search for a Definition," in M. Hartford, editor, *Working Papers Toward a Frame of Reference for Social Group Work* (New York: NASW, 1964).

10. Margaretha Williamson, *Social Worker in Group Work* (New York: Harper and Brothers, 1928), quoted in M. Hartford, *op. cit.*

11. Margaret Hartford, *op. cit.*

12. R. B. Pernell, "Implications of the Statement: A Frame of Reference for Social Group Work Practice," in M. Hartford, editor, *Working Papers Toward a Frame of Reference for Social Group Work* (New York: NASW, 1964).

13. David, *op. cit.*

14. Grace Coyle, "Group Work Agencies in Relation to Community Forces," Minnesota Conference of Social Work, September, 1936 (mimeographed).

15. Emanuel Tropp, "Group Intent and Group Structure: Essential Criteria for Group Work Practice," in *A Humanistic Foundation for Group Work Practice* (New York Associated Education Services Corp., 1969).

16. *Ibid.,* p. 17A.

17. Kaiser, *op. cit.*

18. M. Brewster Smith, "Competence and Socialization," in John A. Clausen, *Socialization and Society* (Boston: Little, Brown and Co., 1968), pp. 272–320.

19. John A. Clausen, "Perspective in Childhood Socialization," in J. A. Clausen, editor, *Socialization and Society* (Boston: Little, Brown and Co., 1968), pp. 172–174.

20. Orville G. Brim, Jr., "Adult Socialization," in J. A. Clausen, *Socialization and Society* (Boston: Little, Brown and Co., 1968), p. 184.

21. Brim, *ibid.*

22. Brim, *ibid.*

23. Orville G. Brim, Jr., and S. Wheeler, *Socialization After Childhood: Two Essays* (New York: John Wiley and Sons, 1966).

24. J. L. Kuehn and F. M. Crinella, "Sensitivity Training: Interpersonal 'Overkill,' and Other Problems," *American Journal of Psychiatry,* Vol. 126, No. 6 (December, 1969).

25. William Ryan, *Distress in the City* (Cleveland: Case Western Reserve University Press, 1969); Leo Srole *et al., Mental Health in the Metropolis: The Midtown Manhattan Study* (New York: McGraw Hill, Inc., 1962); Thomas S. Langner and Stanley T. Michael, *Life Stress and Mental Health* (Glencoe, Illinois: The Free Press, 1963).

26. Henry Maier, "A Sidewards Look at Change." Seattle, University of Washington, 1970 (mimeographed).

CHAPTER 9

1. Robert Chin, "The Utility of System Models and Developmental Models for Practitioners," in Warren G. Bennis, Kenneth D. Benne and Robert Chin, editors, *The Planning of Change* (New York: Holt, Rinehart and Winston, 1966), pp. 201–214.
2. Jack Rothman, "Three Models of Community Organization Practice," in Fred M. Cox, John E. Erlich, Jack Rothman, John E. Trapman, editors, *Strategies of Community Organization* (Itasca, Ill.: F. E. Peacock, 1970) pp. 20–36.

CHAPTER 10

1. See Amitai Etzioni, "Human Beings Are Not Easy to Change After All," *Saturday Review,* June 3, 1972.
2. See Herbert J. Gans, "The New Egalitarianism," *Saturday Review,* May 6, 1972; also James Benet, "The California Regents: Window on the Ruling Class," *Change,* February, 1972.
3. See Charles L. Schultze, Edward R. Fried, Alice M. Rivlin, and Nancy H. Teeters, *Setting National Priorities: The 1973 Budget* (Washington, D.C.: The Brookings Institution, 1972).
4. Bruce Porter, "Welfare Won't Work, But What Will?" *Saturday Review,* July 3, 1972. Also see Peter Kihss, "State to Reorganize Welfare Setup," *New York Times,* June 20, 1972, pp. 77c; Joseph Lelyard, "City's New View of Welfare: A Job for Businessmen," *New York Times,* February 1, 1972, p. 1; Peter Kihss, "City 'Shakes Up' Welfare in a Bid to Save Millions," *New York Times,* April 12, 1972, p. 1.
5. Bernard Neugeboren, "Developing Specialized Programs in Social Work Administration in the Master's Degree Program: Field Practice Component," *Journal of Education for Social Work,* Fall, 1971.
6. See Boyce Rensberger, "Impending Ruling by Federal Judge Promises Hope for Neglected in Mental Institutions Around Country," *New York Times,* March 26, 1972, p. 35; Elizabeth Wickenden, *Social Welfare Amicus Brief in Dublin Case,* National Assembly for Social Policy and Development, New York, N.Y., February 29, 1972.
7. Rosemary C. Sarri, "Administration in Social Welfare," *Encyclopedia of Social Work,* Vol. I, 1971 (New York: National Association of Social Workers, 1971), pp. 42–43.
8. "Wanted: Qualified Administrators," from the May, 1972 issue of *College Management* magazine, p. 4, with permission of the publisher. This article is copyrighted © 1972 by CCM Professional Magazines, Inc. All rights reserved.
9. Warren G. Bennis, "Post-Bureaucratic Leadership," in Donald N. Michael, *The Future Society* (Transaction Books, Published by the Aldine Publishing Company, 1970), p. 41.
10. Bennis, *ibid.,* pp. 53–54.
11. Bennis, *ibid.,* p. 33.
12. Warren J. Haas, "Dealing with the Growth of Recorded Information," *Columbia Reports,* March, 1972, p. 2.

CHAPTER 11

1. Henry S. Mass, editor, *Five Fields of Social Service: Reviews of Research* (New York: National Association of Social Workers, 1966).
2. Arnold Gurin, *Community Organization Curriculum in Graduate Social Work Education* (New York: Council on Social Work Education, 1970).

3. Harvey Cox, *Technology and Culture in Perspective* (Cambridge, Massachusetts: The Church Society for College Work, 1967), p. 8.

4. Reference source unknown.

5. J. Samuel Bois, *Explorations in Awareness* (New York: Harper and Row, 1957), pp. 1–25.

6. For clarity of conceptual presentations on social systems and subsystems pertaining to community and social planning, see: Roland Warren, *The Community in America* (Chicago: Rand McNally, 1964), and his *Truth, Love, and Social Change* (Chicago: Rand McNally, 1971).

7. Peter F. Drucker. *Landmarks of Tomorrow* (New York: Harper and Brothers, 1959), pp. 269–270.

Additional References

Berelson, Bernard, "Beyond Family Planning," *Science,* Vol. 163, February 7, 1969, p. 564.

de Chardin, Pierre Teilhard, *The Future of Man,* translated by Norman Denny. New York: Harper and Row, 1964.

deVries, Egbert, editor, *Essays on Unbalanced Growth: A Century of Disparity and Convergence S-Gravenhage.* Moulton and Co., 1962. Especially Chapter VIII by Jac P. Thrujsse.

Ecklein, Joan, and Lauffer, Armand, *Community Organizers and Social Planners: A Volume of Case and Illustrative Materials.* New York: John Wiley and Sons and Council on Social Work Education, 1971.

Halpern, Manfred, "A Redefinition of the Revolutionary Situation," *Journal of International Affairs,* Vol. No. 1, 1969, pp. 54–75.

Kahn, Alfred J., *Theory and Practice of Social Planning.* New York: Russell Sage Foundation, 1969.

Kahn, Herman, and Weiner, Anthony J., *The Year 2000: A Framework for Speculation on the Next Thirty-Three Years.* New York: Macmillan Company, 1967.

Mayer, Robert R., *Social Planning and Social Change.* New Jersey: Prentice-Hall, 1972.

Meadows, Donella H., *et al., The Limits of Growth.* New York: Universe Books, 1971, A Potomas Associates Book.

Perlman, Robert, and Gurin, Arnold, *Community Organization and Social Planning.* New York: John Wiley and Sons, and Council on Social Work Education, 1971.

"Social Planning and Community Organization," *Encyclopedia of Social Work, 1971,* pp. 1324–1361.

Symposium on Changing Styles of Planning in Post-Industrial America. *Public Administration Review,* Vol. 31, No. 3 (May/June, 1971).

Warren, Roland L., *Truth, Love and Social Change and Other Essays on Community Change.* Chicago: Rand McNally and Co., 1971.

CHAPTER 12

1. See John C. Kidneigh, "The New York Conference Story," in *The Social Welfare Forum, 1969* (National Conference on Social Welfare, Columbia University Press, 1969).

2. Kurt Reichert, *Journal of Education for Social Work,* Fall, 1971, pp. 39–50.

3. Gordon Hamilton, "Education for Social Work," in *Social Work Yearbook 1945* (New York: Russell Sage Foundation, 1945), pp. 137–146.

4. Sue Spencer, "Education for Social Work," in *Social Work Yearbook 1949* (New York: Russell Sage Foundation, 1949), pp. 173–183.

5. Ernest Witte, "Education for Social Work," in *Social Work Yearbook 1960* (New York: National Association of Social Workers, 1960), pp. 223–240.

6. Werner Boehm, "Education for Social Work," in *Encyclopedia of Social Work,* Sixteenth Issue, Vol. I (New York: National Association of Social Workers, 1971), pp. 257–273.

7. Louis Lowy, Leonard M. Bloksberg, and Herbert J. Walberg, *Integrative Learning and Teaching in Schools of Social Work* (New York: Association Press in cooperation with the Council on Social Work Education, 1971).

8. See a sample of attempts at achieving this in *Social Work Education in the Post-Master's Program,* No. 1, *Guiding Principles;* No. 2, *Approaches to Curriculum Content;* and No. 3, *Field Work and Related Issues* (New York: Council on Social Work Education, 1953–54–55).

9. See John C. Kidneigh, "Restructuring Practice for Better Manpower Use," *Social Work,* April, 1968, pp. 109–115; James Bridges, *Job Purification and Job Satisfaction in Social Work,* 1970 Univerisity of Minnesota Doctoral Thesis; David Jan Johnson, *Job Complexity, Job Attitude and Self Concept Among Probation Officers,* 1971 University of Minnesota Doctoral Thesis; also Thomas L. Briggs, Donald E. Johnson and Ellen P. Lebowitz, *Research on the Complexity-Responsibility Scale* (School of Social Work, Syracuse University, 1970).

10. See Edward E. Schwartz, editor, *Manpower in Social Welfare* (New York: National Association of Social Workers, 1964); also *The Admission Process in Schools of Social Work* (New York: Council on Social Work Education, Monograph 64-10-18, 1964).

11. See Anne W. Oren, *The Construction of an Instrument for the Measurement of Social Worker Attitudes Associated with Aptitude for Interpersonal Relations,* 1957 Doctoral Thesis, University of Minnesota; Edward W. Francel, *Factors Associated with the Successful Outcome of Professional Training for Social Work,* 1960 Doctoral Thesis, University of Minnesota; Horace W. Lundberg, *Some Distinctive Characteristics of Students Entering Graduate Social Work Education,* 1957 Doctoral Thesis, University of Minnesota; Joseph Meisels, *Self-Conception, Job-Perception and Job Satisfaction of Social Workers,* 1962 Doctoral Thesis, University of Minnesota; also see John D. Kidneigh, "The Vocational Interest Patterns of Social Workers, *Social Work Journal,* October, 1954.

CHAPTER 13

1. Henry J. Meyer, "Social Work," *International Encyclopedia of the Social Sciences,* David Sills, editor (New York: Macmillan Company and The Free Press, 1968), Volume 14, pp. 495–506.

2. Mary E. Macdonald, "Social Work Research: A Perspective," in *Social Work Research,* Norman A. Polansky, editor (Chicago: University of Chicago Press, 1960), p. 13.

3. Indeed, one projection of the growth curve in doctoral training from a base of five decades indicates that by 1993, more doctoral degrees in social work will be awarded than there are social workers to receive them! Data on doctoral degrees in social work are presented by J. J. Bladi, "Doctorates in Social Work, 1920–1968," *Journal of Education for Social Work* (Winter, 1971), pp. 11–22.

4. Paul Neff Verlal, *The Royal Art of Alchemy,* translated by R. H. Weber (Philadelphia: Chilton Book Company, 1964).

5. A typical, and accurate, description of research includes the ideas of a systematic investigation, using standardized procedures to address a problem formulated to allow its formal examination. See Ann W. Shyne, "Social Work Research," *Encyclopedia of Social Work* (New York: National Association of Social Workers, 1965), pp. 763–772.

6. A number of the problems in collaboration are identified by David Fanshel, "Sources of Strain in Practice Oriented Research," *Social Casework* (June, 1966), pp. 357–362.

7. Selma Fraiberg, "The Muse in the Kitchen: A Case Study in Clinical Research," *Smith College Studies in Social Work* (February, 1970), pp. 101–139.

8. Geraldine L. Connor, "Research Consultation to Social Work Practitioners: Parts and Processes" (New York: National Association of Social Workers, 1966), pp. 33–45.

9. Ann W. Shyne, "Warm Bodies and Lively Minds: Recruiting and Retaining Research Staff," *Social Work* (January, 1969), pp. 107–113.

10. *Race Research and Reason: Social Work Perspectives,* Roger R. Miller, editor (New York: National Association of Social Workers, 1967), pp. 179–182.

11. An overview of the attainments and limitations of social work research is available in *Research in the Social Services: A Five Year Review,* Henry S. Maas, editor (New York: National Association of Social Workers, 1971).

12. Roger R. Miller, "Student Research Perspectives on Race," *Smith College Studies in Social Work* (November, 1970), pp. 10–23.

13. Edward J. Mullen, *et al., Preventing Chronic Dependency* (Institute of Welfare Research, Community Service Society, New York, 1970). See especially, "The Practitioners View of the Study Findings," pp. 213–220.

14. Alvin Toffler, *Future Shock* (New York: Random House, 1970).

15. *The Future Society,* Donald N. Michael, editor (New York: Aldine Publishing Company, 1970), p. 5.

EPILOGUE

1. Emmanuel G. Mesthene, *Technological Change: Its Impact on Man and Society* (Cambridge: Harvard University Press, 1970), p. viii.

2. *Ibid.,* p. 36.

3. James Reston, "Peace in the Heart," *New York Times,* December 26, 1971, p. E9. © 1971 by the New York Times Company. Reprinted by permission.

4. Donald N. Michael, *The Unprepared Society: Planning for a Precarious Future* (New York: Basic Books, Inc., 1968), pp. 16–17.

5. "In '71, 32% of Blacks Lived in Poverty, The Census Finds," *New York Times,* July 13, 1972, p. C11.

6. *Social Speculations—Visions for Our Time,* Edited with an Introduction by Richard Kostelanetz (New York: William Morrow and Company, Inc., 1971), p. 19.

Selected Readings

"Are Our Cities Doomed?" "Yes" by Eugene Raskin; "No" by Samuel Tenen-
    baum. *New York Times,* Sunday, May 2, 1971, Section 8.
Bennis, Warren G., and Slater, Philip E., *The Temporary Society.* New York:
    Harper and Row, 1968.
Benson, Robert S., and Wolman, Harold, editors, *Counterbudget: Blueprint for
    Changing National Priorities 1971–76.* Washington, D.C.: The National Ur-
    ban Coalition, 1971.
Burns, James MacGregor, *Uncommon Sense.* New York: Harper and Row, 1972.
Drew, Elizabeth, "Contemplating the National Navel," *New York Times Maga-
    zine,* June 4, 1972.
Drucker, Peter F., *The Age of Discontinuity.* New York: Harper and Row, 1969.
Drucker, Peter F., "The Surprising Seventies," *Harper's Magazine,* July, 1971.
Eurich, Alvin C., editor, *Campus 1980, The Shape of the Future in American
    Higher Education.* New York: Delacorte Press, 1968.
Ewald, Walter R., Jr., editor, *Enrichment for Man—The Next 50 Years.* Bloom-
    ington: Indiana University Press, 1967.
Harrison, George Russell, *What Man May Be.* New York: William Morrow and
    Company, 1956.
Kahn, Herman, and Briggs, B. Bruce, *Things to Come—Thinking About the 70's
    and 80's.* New York: The Macmillan Company, 1972.
Kahn, Herman, and Weiner, Anthony J., "The Next Thirty-Three Years: A Frame-
    work for Speculation," *Daedalus,* Summer, 1967.
Kahn, Herman, and Weiner, Anthony J., *The Year 2000: A Framework for
    Speculation on the Next Thirty-Three Years.* New York: Macmillan, 1967.
Lamm, Richard D., "Urban Growing Pains—Is Bigger Also Better?" *New Re-
    public,* June 5, 1971.
Lowi, Theodore J., *The End of Liberalism.* New York: Norton, 1969.
Mesthene, Emmanuel G., *Technological Change: Its Impact on Man and Society.*
    Cambridge: Harvard University Press, 1970.
Michael, Donald N., *The Future Society.* Transaction Books. Published by the
    Aldine Publishing Comany, 1970.

National Priorities—Military, Economic and Social. Washington, D.C.: Public Affairs Press, 1969.

Nemy, Enid, "For Them the Four-Day Week Has Arrived—and They Love It." *New York Times,* December 27, 1971.

Population and the American Future. Report of the Commission on Population Growth and the American Future, Washington, D.C., 1972.

Population—The U.S. Problem the World Crisis. Supplement to *New York Times,* April 30, 1972. Section 12 sponsored by the Population Crisis Committee with the Planned Parenthood Federation of America.

"Projections of the Population of the United States by Age and Sex: 1970–2000." *Current Population Reports,* Series P-25, No. 470. U.S. Census Bureau, Department of Commerce, Washington, D.C.

Reinhold, Robert, "Problems of the 21st Century Confound a Parley of Thinkers," *New York Times,* April 10, 1972.

Samuels, Gertrude, "Thank God It's Thursday! Coming Soon? The Four-Day Week," *New York Times Magazine,* May 16, 1971.

Schrag, Peter, "What's Happened to the Brain Business?" *Saturday Review,* August 7, 1971.

Shalala, Donna E., *Neighborhood Governance Proposals and Issues.* National Project on Ethnic America, a Depolarization Program of the American Jewish Committee, 165 East 56th Street, New York, N.Y., 1971.

Social Speculations—Visions for Our Time. Edited and with Introduction by Richard Kostelanetz. New York: William Morrow and Company, Inc., 1971.

Still, Henry, *Man: The Next 30 Years.* New York: Hawthorn Books, Inc., 1968.

Toffler, Alvin, *Future Shock.* New York: Random House, 1970.

"Toward the Year 2000: Work in Progress," *Daedalus,* Summer, 1967.

The Contributors

Government and Social Welfare

WAYNE VASEY, Professor, School of Social Work, University of Michigan, Co-Director, Institute of Gerontology, University of Michigan—Wayne State University. M.A. Social Work, University of Denver; B.A. William Penn College. Previous positions: General Manager, Human Development Corporation of St. Louis; Dean and Professor, George Warren Brown School of Social Work, Washington University, St. Louis; Dean and Professor, School of Social Work, Rutgers University; Director and Professor, School of Social Work, University of Iowa; Research Associate, Russell Sage Foundation; Director, Contra Costa County (California) Social Service Department; Regional Public Assistance Staff, Social Security Board, San Francisco; Field Representative, Colorado State Department of Public Welfare; numerous consulting assignments. Leadership roles in professional and community organizations including Past-President, National Conference on Social Welfare. Author of papers, articles, books, and chapters in books.

Child Welfare Services

PARDO FREDERICK DELLIQUADRI, Dean, School of Social Work, University of Alabama, Tuscaloosa. M.S. in Social Work, School of Social Work, University of Nebraska; B.A. University of Colorado. Previous positions: former Dean, School of Social Welfare, University of Wisconsin, Milwaukee. Consultant to Commissioner of Social Security, Department of Health, Education, and Welfare, Washington, D.C.; Chief of Children's Bureau, Social and Rehabilitation Service, U.S. Department of Health, Education, and

Welfare, Washington, D.C.; Dean, University of Hawaii, School of Social Work; Dean, Columbia University, School of Social Work; Director, Division for Children and Youth, Wisconsin Department of Public Welfare, Child Welfare work in Illinois, Wyoming, and Washington. United States Representative to Executive Board of UNICEF; Chief Delegate to UNICEF Conferences in Bangkok and Addis Ababa; other international assignments, leadership roles in national organizations, former Chairman, Program Committee, National Conference on Social Work and former Vice-President, Consultant to Government agencies, author of research studies, reports, articles in professional publications.

Services for Youth

HERBERT MILLMAN, Executive Vice-President, National Jewish Welfare Board. Ed.M. Harvard University; B.S. Springfield College. Professional experience in Jewish Community Centers and YM-YWHAs and camping. Past-President, Association of Jewish Center Workers; former Chairman, Editorial Committee of National Conference on Social Welfare.

and

ALVIN KOGUT, Associate Professor, Adelphi University, School of Social Work. M.S.W. and D.S.W. Columbia University, School of Social Work. Professional experience in YM-YWHAs and settlement houses; former Consultant, Office of Juvenile Delinquency and Youth Development, Department of Health, Education, and Welfare, Washington, D.C. Author and co-author of books and articles.

Family Social Work

CLARK W. BLACKBURN, General Director Family Service Association of America. M.Sc. School of Applied Social Services, Western Reserve University; A.B. Yale. Previous positions: Executive, Family and Children's Service of Minneapolis; United Family and Children's Society, Plainfield, N.J.; Family Service Society, Hartford, Connecticut. Staff member, Family Service Association of Cleveland; Public Welfare, Cuyahoga County; Relief Administration, North Carolina State Board of Charities and Public Welfare. Active on national and regional boards, committees, commissions.

and

JANICE MARUCA, public relations and writing for Family Service Association of America.

Services for the Aged

BERNARD E. NASH, Executive Director, American Association of Retired Persons, National Retired Teachers Association. Master's degree, School of Social Work, University of Minnesota; post-master's work in sociology, University of Minnesota; graduate of the Federal Executive Institute, Charlottesville, Virginia. Previous positions: Deputy Commissioner, Administration on Aging, S.R.S., Department of Health, Education and Welfare, Washington, D.C.; Director, Foster Grandparent Program, Administration on Aging, Department of Health, Education, and Welfare, Washington, D.C.; Director and Chairman, Department of Community Development, University of Missouri; Executive Secretary, Governor's Council on Aging, Minnesota. Author of articles and chapters in professional journals and books on subjects pertinent to older Americans. Leadership roles in national and international professional societies and organizations.

Corrections

MILTON G. RECTOR, Executive Director, National Council on Crime and Delinquency. B.A. University of Southern California; graduate study University of California and Columbia University. Previous positions: NCCD Western Consultant and Assistant Director; Probation Officer, Los Angeles County Probation Department; Delegate, United Nations, Second, Third and Fourth World Congress on Prevention of Crime and Treatment of Offenders; U.S. Representative to Social Defense Section, United Nations; member President's Advisory Council on Juvenile Delinquency; Consultant, President's Crime Commission; member, Advisory Committee, National Commission on Reform of Federal Criminal Laws; Chairman, Board of Directors, Joint Commission on Correctional Manpower and Training. Board and commission member in other areas of corrections field.

Social Casework

CAREL B. GERMAIN, Professor, School of Social Work, Columbia University. D.S.W., M.S. Columbia University, School of Social Work; A.B. University of California. Previous positions: Professor and Acting Dean, School of Social Work, University of Connecticut; Assistant Professor, University of Maryland, School of Social Work; Assistant Professor of Psychiatric Social Work, University of Maryland, School of Medicine; work in public welfare, adult probation, child guidance. Articles in professional journals.

Social Group Work

RUBY B. PERNELL, Professor, Grace Longwell Coyle Chair in Social Work, Case Western Reserve University, School of Applied Social Services. B.S., M.S.W. University of Pittsburgh; Ph.D. University of London (London School of Economics and Political Science). Previous positions: Professor of Social Work, University of Minnesota; Social Welfare Attaché, United States Embassy, New Delhi, India. Visiting Professor, University of Denver, Atlanta University and University of Washington; Leadership Training Consultant for the United States High Commission for Germany; Training Consultant for Girl Scouts of the United States of America. Leadership roles in professional and community organizations. Articles in professional journals.

Community Organization

ELIZABETH L. PINNER, Associate Professor, School of Social Work, University of Connecticut. Ph.D. Bryn Mawr College, School of Social Work;

M.S.S.W., School of Social Work, University of Pittsburgh; A.B. Bucknell University. Previous positions: Teaching Assistant, Bryn Mawr College, School of Social Work; Fellow, Lilly Foundation; Director of Special Services, Girl Scouts of Philadelphia; Field Adviser, Baltimore Area Girl Scout Council; Fellow, Danforth Foundation. Active in professional organizations and community agencies.

Social Work Administration

HARLEIGH B. TRECKER, University Professor, School of Social Work, University of Connecticut. A.M., School of Social Service Administration, University of Chicago; B.S. George Williams College. Previous positions: Professor and Dean, University of Connecticut, School of Social Work; Associate Professor and Professor, School of Social Work, University of Southern California; Instructor and Director of Field Work, George Williams College; Director, Chicago Leisure Time Service. Author of books, monographs, articles; leadership roles in national, state, and local professional and community organizations. Monographs and articles in professional journals.

Social Welfare Planning

JACK E. A. STUMPF, Professor, School of Social Work, San Diego State University. Ph.D., Forence Heller Graduate School of Andvanced Studies in Social Welfare, Brandeis University; M.S.W., School of Social Work, University of Southern California; B.S. George Williams College. Previous positions: Executive Director, San Bernardino County Council of Community Services; Consultant, Health and Welfare Council, Inc. of Philadelphia, Delaware, Montgomery Counties, Pennsylvania; Research Director and Council Executive, Community Chest and Council, Inc. of Pasadena-Altadena, California. Study Director and Consultant on many community studies, evaluations of organizations and programs and development of social welfare services. Leadership roles in professional and community organizations. Articles in reports and journals.

and

BEN P. GRANGER, Professor and Associate Dean, College of Social Professions, University of Kentucky. Ph.D., Florence Heller School for Advanced Studies in Social Welfare, Brandeis University; M.P.A., School of Public Administration, University of Southern California; M.S.W. University of Southern California; B.A. Whittier College. Previous positions: Special Research Fellow, Brandeis University; Survey Consultant, Child Welfare League of America; Assistant Professor, School of Social Work, San Diego State College; Social Worker, Family Service Association of San Diego; Director of Treatment, San Diego Children's Home Association; Supervising Social Worker, California Youth Authority; Deputy Probation Officer, Los Angeles County Probation Department. Monographs and articles in professional journals.

Social Work Education

JOHN C. KIDNEIGH, Professor and Director, School of Social Work, University of Minnesota. M.A., Social Work, University of Denver; graduate education in Social Work, University of Utah; B.A. University of Utah. Research, teaching, consultation in Canada, Korea, Mexico and South Africa. Previous positions: Associate Director, School of Social Work, University of Minnesota; Personnel Consultant, Assistant Regional Director, Social Security Board, Minneapolis; Merit System Supervisor, State of Colorado; Supervisor, Department of Public Welfare, State of Utah; Supervisor of Community Services, Salt Lake City. Author of numerous research studies and articles. Past-President, National Association of Social Workers, American Association of Schools of Social Work; Chairman, Commission on Accreditation, National Council on Social Work Education; leadership roles in other professional and community organizations.

Social Work Research

ROGER R. MILLER, Professor-Research, Smith College, School for Social Work. D.S.W., M.Sc. (Social Administration) Western Reserve University. Advanced Research Trainee, Hampstead Child Therapy Training Center and Woodbury Down Child Guidance Center, London. Previous positions: Instructor, Assistant Professor, School of Applied Social Sciences, Western Reserve University; Research Associate, School of Medicine, Western Reserve University; Chief, Social Work Section, U.S. Army Hospital, Frankfurt, Germany; Psychiatric Social Worker, University Hospitals of Cleveland. Monographs and articles in professional journals.

Index